D1395537

£22-50

N6L.

The Last Wali of Swat

The Last Wali of Swat

An Autobiography as told to
Fredrik Barth

Norwegian University Press/
Universitetsforlaget AS

Norwegian University Press (Universitetsforlaget AS), 0608 Oslo 6
Distributed world-wide excluding Scandinavia by
Oxford University Press, Walton Street, Oxford 0X2 6DP

London   New York   Toronto
Delhi   Bombay   Calcutta   Madras   Karachi
Kuala Lumpur   Singapore   Hong Kong   Tokyo
Nairobi   Dar es Salaam   Cape Town
Melbourne   Auckland

and associated companies in
Beirut   Berlin   Ibadan   Mexico City   Nicosia

© Universitetsforlaget AS 1985

All rights reserved. No part of this publication may be reproduced, stored in a
retrieval system, or transmitted, in any form or by any means, electronic,
mechanical, photocopying, recording, or otherwise, without the prior permission
of the Norwegian University Press (Universitetsforlaget AS).

ISBN 82-00-07079-4

(Published simultaneously in the United States and Canada
by Columbia University Press.)

Illustrations (between pages 56 and 57):
Photographs Nos. 1, 2, 3, 4, 7, 8, 14
  are all from The Wali's private collection.
Photographs Nos. 9, 10, 11, 12, 15, 16, 17
  are all reproduced by courtesy of Fredrik Barth.
Photograph No. 5: courtesy of The British Library, London.
Photograph No. 6: courtesy of National Army Museum, London.
Photograph No. 13: courtesy of Popperfoto, London.

Cover design: Tor Berglie

Printed in Norway by
Nye Intertrykk as

Contents

Preface

History has moved very swiftly in some parts of Asia, and the personal recollections of Miangul Jahanzeb, the Wali of Swat, span a breathtaking series of transformations of which he himself was partly architect, partly prominent participant or privileged spectator. When he was born in 1908 the Swat valley formed a complex but stateless society of several hundred thousand members, linked to the archaic cosmopolitanism of Inner Asia but hardly touched by the centuries of external influence and British presence in the neighbouring India. Indeed, the Swat valley had never ever been *seen* by an Englishman until 13 years before the Wali's birth. During his childhood, his father emerged as the creator and ruler of a new state in this tribal territory, a state which thereupon became progressively more closely linked, economically and politically, to British India and subsequently to Pakistan. For twenty years, from 1949 till 1969, Wali Sahib himself ruled this state, until it was merged into the regular administration of Pakistan through a peaceful transfer of authority.

The following text gives the Wali's inside account of these events, and his own life in the midst of them, and thus encompasses the total history of the State of Swat from 1917 to 1969, as well as its historical roots in events preceding its inception, and a view of the politics and changes following its merger. The materials on which the text is based were collected through intensive interviews with the Wali, conducted in English, for a few hours each day in the period 10–26 April 1979, totalling c. 60 hours of taped recordings. These materials have the form of questions and answers, conversations, and occasional longer passages of connected account by the Wali of crucial experiences, moments, and chains of events.

I came to these interviews with the background of having previously done anthropological fieldwork in Swat. I was there through most of the year 1954 and have subsequently revisited the area a number of times, and have published extensively on the society and culture of Swat. I was thus already familiar with many aspects of local circumstances and the major outlines of historical events; some of the events and incidents I knew in detail from accounts that had been told me by other participants on previous occasions. I was therefore often in a position to put specific questions to Wali Sahib, and to relieve him of the need to explain extraneous context and circumstances for the events he wished to recount. At other times in our interviews, I could put such questions of context to him, so as to have his own accounts also of them. Cooperating in this way, both Wali Sahib and I made conscious efforts to assure that the account would be complete, in the sense of covering a continuous time sequence and comprising all major events judged by him to be important.

In editing the text from the taped materials, I have sought to retain Wali Sahib's own expression and turn of phrase as much as possible; but I have interposed and strung together different accounts of the same incidents given during conversations that took place on different days, since we often chose to return to certain topics so as to clarify them or elaborate them. Apart from such sequential re-editing, most of the text is given verbatim as told by Wali Sahib. Where I have paraphrased him to link passages or given background materials or concentrated materials, this is indicated by setting such non-verbatim text in slightly smaller type. Wali Sahib has thereupon read the entire manuscript and made detailed corrections of style and content both of the verbatim text and my paraphrase — without thereby at any point changing the substance of the account or suppressing any incident I had included. The transcription of all Pashto terms and names is likewise his. The epilogue, on the other hand, is entirely my own text, though it has likewise been read by him. It presents my own understandings and reflections on the materials he gives. I have also introduced a few footnotes to supplement the Wali's account, or corroborate it, especially for the early period before his firsthand recollections. But I have wished to avoid the questionable method of annotating the Wali's account and insights, or appropriating any part of his life story by harnessing it to my own analysis or argument. My purpose has been to serve as his scribe and medium, to make available his impressive life story and his unique political and social insights to a broad audience of social scientists, historians, and interested public.

The question inevitably arises as to the historical objectivity or factuality of the resulting text. I have definitely made no systematic attempts to critically verify, from documentary sources or the oral accounts of other participants to the events, the veracity of the account which Wali Sahib gives: it is his story, as he has chosen to tell it. In judging it as an historical document, however, I would suggest that the critical reader have the following points in mind. When I first suggested to Wali Sahib, in 1978, that he should write his memoirs, we discussed it in terms of the shared awareness that the archival materials which will be available to future historians have nearly all been written by "the other side", i.e. by British and Pakistani agents and officials. While this indicated to him that there might be a need to re-establish a balance in the available accounts, he was also fully aware that whatever account he himself provided would only affect the ultimate historical picture of Swat State, himself, and his own and his father's achievements, to the extent that it could stand up and effectively confront the facts as given in contemporary documents. Secondly, the Wali must also have been aware of my own not inconsiderable (and rather unpredictable) knowledge of many of the events, deriving from accounts given to me by a wide variety of other persons in Swat who, as his subjects, represented "the other side" in another sense than the above on many issues. Besides his own wish to give a genuine account of his own life and achievements, he was thus constrained by these external circumstances to keep close to the real facts as he knew them and recollected them. It is my own judgement that he has succeeded in this, and that his account provides the most informed and informative account of state-building and government in Swat, as well as a picture of a singular and fascinating life and fate.

Oslo, August 1983   *Fredrik Barth*

CHAPTER I:
"A time of transition"

I was born on the 5th of June 1908.

My very earliest memories are of gunfights between my father and my uncle Shirin Sahib — that is, mainly between their retainers — here in Saidu, and in the fields where Jahanzeb College now stands. Every week or every month, there would be battles; but I could not understand *why* they were fighting. Eventually, Shirin Sahib was defeated and turned out of Saidu. So he lived near the river in Pir Amanderai, beyond Nawe-kelli, and he remained there till our exile in 1915. Then afterwards, when the State was founded in 1917, he came back here and resumed his share of the village, and was my father's Commander-in-Chief, and was killed in the battles against the Nawab of Dir in August 1918. But *if* he had lived, I think there would have been a clash between him and my father. And one of them would have been eliminated.

Otherwise, I remember living with my mother, and going to see my father in the morning. And at the age of four and a half I was put under a mullah, to be taught the Holy Koran. He was Imam of the Mosque here in Saidu — the grandfather of this man who is now my butler.

At that time, of course, there was no State here, my father and our whole family was just one of the Saintly families living in this area, among the Yusufzai Pakhtun chiefs and landowners.

There was no education, not even any *opportunity* for education, as those few mullahs who could read and write did not encourage education. They just taught their own children and nobody else — they wanted to keep their advantage for themselves, and remain dominant.

After he brought peace to the area, my father started building roads, and two or three schools, and improving the condition of the people; and at the same time breaking the power of the Khans so that they should not rise against him and remove him. Gently, he did it. But he

11

did it through the feudalistic system: he gave all power to the Khans. If one Khan would not yield, his cousin or his brother or some big leader of the *other* faction would be raised up, by my father, to become the local headman. But not with *less* power — with *the same* power as the previous Khan had exercised.

When I became Ruler, I started making more schools, hospitals, roads — though my father had made many roads by then, and had also installed the telephone system. But I made it much more extensive; and people recognized that. They always said that of all the states in the Frontier, Swat State was the most civilized. And that is why so many people from Swat are in America, England, Libya, and Saudi Arabia: because of the education they got here. I gave them the educational facilities, and finance and help — so now we have *surplus* doctors and engineers and professors, and some of them earn their livelihood in America and Canada and such places, where they even have adopted citizenship of those countries and settled there.

Then, around 1950, I started breaking out of this feudal system. All the common people used to have to contribute to the Khan's *hujra* (guesthouse and headquarters), where those Khans would entertain their guests and retainers at the expense of the whole population of their ward and village. So I decided I would have to break that system. My father, after he abdicated and I became Ruler, would sometimes give me private advice, and he always used to say: "This will not work, you *must* make use of the feudal system for your own ends, to maintain the State." But I answered: "The time has come. How can people, when they become educated, obey uneducated Khans?" So I released the people from their feudal bondage, and then in 1951 some of the Khans rebelled, and sought the help of the then Chief Minister of the Northwest Frontier Province, Khan Abdul Qayyum Khan, that Swat State should rather be merged with Pakistan. But they did not succeed and had to run away from Swat — and finally, they came begging me to be allowed to come back home again.

Of course, I was also very patriotic about Pakistan. I supported, I contributed whatever I could, in money and in people. We joined Pakistan, we sent our army to fight in Kashmir. The Muslims must have their own land. I was *always* in favour of the creation of Pakistan.

And I knew, all the time, that sooner or later this state would be merged into the bigger union of Pakistan. So that was also one reason why I hurried education and other development, so that the people of

Swat should not suffer in the future. And I wanted the merger to be peaceful and orderly — which thanks to God, it was. We *cheered* when it was announced that Swat was merged.

All this, I have done by my own judgement. I had officials, of course, and they behaved very loyally — at least up to the last couple of months before merger. In the last two years before merger, there was a little corruption. And I could not touch most of those officials, because they all belonged to the Khan families, and if you dismiss one person, the whole family turns against you. So I had to be a little careful. When you are Ruler, then all around you are either enemies, who are against you, or flatterers, with whom you cannot enjoy any society. When you propose something to them, they say "Yes Sir, yes Sir, that is *very* good!" So I have had to think for myself; there was little advice they could give me.

My whole life has been a time of transition — so it has been difficult for me, and for my people. But we created something *new:* my father created the State of Swat, and that is the greatest achievement. Anyone who invents something, discovers something or creates something will feel elated and happy. To create a new state, and then start building it and improving it — that is the greatest pleasure. Sometimes people asked me: "Don't you ever get tired?" I said: "No, this is my hobby and my pleasure!" And it is of this work, and this life, I shall tell.

CHAPTER II:

Family origins 1800–1895

"Not by force of arms, but by influence
and rule of law from *spiritual* power"

I must start with the story of my great-grandfather, as it is through him that our family gained all its influence, and by him that the foundations for the State of Swat indirectly were laid — though he himself never wished to rule a state, and advised his own son against the attempt.

His father, whose name was Abdul Wahid, was of the small Safi tribe from the Mohmand area across the border in Afghanistan; and he settled somewhere in Upper Swat, where my great-grandfather, Abdul Ghafur, was born in 1795 or 1796. Perhaps his father died when he was a child — in any case, my great-grandfather left Swat and started studying religion.[1] He sought knowledge from different scholars — what we call *alims;* and ultimately he settled in Saidu, which was just a very small village at that time. He had a very good character, and wisdom, and knew the Holy Koran by heart. People came to him, and thought he was a Saint; so he was recognized as the Akhund of Swat. People started to come to him for advice, and he used to give them food also. For this reason, people with property would contribute to his kitchen, and after a while he became very well off because every tribe gave him some land, to support his charity. Today there are about 10 million people who still believe in him, from Swat and Dir all along the Frontier to South Waziristan, and in parts of Afghanistan, and also in the Frontier Province in Bannu District, and in parts of the Panjab.

Saidu Baba, as he is now called by the people, had many *sheikhs* (followers) and *murids* (disciples), and wielded great influence. And people used to tell him that they wanted peace and justice. "You will not become our Ruler, because we cannot follow your strict religious standards. But we can beg you please to find us a Ruler!" He answered: "It is very difficult here, because if I chose a ruler from one tribe, another tribe will be angry. And if he is from one faction *(dǝlla),* the other faction will not accept it. But there is a Sayyid, a descendant of Pir Baba,[2] his name

14

is Sayyid Akbar Shah — if you agree, we will bring him." Being of a Sayyid family living elsewhere he was neither identified with a particular tribe or a particular locality, and he was personally very pious and a very good man. So the tribes in Swat accepted Sayyid Akbar Shah as their ruler.

To administer the State he brought in people from his home area; and they did not behave well and did not always obey his orders. My great-grandfather used to request him to amend this or that — and Sayyid Akbar Shah would not listen. I don't remember how long he ruled, but it was more than a decade.[3] And when he died, his son wished to succeed him; but Saidu Baba did not wish to support him and told him it was up to the people of Swat to make the choice — and the people rejected him.

During Saidu Baba's lifetime, the British defeated the Sikhs and took over the administration of Panjab and Peshawar District. In the hills east of Buner there is the colony of Hindustani *Mujahidin,* and they made trouble across the border into the areas administered by the British. So in 1862 the British decided to punish the Mujahidin. To reach their village of Malka the British had to go through the Chamla valley; and the tribes of Buner would not allow them, and made a *jehad* (holy war). They came to my great-grandfather and requested that he should support the *jehad* — the people of Swat, Dir and Buner all gathered in the *Ambela* Pass and met the British Indian Army.[4] It was a great and unequal battle, but none was conqueror, and peace was made. But the British said: "For our prestige's sake you must allow a few people of our army to go to Malka and burn two or three houses, and we promise not to occupy it and go straight back again." So my great-grandfather accepted that agreement and the British abided by it and never made another effort. It was very wise of my great-grandfather to make peace with them. He was a very intelligent person, and understood the changes that were taking place and the necessity to make adjustments.

In 1877 Saidu Baba died, and Swat reverted again to anarchy. Saidu Baba left two sons; the senior Miangul Abdul Hanan, and the junior, Miangul Abdul Khaliq, who is my grandfather. The elder son aspired to become Ruler, as Sayyid Akbar Shah had been, but Saidu Baba never gave him any encouragement or help. The younger son, my grandfather, followed in the footsteps of his father: he lived in the mosque and kept the religious tradition alive, and as time went on he wielded great power in enforcing the Shariat (Muslim law) in Swat. His servants and retainers were called *sheikhs* also. They carried no arms; but when such a *sheikh* came to a village, *he* would sit on the bed and the Khans (tribal chiefs) would sit on the ground. When a murderer is executed for his crime in accordance with Shariat, it is called *qiṣṣaṣ;* and there were many cases settled by *qiṣṣaṣ* in Swat by his order. It was not by force of arms, but by influence and rule of law from *spiritual* power *(barakat).* My father told me that, if he had lived long, he would have *surpassed* Saidu Baba in spiritual power.[5]

But both sons of Saidu Baba died at the age of 35, with the same six years' interval that there had been between their births: Abdul Hanan died in 1887, and my grandfather died in 1893.

With the death of my grandfather, there were only four young boys left in our family of Mianguls: my father, Miangul Gulshahzada Abdul Wadud, who was only 11 years old, and his brother Miangul Abdul Manan, known as Shirin Sahib, who was 5 years old; and their cousins Miangul Abdul Razak, known as Said Badshah, 13 years old, and Miangul Abdul Wahid, known as Amir Badshah, 9 years old. My grandfather had served as guardian also for the latter two, and for their mothers, the three widows of his brother Abdul Hanan, one of whom was from a Sayyid family, the other a princess of the Khushwakht dynasty of the state of Chitral, north of the Swat valley, and the third from Jambil village.

My grandfather was also survived by his only wife, my grandmother, who was the daughter of the ruler of Chitral, Mehtar Aman-ul-Mulk, and half-sister of his successor, His Highness, Sir Shuja-ul-Mulk. With my grandfather's death our family property was divided. The large landed properties deriving from Saidu Baba, the Akhund of Swat, which my grandfather had partly owned, partly administered on behalf of his nephews, were now divided and allotted to each of the four boys. What is more, my father, being only 11 years old at the time of *his* father's death, had *no* religious education and was uneducated also in the sense of being illiterate. It was not till after his abdication and retirement as Ruler of Swat that he had the time to remedy this.[6] Thus the religious tradition from my great-grandfather the Akhund of Swat, continued by my grandfather, was lost; though the *influence* deriving from our descent from such a great Saint and scholar continued.

Instead of pursuing that scholarship, my father went into the civil wars at the age of 13, and became head of *one* of the parties or factions *(dalla)* in Swat, while my uncle soon was to become head of the *other* party.

But first my father had to gain effective control of his own property. My grandmother, as I said, was the daughter of such a prominent person as the Mehtar of Chitral; and so she wielded some influence over her son while he was a child, in the lifetime of my grandfather. At the age of

11 my father wanted to look after his land and manage his own affairs; but she did not want to part with that power. For a whole year my father waited — then he told the tenants and servants not to consult his mother as that was improper. Thus they had to report to him instead, and that gave my father all the power of management by himself! And when he later became Ruler, in 1917, he told his mother: "If you think that *you* can rule this country, then you should come out and rule it, and I shall be an obedient son and servant to you. But if you cannot do so, then please do not interfere in my affairs!" Thus he took over all property and power himself. But still, there were some occasional quarrels between them about some affairs; and in such cases I quite remember that my father reacted by cutting off his visits to her, and not going to see her for perhaps six months or even a year.

CHAPTER III:

The emergence of Badshah Sahib and the foundation of Swat State: 1895–1917

"The Swat people do not want to be
under anybody for a long time."

In 1895 events took place that fundamentally changed the political scene in the whole area. In the valleys west of Swat there had long been a few powerful Khans, among them Mohammed Sharif Khan of Dir.

Though his family had ruled from the village of Dir for many generations, he was not a recognized ruler and Dir was not recognized as a state by the British Indian Government — he was just a Khan, but a *powerful* Khan. In Jandul, west of Dir, there was another big Khan named Omara Khan. First he started raiding into Dir and for the next ten years progressively conquering territories from Dir, and finally Mohammed Sharif Khan was exiled. He came and took refuge in Mingora (the neighbouring and larger town adjoining Saidu). There is still a group of houses in Mingora called Dir Cham — *cham* or *mahalla* means quarter. I don't remember how long, but he lived for some time here; it must have been a year or two.

When Omara Khan took over Dir, the British Government sent him a letter of congratulation — congratulating him on his success and so on. So his advisers said: You should conquer Chitral, and the British will *again* send you congratulations. One of his advisers was an intelligent person, and he told him *not* to attack Chitral. The situation there, of course, was quite different: it was a recognized state, and there was a British garrison there.

The British sent him many messages not to do it, but yet he attacked and besieged the fort in Chitral, with the British representative in it.[7]

So the British sent two columns to the rescue: one from Gilgit, and the other via Malakand, up the Dir valley and to Jandul where the residence of Omara Khan was. The mullahs and religious people got excited and said we must not allow the British to go through Lower Swat; and the

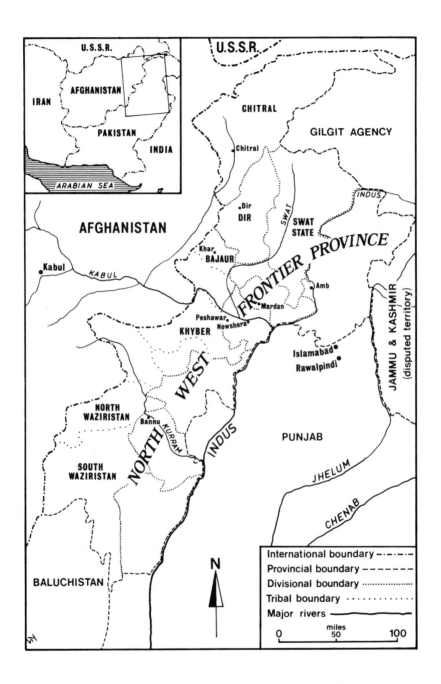

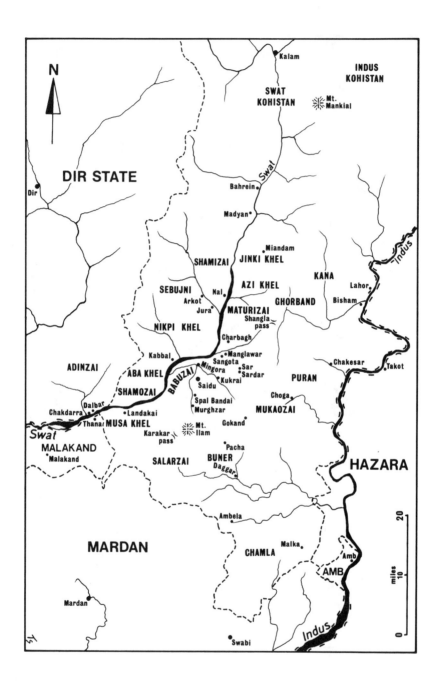

tribes were mobilized and there was a great battle at Malakand.[8] The British Indian Army broke through eventually, and entered and crossed the Lower Swat valley. When they proceeded towards Dir, Mohammed Sharif Khan went to the British and cooperated with them by bringing his whole *lashkar* (tribal army) in their support. So when Omara Khan was defeated, Mohammed Sharif Khan was reinstalled in Dir, and also given Jandul. And I do not remember exactly, but after a short while he was recognized and made Nawab, and given an annual subsidy of 50 000 Rupees by the British.

It is from *then* on that he became more powerful.

At the same time, the British also established the Malakand Agency, up to what later became the borders of Swat State, as a protected tribal area. Beyond that point, they left the Swat valley free and uncontrolled. They established their garrisons in Malakand, at the top of the pass leading into the Swat valley, and at Chakdarra, by the bridge that leads across the Swat River and gives access to the valley of Dir and the road to Chitral.

The Khans of Thana also cooperated with the British as the Khan of Dir did, so they were likewise rewarded with allowances. Even today, four of the big Thana Khans are still enjoying 3 000 Rupees a year. I think it was through the *jirga* of Mardan that the British had contacted them, telling them that their purpose was just to push through to relieve the garrison in Chitral. So those four or five people, who were intelligent, understood and cooperated. But the rest of the people — you cannot convince the masses — they fought.

After two years, in 1897, there was new unrest. There was a mullah in Fatehpur — some people call him Lewanai Fakir (Mad Fakir), or Sartor Fakir (Bareheaded Fakir) because he did not wear a turban. He raised a flag and said: "Let's go and make *jehad!*" The general public know nothing about fanaticism; but then they were just like sheep. When a fanatical mullah came out and preached and excited their sentiments to make *jehad* in Malakand, they merely followed. It was only the mullah who led them like that. Now I may be asked: then why did my great-grandfather fight *jehad* as he did in Ambela? The answer is, the British invaded Buner, and he wanted to defend the people; and then he made a *treaty* with the British and abided by it till his death. Many a time, people would come to him and say: "Let us make another *jehad!*" But he would answer: "For God's sake — the British are more powerful. Leave us alone — if they don't want to attack us, we will *never* fight."

21

Whereas the Lewanəi Fakir, he was just that: a *mad* mullah. He had no descendants, he had no tribe — so he played with the sentiments of the people, how we had been defeated two years earlier and must have our revenge. In that way, he raised a *lashkar* and attacked Malakand.

My father and his cousins also joined the *jehad* — my father did not actually do anything, he stayed behind the lines; but he felt compelled by the people to join, or else he would have been declared an infidel or something.

The *lashkar* was unsuccessful in the attempt at Malakand — the place was already occupied and well fortified, and the *lashkar* was defeated. The British pursued them up the Swat valley as far as Charbagh. They occupied Mingora and Saidu for several weeks. I don't know what their policy was — apparently they did not want to conquer it; perhaps they just wanted to show their flag. Afterwards, they went back. They came on foot, and they returned by way of the river, on rafts.

Meanwhile the people of Mingora and Saidu had fled and hid in the hills — not the shop-keepers and so on, but the Pakhtuns and especially the Khans, they went and hid in the small valleys all around. My grandmother also — she was taken to Murghzar for safety.[9]

Society in Swat before the inception of the State was more divided, in some ways, than it is now.[10]

There were not so great differences between poor and rich, but the land-owning classes belonged to different categories: one was Pakhtun and the other was the descendants of Saints like my family. Though they spoke the same language and in most respects lived the same sort of lives, their respective positions in society were different.

The common people — the craftsmen and labourers and traders — were their clients and tenants. The *Gujars* likewise, who keep water buffalo and other animals and are mostly hill people, were under the Pakhtun tribes.

The Pakhtuns of Swat are of the Yusufzai tribe; but there are some other tribes who came with them. The ancestor of Khan Bahadur of Jura was a Shinwari, and there are some others in Upper Swat who were Khattaks, and some of the Khans near Shangwatəi are from Bajaur. When the Yusufzai people conquered this valley in the sixteenth century they turned out the original Swatis, who were also Pakhtuns and came with

22

Mahmud of Ghazni. Some of them fled to Hazara and the Black Mountains, where they are landowners, and others became tenants here in Swat. Other Pakhtuns who lost their land have likewise become tenants. And there are also mullah families, and traders and others.

By virtue of conquest, all the land here became the property of the Yusufzai and their allies.

The houses of poor people also belonged to them — they used to pay a small rent of 2 Rupees a year. Even the shops were very cheap, they used to pay only 20–40 Rupees a year. Whoever lived in the house of a Pakhtun was called faqir = tenant, and he was that man's subject. And as a matter of honour, the Pakhtun was responsible for protecting his house tenants from the aggression of other people — an obligation we call *nangwali*.

In the Pakhtun villages, they kept men's houses or clubs, what we call *hujras*. The poor people had to contribute to the *hujra*, and sit in the *hujra* of their house-owner — a poor man could not frequent the *hujra* of another landowner.

But he was free to try to get the lease of land for cultivation from other landowners — that was his own affair.

All the Khans were of the Pakhtun category — the biggest landowners among them. But before the State, they used to live a very simple life: except for entertaining people, there were very few expenses in those days. There were no luxuries, such as bungalow houses and expensive clothing, or expensive habits of other kinds. So when they sat down to eat, the servants sat down with them, and they all ate together. In that sense there was no class difference — because perhaps the next day, they would be killed together in the tribal fights.

Though they did not have very great *personal* consumption, the Khans were very *spendthrift*. They used to spend all they had on rifles, cartridges, and also on entertaining to become popular. I don't think the biggest landowner then would have had as much as two thousand Rupees in cash — all their transactions were in kind: in land and grain and hospitality. But they kept hundreds of servants: Khan Bahadur of Jura kept 90 armed men, as servants and bodyguards; and Darmai Khan kept about 120 to 150. They were called *Tayar-khor*, meaning people who "eat ready-made food", who don't keep their own household but live as dependents around a Khan. So many of the Khans kept from 10 to 90 such servants as a private army, besides the followers they could amass in their *hujras* (men's houses).

In Upper Swat, where the Khans were more powerful, the other category, the Mians or descendants of Saints, were not aggressive; they were calm and quiet and had no power. But in the parts where they had power, especially in the side valleys like here, above Saidu, and in the inter-mountain valleys between Swat and the Indus, the Mian families were powerful and aggressive. Like the Sar and Sardari Mians — they used to come and raid the villages, even the big villages of the Pakhtuns, like Manglawar; and they raided our valley here, like Sheratrap. They looted the people and were like robbers. And they kept up the same standards of entertainment as Khans, even if they had no *hujras;* and they kept the same arms and cartridges and ammunition.

There was a certain Mian of Sardari, his name was Shah Madar. He was *very* famous for his generosity. What *he* did was to raid southward, to the Buner side, and take, for example, a few cattle — and if a man from Swat went to the Mian and said I have a marriage ceremony coming up, or I need a bullock to plow my land — then he *gave* those cattle to the man, as a gift. And then he would raid on the Swat side — and give to the Bunerwals! So he became very famous, for his generosity! He became the first Commander-in-Chief of my father's army, under my uncle Shirin Sahib, who also shared the central power more or less equally with my father, so Shah Madar was the Acting Commander-in-Chief, until he was killed in the war with Dir.

But there was one big difference, before the State, between the Pakhtuns and the Mian families, and that was in terms of land ownership.

When the Yusufzai conquered the valley, Sheikh Malli made the system of land tenure for the tribes: they did not permanently divide the lands that they had conquered, but made what we call *wesh*. By that system, all the land was redistributed every ten years between the branches of each tribe — so every ten years, all the landowners would move, and settle in the villages that had been allotted them for the next ten-year period, and divide those lands and houses between themselves. The Mians and other religious families, on the other hand, when *they* were given lands by the tribes, that land was called *siri* land, in permanent private ownership. So the Mian families did not move, but remained permanently on their own lands and in their own houses and villages.

It was a great spectacle when the Pakhtuns moved! All those people, with all their paraphernalia, some going up and some coming down the valley, and the tenants waiting in the villages, to meet the new landowners and masters who would be arriving! Sometimes the Pakhtuns occupied the *siri* houses of Mians and Sayyids, and turned them out of their homes for one or two months while they were settling the new allotment of lands and villages. Then, when that was all cleared, the Pakhtuns would settle in the new place, and let those Mians have their own houses back.

Before the State came into existence, might was right. So everyone had to join one or the other of the *dalla* parties, to have allies who would support him. Within the families, between cousins, there would be vendettas, and so the two sides would each align with opposite *dallas*. Even the Mians and Sayyids also belonged to one party or the other, and took part in the party feuds, and would kill each other. A story is told from those days, for example, of one of the Sar Mians, a young man, who killed a person from Sardari. He was of the same family, but of the other party; and the murdered man's sister was his wife. So when he came home to his house, he told her: "I have killed your brother. You can go for the funeral; and then after a month you can come back here!"

Most of all, people used to fight with their own cousins, or second cousins — what we call *tarbur,* which means both 'cousin', and 'enemy'. Before the State, when his rival or *tarbur* managed to turn a person out of his village, that person would have to take refuge in another village, with *his dalla.* So long as he was there, he was called *sharune,* exile. But people who were exiled usually were able to come back, within a year or two, as the other party would split and fall apart, and then *their dalla* would become the stronger.

In Western countries too, people may change from one party to another. Even Churchill once joined the Liberal Party, and then later he returned to the Conservatives. But in such cases, party loyalty changes in accordance with policy. If a man is of a determined mind, and a man of principle, then he changes his party loyalty because the old party no longer conforms to his principles. But here, both before the State and today, it reflects people's untrustworthiness, because it is done out of opportunism. If a man sees that his party may be going to fall — then he goes to the other party.

My father always used to say that during those first few years after he joined the civil wars, he received practical training which was to prove very valuable in days to come. At a time when others of his age would have been content to amuse themselves with games, he recruited retainers and had to be always alert and fore-sighted. To survive as a property-owner in an anarchic world, he had to develop qualities of leadership, foresight and decisiveness. Very soon, rivalries developed between himself and his cousins that tested his determination and intelligence.

His cousin Said Badshah was the first among them to cherish the ambi-tion to become Ruler — as had his father Abdul Hanan before him. Said Badshah was the eldest, about two years older than my father, and his mother came from a Sayyid family, so all the Sayyids were on his side, particularly the Mians of Sar. Said Badshah decided he would kill his brother and two cousins, all of them, so he would become sole owner of the property and subsequently become Ruler. But my father came to know about it; and he, and my uncle Shirin Sahib and their cousin Amir Badshah, all got together and killed Said Badshah instead.[11]

That was in 1903. My father had been married to Said Badshah's sister; but when Said Badshah was killed, she went back to her natal house, and shortly after that she died there. It was some illness, maybe pneumonia. Pneumonia in those days was very dangerous, since there was no medicine for it. She had only one daughter, who died in child-hood — I think she lived for about six months.

Said Badshah had one more sister, and she remained a spinster till her death ten years ago. When her sister went back, she on her part vowed she would never marry. And she lived a very pious, religious life. Later, my father used to go to her sometimes, and tell her to take some money, or some land. But she always refused.

After the death of his first wife, my father remained single, and he did not think of marrying at all. But then my grandmother insisted, and my mother was married to him. She was also from a Sayyid family, from Kukrai up the Murghzar valley. Actually, she was born in Zaida in Swabi, down in what was then Peshawar District; but they came and settled here. Because the family on my mother's side also had *wesh*. So they used to alternate in residence: for ten years my grandfather would be in Kukrai, then ten years down there in Swabi while his cousins and other relations came here. Although they were Sayyids, descendants of Pir Baba in Buner, they had *wesh* inside the family — uniquely, I don't know of any other example like that. But eventually, my maternal

26

grandfather asked his relations to make a permanent division and allotment. So they chose to settle in Swabi, and he settled here.

After Said Badshah died, his half-brother Amir Badshah inherited his whole property. He became wealthy — and so he developed the same aspirations as his late brother and father: to become Ruler. My father always told him that they should *not* hold such aspirations. But one of Amir Badshah's two wives was of a powerful Mian family in Jandul, and her family there egged him on. He bought horses, and formed a sort of cavalry of 20–30 armed men; but he realized that he could not become the Ruler unless he bumped off my father. My father was always very shrewd, and understood and could foresee things. So he acted first, and killed Amir Badshah on a hunting trip — right across the valley here, west of Saidu.[12]

Amir Badshah left two wives. *My* father did not believe in second marriages; but in those days it was *sharm* — shame and disgrace — to let a widow from one's own relatives go as a wife to someone else. So one was married to my father, the other to my uncle Shirin Sahib. My stepmother was hardly 14 or 15 when she was married to my father — I don't think she was of age even. By her, my father had two sons and four daughters; and my mother had two sons and two daughters. One was three years younger than me, but he died in childhood. One of my sisters died while she was married in Nowshera. The other one is still alive, married to Major Bahri Karam, the grandson of Shirin Sahib.

My father saw very clearly the importance, even at this early stage, of establishing good relations with the British. W.R. Hay tells in his little booklet (Hay 1933) how my father arranged once in 1903 to have a stolen government rifle returned to Chakdarra, without compensation — (though such things were very highly valued by the tribesmen then). He also attended the big durbar at Chakdarra in April 1905, on the occasion of the instalment of Badshah Khan as the new Nawab of Dir. And he always used to say that maintaining good relations with the British was a matter of first importance. But they were very shrewd, and remained suspicious for a long time.[13] When Sartor Fakir reappeared in 1908 and tried to make new *jehad* against Malakand, my father managed to stop him and disperse his *lashkar* peacefully; but still they remained suspicious.

In those days before the State, my father just kept his own private retainers; but compared to the big Khans even, he had more servants. He used to keep 160 armed men, and my uncle kept 140. My uncle said: You are the elder, you take more — so that made the difference of 20 servants. But at any one time, there would be only 4–5 present with my father, the rest of them would be in their own homes. When there were battles, they were called up to fight; and often there would be battles every month.

I do not think that my father and my uncle ever quarrelled; but they were divided in their real interests and they were leaders of opposite *dallas;* and so they fought against each other often, with their retainers and supporters. Yet the Babuzai and some of the other tribes kept asking my father and Shirin Sahib to become joint rulers — but my father always refused, because he did not believe in a diarchy whereby he and his brother were to divide the authority between them.

I was only ten years old when my uncle Shirin Sahib died, but I still remember his face very clearly. As for his character, it is not so easy for me to characterize him, as compared to my father. They were both very brave men; and Shirin Sahib died because he did not want to surrender. He was surrounded by the Dir forces, one to ten, and yet he would not surrender. Then he was killed. But otherwise he was *not* as religious and principled as my father. I can certify that he was not a fanatic, my father: never bigoted or fanatical; but he was strict in his observation of prayer and fasts. He never smoked, he never drank, he never took opium or any drug at all in his whole life. My uncle, on the contrary, was lax about praying, and he also smoked.

He was a big bulky person, and people admired him because of his physique, recklessness, and sociability. He mixed with everybody. He went to the *hujras* of the people, and he had a *great* sense of humour: always smiling and laughing.

He was very close with many of the Babuzai Khans, particularly Jamroz Khan, and he married Jamroz Khan's daughter, as his third wife: his first wife was his cousin, Amir Badshah's sister, by whom my children's mother was born; then his second wife was one of Amir Badshah's widows, who died shortly afterwards; after that he married Jamroz Khan's daughter, by whom he had only one daughter, who is married to my half-brother Sultan-i-Room.

Jamroz Khan was prominent, but his father Taj-al-Nur Khan was *more* prominent. And some people say, even within that family, that Taj-al-Nur Khan had the blessing of my great-grandfather, the Akhund of Swat, and *that* was why he rose to such power. To most people, he is popularly known as Malak Baba, out of respect — those in the first generation below him called him Malak Kaka, "Uncle Malak", and the next generation called him Malak Baba,[14] "Grandfather Malak". He became the greatest Khan of the Babuzai. After his death, his children split up. The sons from one wife — the first among them was Mir Abdullah Khan, the father of Nowsherawan Khan — they were of my father's *dəlla*. And Jamroz Khan and his brothers from another wife — Haji Nawab, Amir Nawab, and Said Nawab — were of the other *dəlla* — they were closely united. *Being* united, they had more power than my father's *dəlla* at that time (but see sequel pp. 67 ff.).

The eldest son of Malak Baba was from a third wife, his name was Janas Khan, and he was her only son. But being the son of a poor woman, he was never considered as a successor to Malak Baba.

Since he was alone, he could align with either side; and he and particularly his sons, who were of my generation, were very useful to the State.

As our neighbours, these Babuzai Khans were very important in the *dəllas* and thus in the battles between my father and my uncle. But more important for the long-term development of the State was what was happening on the right, or west, bank of the Swat river. On that side, some of the Khans were rather bigger and more powerful than they were on this side of the river, particularly in the territories of Shamizai and Sebujni, and several Khans of Nikpi Khel. But they were also divided by *dəlla,* and fighting each other and evicting each other. Meanwhile the power of the Nawab of Dir was growing, due to his recognition and subsidy from the British. So the losing party among those Khans started seeking help from the Nawab against the opposite *dəlla.*

In that way, the Nawab as ruler was brought into Nikpi Khel territory — not to rule so much, but to exercise influence, until both *dəllas* became fed up with his interference and turned him out. In one such period, in 1908, the Nawab also built a fort at Nal in Shamizai, which he garrisoned with his own troops, and later also at Kabbal, right across the river from here. Taj Mohammed Khan of Arkot in Sebujni likewise was very friendly with the Nawab of Dir and favoured him, whereas the Darməi Khan of Shamizai was of our *dəlla.* As the Nawab's interference increased, more people turned against him; and in 1914 all those Right Bank tribes rose in rebellion. It was difficult for them to unite behind Khans who were divided by *dəlla,* but by lucky coincidence there was a religious fanatic of considerable influence present among them at that time. He was born in the Chakesar area, in a village called Sandakai, and was known as Sandakai Mullah. He had travelled widely in pursuit of religious inspiration and religious study, and had settled for a while

29

in the village of Tahkal, close to where the University of Peshawar now stands. Then he went to Bajaur, where he installed the Khan of Khar as Nawab of Bajaur. How and why he came to Upper Swat I do not know — but once he came, many people became his disciples.

One of the Mians of Ningulai, a small village in Nikpi Khel, whom the Nawab had victimized, drew the attention of Sandakai Mullah to the oppression of the Nawab, and the discontent of the people, and how they needed a leader to overthrow the tyrant. So rather than continue to incite the people against the British, Sandakai Mullah gathered the people and stormed the Nawab's fort at Nal, while my father and uncle led the *lashkar* that took the fort at Kabbal, on the flats just across the river from here.

Thereupon all the people, and the elders and Khans gathered and again offered the rulership to my father and uncle, each as the leaders of their *dəlla,* to defend Swat against the Nawab of Dir. But my father again said "Impossible! There should only be *one* Ruler!" Thereupon Sandakai Mullah and those Khans brought in Sayyid Abdul Jabbar Shah of Sitana from Amb, to be their Ruler.

This Sayyid Abdul Jabbar Shah was the grandchild — the son of the daughter — of Sayyid Akbar Shah, the man who was made King of Swat by my great-grandfather the Akhund of Swat. He was about the same age as my father. I never met him here; but later I have met him elsewhere, many times. He was always very polite, rather a paternal-looking man. He was a good scholar and orator. But he was a stranger to these parts; and though he came, and very swiftly set up some kind of state administration, he never brought his wife and family here. I think he was not confident that he would remain here.

Sayyid Abdul Jabbar Shah made his centre at Kabbal in Nikpi Khel; but the tribes on *this* side also submitted to him. Now my father and my uncle were reconciled and joined together against him — because of the circumstances. Both Abdul Jabbar Shah and the Babuzai Khans put pressure on them, and they had to destroy all their forts in this area, except *one* fortified tower for each. And they were told by the *jirgas* of Swat that they must either pay allegiance to Abdul Jabbar Shah or leave Swat. My father and uncle refused to submit, and preferred rather to leave. So they went into exile to Dalbar, near Chakdarra, where we had some land inherited from my great-grandfather. That was towards the end of 1915.

To reduce our position further in my father's absence, Abdul Jabbar

Shah also supported a rival to our property, the Shaghalai Miangul or "False Miangul". The story behind this was as follows. Whereas my grandfather married only one wife, his brother, the senior Miangul, married several: the mother of Said Badshah of Sayyid family from Bara Bande in Nikpi Khel; the one of Khushwakht family who was mother of Amir Badshah; and a third wife, the daughter of a local person. That makes three — but he also kept another woman, a concubine whom he did not marry. But after he died, there was a child produced by this woman — several years later. Yet she claimed that she had this son by him, the senior Miangul; and when Abdul Jabbar Shah came, he brought this man out into the open, and supported his claim to his share in the property. Nobody took much notice and it made no difference. When my father came back, this man ran away and settled in Dir, on our lands there. Then my father gave money to someone, and had him eliminated. But his children are still there, and even now, after merger, they again claimed that their father was a Miangul and their grandfather was Abdul Hanan. But the government took no notice of it.

Abdul Jabbar Shah was made King of Swat in 1915. Our exile in Dalbar was a great setback to my father; I think he felt that he had been driven out into the wilderness; but he was always confident that he would come back. For this purpose he made an alliance with the Nawab of Dir, that they should attack Abdul Jabbar Shah together. We also had support from the Mians of Sar and Sardari. So the Nawab brought his army — but his ambition was only to conquer the Right Bank, and he failed to cross to the Left Bank and support my father. We did not know at the time that he could not cross to this side because there was a stipulation in his treaty of recognition by the British government that he would refrain from any interference across the Swat river: I think the British simply wanted to limit the potential growth of the state of Dir. But in any case, the Nawab brought pressure from that side, and the Babuzai were more inclined to accept my father. The *lashkar* of the Nawab came as far as Parrai, which is about 10 miles down the river from Saidu, on the other side. My father and my uncle, with their combined force of servants — hardly more than two hundred — crossed the river and fought a battle at Tindodag. Their opponents were not united, so the Babuzai fought very half-heartedly. Then my father dispatched his Wazir, Hazrat Ali, with some men across the hills just south-west of here, and occupied Saidu from behind. When the Babuzai forces discovered that, they melted away, and my father reoccupied Saidu and his properties here. And there was an understanding — not a treaty, but an understanding — between the *jirga,* Abdul Jabbar Shah, and my father, that he would rule this side and Abdul Jabbar Shah would rule the other side, on the Right Bank only.

Having re-established himself in Saidu, my father broke with the Nawab of Dir and joined Abdul Jabbar Shah in the defence of Swat against the Dir forces. But things were developing against Abdul Jabbar Shah. One reason was that he had brought many of his relations into Swat — none of his female relations, but men that he trusted more and used to staff his administration. And they did not behave well — they took taxes by force. The other reason, which was more important, was religious: it was discovered that Abdul Jabbar Shah was a believer in the Ahmadia sect. So Sandakai Mullah and other mullahs agitated against him — these people hate the Ahmadias and other heterodox groups: because they are all Sunnis in Swat. They told him: "Either you swear that you are not a believer in Mirza Ahmad, or you go." He said: "You brought me peacefully, you should send me peacefully, without molesting my relatives and servants." So they turned him out — peacefully.

I do not know how he was found out — but perhaps it was by the way he offered his prayers. Ahmadias pray at the same time as Sunnis, but there may be some deviation in the form of the prayer. Or else somebody may have come to know from Amb that he is Ahmadia. But in a sense, all this was an excuse, I think. Basically, the Swat people simply do not want to be under somebody for a long time. So I would say what they wanted was a change of person. And my father, being born and bred here, and being the leader of one of the *dallas,* he knew the temper of the people and how to tackle them.

So the big *jirga* of all the tribes gathered, first on this side and then across the river, at Kabbal, where the golf course is now situated. They tied the turban on his head and made him a King or Badshah. That was in September 1917.

CHAPTER IV:

My early life: 1908-1926

"He thought to make me strong and
self-reliant"

I do not myself remember the crowning of my father as Badshah, for I
was at school and have only heard his account of it. For several years,
already, I had been away from Swat most of the time, apart from summer vacations. It came about as follows:

My father had gone for a visit to what we call our *pirkhana,* that is,
the home of our spiritual leader in Torder in the Swabi subdivision of
Mardan district. Saidu Baba received his inspiration there, from Molana
Mohammed Shoaib. He was long dead of course, but my father wanted
to visit his *ziarat,* his shrine. This was in 1912 before the State was
founded, and there were no roads, and my father stayed near Mardan
with Nawab Mahabat Khan of Toru. There was this Molvi there visiting
him too, and they started conversing. The Molvi was a very good speaker — he was not a fanatical person, but he had a great deal of knowledge
about Islam. In practice he was not very particular, as I came to know
by being in his home; but that was later. My father was very much impressed with him. During the conversation, he also learned that a school
was going to be opened in Peshawar, by the British, for the people of
the Frontier. The school would be part of Islamia College, that is why it
was called Islamia Collegiate School; and this Molvi was to be the Dean
of the College. So my father said: "All right, I will send my son there to
study. Will you take care of him and keep him as your ward?" Being
impressed with the Molvi and seeing that in this way I could simultaneously receive religious instruction and English education, my father decided then and there. So that was the start of it — all settled during that
one evening. It was in 1913; I was five years old, and my father sent me
to Peshawar.

It was a very bold act on my father's part: to send his son away like
that, away from the world that he himself knew, and enrol me in an

English institution. Many people spoke to him, and pleaded for me, that I was too young, only five years old. But my father simply answered: "He is useless to me now, so let him learn to read and write; and when he becomes useful, he will help me!" That was his attitude.

In the beginning, my father made special arrangements for me — I was to live with the Mullah, and in that way I would also learn religion. But unfortunately, the mullah was very harsh. He was a good disciplinarian, but he gave us very bad food, and far too little. For eight years I was there. After four years, my half-brother Shah Room, who was four years younger than me, joined me. After five years my cousin Bahramand, Shirin Sahib's son came, and one year later also the sons of my father's Wazir joined us. We had very cramped quarters — I remember there were two rooms, each about 12 by 14 feet — and a small kitchen and a bathroom and a latrine, and a small storehouse for food and firewood. The mullah kept his wife at home in the village, but had a daughter staying with him to do the housework. And he had three sons, the youngest of them was my age. So the mullah lived with his elder sons in one room and the 4 or 5 of us boys used the other room. In summer we put our beds out in the courtyard; in winter we would sleep inside, to keep warm.

It is very bad to say bad things about one's tutor — but he was a great miser and did not give us enough food — very little milk, and meat only once a week. But one thing I must acknowledge: he treated us and his own children equally. He did not favour them; he gave us all the same food and the same clothing. So he was fair, by his own standards; he did not act from greed towards us as his lodgers.

It was a very bad time for me, because when one is a small boy one thinks the whole world is like that, one is unable to look ahead to something else and better. Whatever position you are put in, you accept it. And so I never dared tell my father how I was being treated. I was too afraid of him. Nor did I venture to tell my mother, because then I thought she would tell him. I think my mother knew it. But I would not complain, lest my father should think me insubordinate. My father was a strict disciplinarian. I cannot remember him ever kissing me, or taking me on his lap, although he did it with my brothers. But being the eldest, I think from the very beginning he thought to make me strong and self-reliant. So he treated me specially; and when I grew up he treated me like a friend or brother. And he was very happy when I was in his company, for an hour or two. He had great affection for me, and when I started developing the State he used to tell his intimates: "I made no mistake by giving him the State!" Simple words, but very gratifying.

My mother likewise had great affection for me — but she never spoiled me. I was her only son, yet she did not show much love or affection. She was a very simple, religious woman, and she truly submitted to God's will. When her first daughter died — she was about ten years younger than I — and when her mother died, and her father, and three brothers, she did not cry, though I could see tears in her eyes. She was so composed. She never embraced me, but kissed me sometimes.

Every summer and sometimes in the spring vacation, I used to come home to Swat; and for those two years while my father was in exile, I would come to him there, in Dalbar. The trip home was always full of excitement and anticipation. We went by *tonga* — the two-wheeled horse-drawn carriages that one still sees around — from Islamia College to the Railroad Station in Peshawar, then by train to Nowshera. There we had to change trains, to the narrow gauge line north to Dargai. From there again by *tonga* up through Malakand Pass to Thana village. We would reach there by the evening, and then spend the night in the *hujra* of one of the Khans of my father's *dalla*. Ponies were already waiting there — my father had sent them, and next morning we went on by pony-back, another six or seven hours to Saidu.

When we arrived we would go first to my father. He would be sitting, waiting in his house. And we would come, respectfully, and salute and give our salaams. After a while, he would say — "You may go and see your mother and grandmother." And they would be very much excited, and blessed us. Then after a while I would come back to my father's house, where we were given a room to stay.

For those two and a half months of summer holidays my father used to order me to bring a tutor, so I should not be idle. In the morning for two hours I had to study; and then we had lunch at 12 o'clock. Thereupon my father used to take us to the riverside for swimming. There were no roads, we had to walk for about four miles, then for an hour we swam, then marched back again. It was very, very tiring; we never had an afternoon rest or nap. And early in the morning my father used to wake me up for prayers. I had no chance of mixing with other people, playing or relaxing. The mornings with my tutor, then half an hour to see my grandmother and my mother, then lunch, and then with my father to the riverside, in the burning sun with an eight-mile walk, then food and so to sleep. All by order. It was very difficult for a small boy

— no choice, and sometimes I felt very tired, besides thinking that soon we will be back in Peshawar again.

Peshawar was worst during those first four years, while I was alone with the mullah. I remember once, there was an order from the headmaster that from now on, everyone should wear a school uniform — a Turkish coat, what we call a trenchcoat now. So I told the mullah, and he said "No. We shall see if we can make one, at a convenient time." After a while I was called before the headmaster: "Why do you not wear the school uniform as instructed?" I explained, and concluded: "What can I do?" He said: "All right, I will show you what." And he held my hands, palms up, and gave me two strokes on each with his cane. My hands were bruised and swelled up — then he said: "Go and show this to the mullah and tell him if he doesn't make you a coat, you will get more." That was the only time I was ever beaten by my teacher. I went to the mullah and showed him, and he said: "I am sorry. I will make you a coat."

I became very thin from undernourishment. For those months in summer, I would eat ravenously at my mother's house, but then it was back to the mullah's fare. When we woke up in the morning, he would give us one cup of tea, with one spoon of sugar and a little milk. That was our breakfast — no bread, nothing else. Then we used to have rice once a week, and meat once a week for our main course — *once* a week! Otherwise we were given some kind of cheap vegetables, and what we call *nan* — one small piece of unleavened bread. In the evening we had no tea — that cup in the morning was the only cup we had.

Some of the others in our school realized that I was being treated badly, and knew about me, I mean who I was. Even though my father was not yet a ruler, he was the grandson of the Akhund of Swat, and he himself had also made some sort of reputation. So they had pity for me and I felt it very much: to be pitiable! But fortunately I never asked anyone to lend me money or share with me — if someone had fruit or sweets or anything. It seems very strange, but nobody ever offered me fruit or sweets. I wonder why.

Now when I look back on it, it strikes me that such living must have been harmful: in childhood you need some nourishment, vitamins and healthy food, which can make you stronger for future life. I felt miserable. But in a way it was good training for me. I have known poverty, and I can understand what it is. If there is a small boy, and I see him there — shoeless, undernourished — I give him some money. Though I wish to help all who are genuinely in need — blind people, cripples, destitute or ill persons in hospital — it is for the small boys I feel pity.

Those first years, I was alone with the mullah's family; but there was his son there, of my age, and we were treated the same way and so there was some companionship in it — we shared our troubles, and grumbled about the food together. Then after four years, my half-brother also came. So the affection and love between brothers was some consolation for us both. Then a year after that again, my cousin Bahramand, the son of Shirin Sahib, joined us. When Shirin Sahib fell in battle, my father became the boy's guardian, and so he sent him to the mullah too. He was also unhappy there — once he became very tired of it and ran away. He was very young at the time, but he tried to find his way all the way home to Swat. He hid in the bushes here and there, as he went along, so he would not be caught. But then two miles this side of Nowshera there is a steep road-cutting, by Sar-i-Pul, and there was no other way, so he followed the road, and the mullah was pursuing and searching for him all the time, and he caught him there. Bahramand dared to do it because, whereas I was very afraid of my father, he was afraid of nobody, because he was an orphan.

I remember once the mullah went to Peshawar and stayed there overnight. His one son, who was the same age as us, myself, my brother and cousin, we made a conspiracy that we must enjoy this evening, since the mullah was away. It was winter — but we took our beds out and slept outside. Though we had our quilts, around midnight it became very very cold. So we brought out the floor carpet too, and put it over us; and till next morning we never went back into our room. That was our little celebration of independence.

Some people, I think, told my father that I was not being treated well. But he answered: "He is my son, not yours!" But our deliverance came one day. The last two years were shared also by the sons of my father's younger Wazir. His boys were twins, and only one year younger than I. They were also sent to the mullah. And I cannot describe their misery: they were treated *worse*. Instead of one piece of bread, they were given a half. Because they were twins, the mullah said: "Having been born at the same time, you should share everything!" So they got half rations, and became like skeletons. And we also commanded them, being three brothers and cousins against just the two of them, so they had two sets of masters.

Finally, they complained to their uncle, the elder Wazir — or rather

37

he asked them: "Why are you so thin?" and they told him. So the Wazir went to my father and reported how badly the mullah was treating us, and finally convinced him. The Wazir did it for his own reasons: he could not just take away his own nephews or my father would be annoyed and ask him why.

It was just before the summer holiday — and the mullah used to accompany us on our journey home. But this time one of my father's clerks, a very decent fellow, turned up and said: "I have come to take you away." We could not believe him, but he brought a letter to the mullah from my father saying that we would not come back to his house in the autumn. We could not believe it! We cried: "For God's sake, swear it is true!" And he swore that after the holiday we would not live with the mullah, but separately. In September when school opened, I was in the 9th class. So all the younger boys were put under my charge: my brother, my cousin, and the two sons of the Wazir. And I brought 4 or 5 boys of about my age, sons of my father's servants, to be our companions and servants, and I engaged a cook. So we had our two separate rooms in the hostel, and entertained some of our friends sometimes with meals.

The mullah was one of the Deans at the College, and we had to go to him and pay our respects and give our salaams to him now and then. He was not particularly angry with us — though he did not show the same affection for us that he had previously. For indeed, though he did not treat us well, he used to have affection for us — like he had for his own children. Except for those two Wazir sons: he disliked them, because he wanted more money. And the Wazir would not give him more but said "That is enough, you do not spend even that!" So he was always angry with the Wazir.

I spent eight years with the mullah, and another five years I spent in the College Hostel, attending the Islamia Collegiate School and studying up to the F.A. level. As time passed I developed some very good friendships with classmates, and three of them are still my very close personal friends; they come here and visit me still. Many others, who have had good careers and become prominent and influential persons in Pakistan, have gone through the same school, so we have known each other from the very beginning. I was very close to my half-brother, since we lived together for nine of those thirteen years and went through many things together, and I was responsible for him.

He was a very capable boy. His sister was given in marriage to the elder Wazir of my father; and the Wazirs had plans to persuade my father — not immediately, but future plans, together with some Khans who were also their relations — to make that half-brother of mine the heir apparent instead of me. But then he died at the age of 17, while he was still in college, of broncho-pneumonia. Fortunately for me, my father was there for the last three days to look after him — otherwise some people would have suspected something and spread harmful rumours that I had somehow been instrumental in his death. On the contrary, we were always on very good terms, and never became *tarboors*. But after he died, and after some time I and the ministers became like *tarboors*.

When my father was made Badshah of Swat by the *jirgas* in 1917, I was only nine years old. And for the next few years, he was very busy building and defending the State. His army fought against Dir, and against Abdul Jabbar Shah, who had returned to Amb and was made minister by the Nawab and who tried to annex Buner on behalf of the Nawab of Amb, and against the Khans and Mians. The fighting with Dir was very severe, and lasted for four or five years.

There were battles every year; sometimes for a month, sometimes two, sometimes they lasted for six months. It was trench warfare with each side continually manning and holding their lines. It went on like that for six months.

Meanwhile I was living my life at school, and with the mullah. I knew of course what was happening in Swat, but it was not something I could participate in, and the thought that I might do so never entered my mind at the time. I knew that my father wanted me to be educated, and so I was there — that was all. I had no feeling about how the state was run, and what would happen.

The realization, the consciousness that I might some day become his successor as Ruler of a State, only came when my father declared me Waliahad — heir apparent. But the British did not recognize me till 1933; my father did it in 1923, after his conquest of Buner. He summoned all the *jirgas* of Swat and declared to them that it was his wish and intention to make me his Heir Apparent, and he asked them their opinion. And they all agreed. It was in June, I had come home for the summer vacation, and the *jirga* gathered in the big hall in my father's old residential quarters. The house is now demolished — it stood close to where the house of my eldest son, Aurangzeb's house, now stands. It contained a big hall, about 20 by 100 feet, and all the tribal elders were sitting there. They tied the turban around my head. It was a very simple affair: the head qazi tied the first loop of the turban, and next the Darmᴈi Khan did it. But then every Khan said "I will also tie one knot!" and so the turban grew so heavy I could hardly hold my head up; it was swaying back and forth. For that reason I could not even understand the words I read as my speech of acceptance: the first speech in my life. Even today I cannot remember the words. But I must have promised that I would obey my father according to your wishes — something like that. I read it out, and I must have said the right things — because it was a written speech.

This was a great moment for me, naturally. And I had no one to share it with, no one who could give me confidence and support. I knew very few people in Swat, and when I returned to Peshawar, I had only very few friends — I mean friends who were personally close. There were one or two of my classmates, whom I told what had happened — and they congratulated me, and were very happy for me. So I told them that the greatest responsibilities were going to face me in the future, and that I didn't know how I should be able to handle it. They said "Don't be afraid" and so on — but I do not think they really understood, and that made me feel lonely.

But I was happy, as a boy, to get education and knowledge. When I was 13, and we moved into the hostel, my father put me in charge of my brother and those other boys. I do not want to boast about it, but at the age of thirteen I was commanding 5 or 6 boys and 4 or 5 servants; and that was good training for me.

My favourite subjects in school were mathematics, and history. I stood first or second in history, and about the same in mathematics. I was interested in many things, but in proper subjects, not just amusements. When I went to the cinema, I wanted to see some historic pictures or war pictures ... Arabic was also one of the subjects my father told me to take — so I learned Arabic, not so I spoke it fluently, but well enough to understand. I read it for four years, starting from the 9th class. And later, when I came back to Swat after finishing school, there was not any special work to begin with, so I had a Molvi whom I employed, and he used to teach me, for one hour every morning, for the subsequent seven years. And I read widely. My father wanted me to have *both* Islamic education and English education. Despite his background, he was very liberal. He used to tell me: "You are more conservative than I

40

am". He had a very open mind. He believed in his religion, but he liked things to develop, so he encouraged English education also.

In sports, I was fond of tennis. I started playing tennis, and I did well for the college, by winning the cup along with Aman Khan as my partner from Edward's College. It was great entertainment for us, what we call *tamasha,* when the Chief Commissioner came and distributed prizes. We had a good time.

In 1925, when I was 17, I was married. Like all marriages at that time, it was an arranged marriage. She was my first cousin, the daughter of my uncle who died in the battle against Dir. She was younger by two and a half years than I. We were married in March, when I came home for the spring holidays; my father arranged the marriage. It was a very simple affair, like all the marriages in our family. There were no *tamashas,* or celebrations. A mullah was called, and my cousin took the consent of his sister and I gave my consent, and the mullah recited a few verses from the Holy Quran with prayers for success. Then I went back to Peshawar, but came to Swat again for the summer vacation in June. Next March I did not come for the spring vacation because my final examination was quite near, so I had to prepare for that, and also for the tennis championship. I tried my best, and succeeded in both, before returning to Swat for good in May 1926.

Our first child, Aurangzeb, was born on the 28th May 1928. I was very happy to have a son, but I was feeling very shy. I made a trip to Muree. A telegram came there that a boy had been born. My mother and grandmother were so happy. My (paternal) grandmother felt more intimacy and affection for me than for any other grandchild — I was lucky to have her blessing. I was more close to my grandmother than I was to my mother — because I was her first grandchild.

My graduation from school in the early summer of 1926 coincided with the formal ceremony when the British recognized my father as the Ruler of Swat — in his personal capacity. I finished my exam by the end of April and came home on the 1st of May; and the Durbar in which my father was recognized was on the 3rd of May 1926. Ataullah, who later became Chief Secretary to my father and then to myself, served as a sort of majordomo of the ceremony. He had come to Swat first in 1923, while he was a student in Law College, as my tutor in place of a more senior person, Professor Abdur Rahim, who was supposed to have come, but was prevented. Ataullah was from Gujranwalla District in Panjab, and he spent the summer learning Pashto, and teaching us English — not so much, because my cousin was very naughty and would always make fun of him. Next year, Professor Abdur Rahim came — he was a very respectable person and a great philosopher. But when I was about to go back to College, my father said: "Next year, why don't you bring that fellow again, that young Ataullah?" So in 1925 I brought him here again. And my father took a liking to him; and later, he told me: "You tell him that if he can get a job elsewhere, that's all right, but otherwise, he can come and be my secretary." So I wrote to him while he was in Lahore at Law College, and he wrote back: "Why should I waste my time in Swat — I will practise law and earn more money here!" But he was a shy fellow, and when he appeared in court, he could not speak. So after a while he wrote to me, to say that if the offer still held, he would come. He started on a salary of 150 Rupees a month, which was reasonable pay at that time. He arrived about the middle of April, two weeks before I came. He made all the arrangements for tents and furniture for the Durbar. Afterwards, he took service with us. My father trusted him, and I trusted him very much. I am sorry to say, in the end after the merger of the State he proved less than loyal. But for many years he worked very closely with me. In due course he also became a very rich man, a multi-millionaire, developing very good business here, and then spreading out into Muzaffarabad, Azad Kashmir.

The Durbar at the recognition of my father was a very big affair. All the elders of Swat came, and officials and prominent people from the Frontier Province. The ceremony was held under a great awning or canopy, what we call *shamiana*. Big tents were put up for the night. So many people came that they could not all stay overnight, as there was little accommodation. So the British representatives, led by the Acting Chief Commissioner of the Frontier Province, Col. J.W. Keen, arrived in the morning, installed my father, had lunch, and then went back. But the other notables from the Province, like Sir Abdul Qayyum and the Nawab of Hoti, stayed the night here.

From then on, my father decided he wanted me to stay here in Swat. My only regret, which I felt keenly, was that I have not been educated more — but the circumstances were such that my father was alone. He had his two ministers, but after all I was his son. So he wanted me to be trained here, in local politics, rather than sending me to U.K. He was very broadminded, but he did not believe that foreign education would be much good here. And I still think, and always have suffered from this mentally, that I should have graduated from Oxford or Cambridge.

CHAPTER V:

The Consolidation of the State of Swat: 1917-1926

> "The Government does not want to create another Afghanistan on our northern borders"

It was a long and uncertain path which led my father from the triumphant moment in 1917 when the *jirga* acclaimed him as Badshah to the formal Durbar in 1926, when the British recognized him as Ruler. In the intervening years he had been forced to meet a number of challenges to his authority and to the State's very existence, both from without and within; and he had worked to design and build up a structure of administration and communications to realize the State, and a network of political relations between the State and its surroundings. There were moments when the fate of Swat seemed poised in the balance.

The first and greatest threat was posed by Dir. The Nawab of Dir continued his attempts to gain control of the areas on the Right Bank of Swat, and still had his partisans among the tribesmen there. The Nawab's party held Shamozai, in the south, and also the area of Adinzai beyond it, surrounding Chakdarra, to which my father laid claim. In the autumn of 1917 my father had news that the Nawab of Dir and Abdul Matin Khan of Jandul, the son of Omara Khan, had fallen out, and he took the opportunity to regain Shamozai, though he failed to proceed farther and conquer Adinzai. In the spring of 1918, he resumed his attacks; but by autumn the Nawab of Dir returned with a considerable force, supported by his *dalla* within that part of Swat and also by a *lashkar* led by the Khan of Khar (who ruled a territory beyond Jandul and was a natural ally of the Nawab). My uncle Shirin Sahib was in command on this front, stationed in a fort in Khazana in Shamozai with a small garrison. The fort was surrounded by the Dir forces, and though the garrison fought bravely with great losses, they finally had to surrender. As Shirin Sahib was led away as prisoner, he was shot by one of the Dir tribesmen. The main Swati force, led by my father, arrived shortly afterwards but were unable to dislodge the Dir forces and were obliged to give up the whole of Shamozai. However, several religious leaders friendly to my father, who were in the territory of the Khan of Khar at the time, heard this news and managed to incite the people of those parts against their Khan. He was thus forced to return with his *lashkar* to Khar, and for this reason the Nawab of Dir did not pursue his success further.[15]

The following year of 1919, the Nawab again attacked, but was repulsed by

43

my father's unexpected tactical use of cavalry. But then in August, again supported by his old *dalla* within Swat, the Nawab crossed over the mountains further north and entered Upper Swat, into the Sebujni-Shamizai valley with a large force.

He conquered the area all the way down to Matta — until suddenly he had news that Abdul Matin Khan meanwhile had attacked Dir. So the Dir *lashkar* tried to withdraw, in unorganized fashion, at night, to reach Dir as quickly as possible. But somehow the Swat people came to know and fell on them in the passes, capturing their arms and horses and everything.[16] Our *lashkar* then went and reconquered Shamozai, and also took Adinzai. After that, fighting continued for several years in the Adinzai area, ending in a long trench war.

Meanwhile, the deposed Abdul Jabbar Shah had returned to Amb State, and was made Chief Minister there. He convinced the Nawab of Amb that this was the opportune moment to extend that State's territory into Buner. His idea was to create a base and then conquer Swat for himself.

When Abdul Jabbar Shah attacked with the *lashkar* from Amb, we had no men to spare — the elder Wazir was in command of a big force near Chakdarra against the Nawab of Dir, and the rest of our forces were facing Dir forces in Nikpi Khel. So my father could send only about 80 people — but he mobilized the people in Aba khel and Musa khel, and they defeated the Amb forces. Abdul Jabbar Shah with his *lashkar* came all the way to Karakar — the steep and narrow pass between Buner and Swat; there he was defeated by our people.

Buner was not conquered by force — *jirgas* came in to my father a year after the battle at Karakar, and declared their wish to join the State.

The Khans in Buner were not very strong, and there are many small tribes and branches. But they were all aligned in two *dallas,* and my father was connected with one *dalla* while Abdul Jabbar Shah was intriguing with the other *dalla.* But the people became tired of the interference from Amb, and so in March 1922 their *jirgas* came and invited my father; so he sent a force and took over the area without a shot being fired, and constructed forts in the central places there.

Sometimes, my father had to field two or three armies at the same time, on different fronts.

But the battles were not so large, measured by the number of soldiers involved at any one time. And in much of the fighting, as for example

44

against Amb, all the people of Swat were united behind my father. On the other hand, during the four or five years of fighting against the Nawab of Dir, he had his *dalla* there on the Right Bank, and sometimes the other *dalla* ran away and fought on that side, and sometimes they were hesitant behind the lines. Generally, the *lashkars* were of the order of one thousand men, say from 800 to 1500. But if the battle lasted for too long, people got tired and went back to their homes. Then my father would have to send more people. That is why it is called a *lashkar* — in a *lashkar* everybody is independent and not organized; they provide their own supplies and fight as long as they themselves wish.

The valley we call Mukhozai, which lies north and east of the main valley of Buner, fell to my father in 1923, along with Buner. This led to a conflict with one of my father's long and close allies, inside his own *dalla,* namely Mian Hamzal-lah of Sardari.

The Mians of Sar and Sardari controlled the high hills between the Swat and Mukhozai watershed; but they were divided by *dalla:* Mian Hamzal-lah and the other Sardari Mians were of my father's faction, while the Mians of Sar were in my uncle Shirin Sahib's *dalla.* So when the State was established, my father told my uncle that they could not keep these two local *dallas* equal, or they would fight all the time: one must be in the more powerful position, one in the lower position. By his tact and reasoning, my father convinced Shirin Sahib that these Sardari Mians were more trustworthy than the Sar Mians, and should be favoured. Now the Sar Mians were holding by force the hamlet of Sheratrap, which belonged to the Mians of Spal Bandai. There were some other considerations too, but mainly for this reason those Sar Mians were ex-pelled. They took refuge in Buner. After a while, when the battle of Shamozai was fought, with my uncle in command, they went there and joined the Dir forces. Shah Madar of Sardari, who was my uncle's second-in-command, was killed there by the Sar Mians — they caught him and shot him. And then when my uncle was being escorted from the fort after surrender, he was also shot — but that was by a person in the Dir *lashkar,* whose brother had been killed in the battle just an hour earlier, and who took his revenge on Shirin Sahib. After that, the Sar Mians returned to Buner; and when Buner was conquered they went to Amb, and from Amb they went to Chakesar and took refuge there and fought against us till Chakesar was conquered.

Meanwhile, my father wanted to counteract their influence; and as he

45

believed in feudalism he always did that by supporting another big man, a Mian or Khan, so as to rule through him. So he supported Mian Hamzallah of Sardari very strongly, and Mian Hamzallah came to him and said he wanted to collect the year's tithe, what we call *ushur,* for the whole mountain area from Karakar to Shangla; and my father agreed. But this made Hamzallah ambitious, and finally he sent a message to my father and said: "When you help me and conquer Purun, you must give that to me. Plus the Gokand valley; and Mukhozai — all three. The rest — you can have." That was a challenge to the authority of my father, and he would definitely not agree. But he called Mian Hamzallah here to Saidu for negotiations and compromise — though he was not prepared to compromise at all. My father arrested him immediately on his arrival, and put his nephew in his place — to become head of the Sardari Mians.

After that, those Sar Mians approached my father through some Khan of Chakesar, and asked to be allowed to come back — on any condition he might impose. And he let them have high jobs in the Army: Shazad Gul, the Sar Mian, was made Naīb Salar, and his son Badshah Gul succeeded him after his retirement as Naīb Salar. The downfall of the Sardari Mian occurred because he became over-ambitious. He wanted to become semi-independent. But he was not an intelligent person. He was powerful; but not clever enough. There are only a few cases of this kind of internal struggle, arising from greed for power, here in Swat. In European history, you see it so often — between the Dukes and Princes of Germany, and then Bismarck came. Here, usually, the conflicts are between persons with opposed interests, who are rivals — not internal between those with common interests. Though it does happen, sometimes, everywhere.

One result of this conflict with Mian Hamzallah, however, was that the *dəlla* of the Sardari Mians among the independent tribes further west in the hills, in Puran, Ghorband, Chakesar and Kana, collected and attacked the new fort at Choga in Mukhozai. But they were repulsed, and my father's forces advanced and occupied Puran while he sent a *lashkar* from Upper Swat to seize Ghorband, with assistance from his own *dəlla* there; while Kana and Chakesar were left independent for the time being.

Now in the days before the State, there was a big Khan in Kana, his name was Pirdad Khan, and the other *dəlla* there exiled him. So he spent a year with my father, in Saidu. He was a very intelligent man.

After that year, he managed to get back to Kana; but then shortly after my father conquered Puran and Ghorband, Pirdad Khan and his *dəlla* asked my father for help. So Badshah Sahib sent an army there — but before going into Kana they suddenly and unexpectedly turned south and entered Chakesar, which was taken by surprise and conquered without a battle, and afterwards they went on to Kana.

There, Pirdad Kahn's opposition ran away and sought refuge in the Black Mountain area, across the Indus. Thereupon, Pirdad Khan was given full power in Kana by my father. Elsewhere, my father always sought to maintain both *dəllas,* so they would balance each other and the influence of the State be secured. But in Kana my father made Pirdad Khan *tahsildar,* and he was a Khan with full powers. His sons and nephews were made subedar and subedar-major. Ever since then Pirdad Khan and his brothers amassed more wealth, and bought more land. Now both he and his brother are dead; but their descendants own one third of all the land in Kana. My father did that because he trusted Pirdad Khan, as he had lived with him for a whole year, and they had talked about all these things and were agreed.

During the first year or two of the State, Sandakai Mullah — who had first supported Abdul Jabbar Shah as king and then driven him out as an Ahmadia — gave his support to my father. He lived as a Pir in Upper Swat, in Sebujni and Shamizai, and had great influence — even Khan Bahadur Sultanat Khan of Jura was his disciple. He never interfered in other parts, but there he interfered, and even had his own Shariat Court and inflicted punishment on people. My father has told me what he did and how he reasoned. He could not kill or destroy the Sandakai Mullah, because all the people of Upper Swat — rather most of the Khans there — were very much in his favour. So my father told one or two persons to go and visit the Mullah, and confidentially let it be known to him that Badshah Sahib was going to kill him. My father deliberately did this — to scare him away. His policy was that he was not so afraid of an enemy who lives outside the State as one who lives inside the State. Though nobody tried to harm the Mullah or catch him, he ran away to Dir. After that he went to Indus Kohistan, to incite those people against us. But shortly after going there, he died a natural death. He had no descendants — I don't think he was married.

My father always used to tell me as advice, that a Pir and a Ruler cannot last together. So one, and one only, should be the Ruler. And if you are the Ruler, you have to limit the influence of the Pir. And if you can't remove his influence, you can at least remove him. When he created the State, he chased out all those Pirs who used to exercise political influence over the people.

In Jinki Khel, the northernmost Pakhtun tribe on this side of the river towards Kohistan, there was a fairly powerful Khan called Habibullah Khan. He was of my father's *dalla* and had a fort at Miandam, which my father allowed him to keep.

He was disloyal to my father and double-crossed him — but he was not a very intelligent person, not even mediocre. He had a dream of making the area of Miandam, and the Upper Swat valley around Madyan and those parts, into a separate state and to become a ruler of that state. He wished to create it with the help of my father, to conquer Bahrein and then keep it for himself. My father said: "How can I give you my state?"

While we were fighting the Nawab of Dir in Adinzai, Habibullah Khan of Miandam raised a *lashkar* from Kohistan and attacked my father's fort at Madyan; and at the same time Abdul Jabbar Shah was advancing towards Karakar. So it was some months before my father had time and people to spare to drive Habibullah Khan out of Churarai; and he let him keep his place in Miandam. Some years later, as I shall describe in the next chapter, Habibullah Khan again turned against my father and joined the sons of the Darmai Khan in an attempt on my father's life. When they failed, he fled with them to Dir.

Much of his land around Miandam he had usurped from the Gujar people. When he ran away, my father returned that land to the rightful owners. Eventually, my father allowed him to come back; and with little land left he had little income to sustain him. He used to come often to me. But he was very simple. Even with that *small* land, he used to keep a retinue of 20 or 30 servants. My father advised him that he did not need to employ so many people, "because you are being protected by *me* now. Five or ten servants are more than enough." But he said: "No. I have *given* them this land (as fiefs), and they will live on that as long as I live. I don't want anything — just two square metres for my grave." So he would not dismiss those people, or retire them. It was a matter of old-fashioned honour, what we call *Pukhtunwali*.

As time passed, my father expanded and strengthened the State, over those first years. The British were watching, they kept themselves informed; and they also had their own interests. First, there was the Adinzai fighting between us and Dir.

The road to Chitral passes through the Adinzai area, and the armies were fighting there.

The British thought that this road should be safe and open; and after a period, when the war there became trench warfare, they told my father that he should vacate that part of the land, and they would guarantee that the Nawab of Dir would not wage any further wars. Unless two thirds of the people of the Right Bank of Swat wanted the Nawab to come back, *and* they obtained permission from the Political Agent, the Nawab would not be allowed to invade Swat. So there was a slight weak point in the agreement — but only theoretical, it could never happen.

In 1922, that agreement was made — not with the Nawab of Dir, but with the British. How they conveyed their decision to the Nawab I do not know. Nawab Badshah Khan was a very tough, brave, and intelligent man. He listened to nobody. He was illiterate, and a leper too. At that time, his elder son Shah Jahan was heir apparent; and the second son, Alamzeb Khan, was Khan of Jandul province. To check the Nawab, my father had an oral agreement with his second son, and also with the Khan of Khar — he was *not* Nawab but he used to call himself so. My father used to pay subsidies to those two in those days: 4000 Rupees to Alamzeb Khan and 5000 Rupees to the Khan of Khar, yearly; and in case there was a dispute between us and the Nawab those two would support us.

In that way, my father sought to build up his strength against the Nawab, but as it turned out it was the agreement made with the British that was most important.

At the time, the agreement on Adinzai in 1922 did not seem favourable. But it became favourable — as it increased the Government of India's confidence in my father and contributed to his formal recognition (see below, pp. 59 f.). It also secured him towards the West but left the way open to the South and East, so it gave my father the chance to take Buner and Ghorband, Kana, Chakesar and those parts.

But then, as he expanded his State so rapidly, the Government of India became concerned about that. And because of the other *dɘlla* in Kana who fled across the Indus, and because Baradar Khan of Takot, who held lands on both sides of the Indus, was opposing us, my father became involved across the Indus, in the Black Mountains. And these were the words of the then Political Agent, H.A.F. Metcalfe. He called the elder Wazir to Malakand and told him: "The Government *does not want* to create another Afghanistan on our northern borders. You *must* retire, and not cross the Indus". He thought that if my father were also to become ruler of the Black Mountain area we would become too big. So the river Indus was set as the limit.

From the very beginning, my father wanted to establish good relations with the British. But they were always suspicious because his grandfather — and he himself, a little bit — had been involved in *jehad*. But his attitude was always friendly, because he was a very intelligent person, and politically he could foresee things. By opposing the British we could gain nothing. By cooperating with them he might survive and also gain something. There was never any direct help from the British — neither with money or other finances, or even 50 or 100 rifles, or anything of that sort. But I think they *looked favourably,* not encouraging him but looking favourably, at the fact that he was establishing himself, and thereby would make this part of the frontier safer for them. Materially, and morally, they gave nothing. The Nawab of Dir received 50,000 Rupees subsidy and was attacking us, and they gave nothing to us. But there was that stipulation that he should not cross the Swat River. When they stepped in in 1922 and stopped the fighting, my father was still not recognized. They were too clever; they thought he might be bumped off, or overthrown by other people. Even when my father was recognized in 1926, he was recognized *in his personal capacity* only. Because they did not know whether I would be able to be tough like my father, or whether I would be soft, being educated. Not until 1933 — on the 15th of May — did the British Government recognize me as heir and successor — and that was again in my personal capacity only.

The difficult job was really done by my father, in the beginning. As Swat people were very brave and disobedient, he had to tackle them carefully. If someone committed a crime, and my father fined him, then all the culprit's friends in the *jirga* would come and say: "You must not take this fine from him." So if my father had not shown his force of character at that time, he would surely have had a rebellion. My father had to show fierceness and ruthlessness in the beginning. Then, after two or three years, when he had established himself in Saidu, the time came when he started going around to the *hujras* of the Khans, especially in Upper Swat. He used to spend two months there in the summer — not for the season's sake, but for going to this Khan to persuade him to do this, then another Khan to persuade him to do that, seeking by persuasion to extend his influence. And, when he felt strong enough, he ruled. And I inherited the ready-made thing.

My father always believed in maintaining the two *dallas,* or parties, and basing his power on the balance between them. One *dalla* was a little bit weaker, and one was his favoured *dalla.* And so it was sort of divide and rule. Whenever the upper *dalla,* the favoured one, made too great demands on my father and suggested something that was impossible and against his interests, then he would give a lift to the other *dalla* and favour them for a while.

The first seeds of my father's administration go back long before the days of the state. From the very beginning of his career, he needed someone who could be his scribe — and there was no one in all of Swat who was able and willing.

So the man who later was to become his Chief Minister, the eldest Wazir, saw the chance and told my father: "Please, let me go to Thana village and learn to write." In a year or two, he learned to write a little Persian — because in those days all correspondence was in Persian. Urdu came afterwards; and then my father introduced Pashto, which I continued. But of course with the outside, the Government of India and later the Government of Pakistan, we have always corresponded in English.

My father had messengers, especially trusted messengers, for carrying letters to Khans and other allies elsewhere. He sometimes sent messages by word of mouth; there were two or three persons who were very, very loyal to him — most loyal I would say. Everybody knew that; so from them they always took the messages verbally, and people trusted them. But otherwise, my father would have his scribes write the message, and he would seal it himself — and the persons who received the message would have their scribes who could read it.

The most trusted messenger of all was a man who had converted from Sikhism — so he was called Shaikh, i.e. convert. His father was born in Rawalpindi but later settled here; and then the boy picked up Pashto like a native speaker. He remained always very loyal. My father sometimes told me stories about him. Once, long before the State, my father was given permission by the Political Agent in Malakand to import shotgun cartridges: my father was always very fond of shooting, but the British were always very reluctant to allow cartridges into the tribal areas. Now at that time, Odigram and Kambar were occupied by the other *dalla* and so they barred the way from Malakand — and my father was wondering how he could get this very heavy box with a thousand cartridges brought to Saidu. And then this Shaikh brought the whole box on his shoulder over the hills and through the high pass into the Guligram valley. My father was so delighted, and gave him *bakshish*. Another time, the Shaikh was sent to Dir with a message to the Nawab. And he came back very tired, having run on foot through the mountains — they mostly went on foot, to be able to pass by the shortest track and relatively unobserved. My father immediately had an urgent answer to the Nawab. And the Shaikh looked at him, and asked: "What are you thinking?" My father told him: "This is what I must say urgently to the Nawab, and I don't trust anyone else but you..." "Truly?" said the Shaikh — and volunteered to go right back with the new message.

His sons were employed by my father as bearers, according to their ability. Eventually, the Shaikh came to my father and said "I am growing old, I am losing my eyesight, I want to retire". So he was given a pension, and the pension was the full pay of a soldier, besides employing his sons. He used to come to me sometimes, and take me aside, and reminisce; and I would give him money, or clothing. But he was a very contented man — he did not aspire to become rich or influential, only wished to remain loyal.

The first beginnings of a state administration were created by Abdul Jabbar Shah when he was elected to rulership in 1915. He set up an army, and he started collecting *ushur*, i.e. land revenue. Previous to this, the tribes had twice asked my father and Shirin Sahib to be rulers — and my father had refused (cf. *The Story of Swat*, p. 33).

There were several reasons for that, but one reason, he told me, was that he saw no way of paying for an army, and collecting *ushur*: "I would have to buy at least 2000 rifles, and I had no money for that." But when Abdul Jabbar Shah became Ruler, he told everybody that "Anyone who produces 20 armed men, I shall make him a *jamadar*. And anyone who can produce 100 men, will be made a *subedar*" — and so on. So my father said: "I had no idea of such things. People brought their own arms, and they were just given the pay. This whole idea I learned from Abdul Jabbar Shah". The collecting of *ushur* likewise was started by him, though he could not collect from everyone within the year or two that his rule lasted. In any case, the system was his. I once heard my father say, jokingly: "Do you know what I thought of Jabbar Shah, and what he thought of me? He was a very intelligent person, and a good writer and orator. I thought: 'I wish I were Ruler and he were my prime minister!' And as for Abdul Jabbar Shah, I imagine *he* thought: 'I wish that I should be ruler and he, that brave man, be my commander-in-chief!'"

Abdul Jabbar Shah brought in his own people as key persons in his administration, and he let the army collect the *ushur* directly, as Sayyid Akbar Shah had done in the nineteenth century when he was King of Swat.

But that way, half of it went into the pockets of those who collected it. So my father decided to change that system, and he introduced the auction method.

The *ushur* to the State was one tenth of the produce, to be paid in kind. We would divide the land into suitable areas, each composed of a few villages — Babuzai, for example, would usually be divided into four parts, Nikpi Khel into two, and so on. Anyone who had some influence and some source of income could bid for the right to collect this tax. He would have to have some income, for if a pauper got the contract he might then just sell it and run away. And he would have to have some influence, or he would be unable to collect it from the villagers. But he could not use force to take more than one tenth, for everyone knew how much they were obliged to give and if they were pressed for more they could appeal to our officials, who were not involved in the collecting, or they could approach me directly. In fact, such complaints never came to me — it was a system that resisted all abuses by itself. The person who made the highest bid got the contract, and then collected the *ushur,* and gave us what he had bid for it, keeping for himself as his profit whatever excess may have been produced that year, or even paying the deficit to us from his own production, if he was out of luck and had bid too high. Then sometimes there might be a hailstorm or other natural damage to the crop. In such cases the contractor could appeal to us, and we would send two or three honest people to inspect and verify the conditions and estimate the loss, and the payments required from him would be reduced accordingly.

The *ushur* would be transported to our storehouses, called *ambar,* in the local area, where it would be kept, and mainly used in payment, also in kind, to Army people and police in that area. The Army commander-in-chief — and after a while I was doing it myself — would write chits that so much wheat and so much rice be paid to so-and-so from this or that *ambar*. The rest of the grain, whatever was left from the local salaries, was auctioned to grain merchants who resold it or exported it. And in some parts of the State where there was less *ushur,* so that the salaries were not fully covered by local produce, some of our officials would be paid in cash, the equivalent of the grain due to them according to market price.

My father got the idea for the auction method from Dir, where they practised it, because the state there was twenty years older than our state.

But he introduced it here, and it formed the cornerstone of the State's economy, and was very just and simple and inexpensive to administer.

Another advantage is that the prices of grain grow higher every year. Though we continued to pay our army in kind, there was always some net surplus left, and the value of that surplus has risen every year. That has been one source of income for the State.

The second source of income that my father developed was the forest.

The vast forests of Upper Swat and Kohistan were not accessible to any regular exploitation before the State came into existence.

In a way the forests were owned by the local villagers, but they could not control them — anyone who could get in there could cut down the trees. The villagers were too few to defend their property and collect any money on it, and it was not a source of income to them. In the old days, Kaka Khel Mians would sometimes come, and they might buy the great deodar trees for one Rupee a tree. So, when the State was organized, my father said that the forests are state property; and whatever the income from it will be, one tenth will go to the local people, and nine tenths to the state.

The third source of income he established was the *octroi,* the export and import dues he imposed on goods crossing our boundaries at Landaki. We could not call it customs duty because we were not independent; but it functioned like customs duties.

In the beginning, of course, there was little income from the State, and it no doubt operated on a deficit. But my father had large properties with which he could support his endeavour.

After the first two years or so, things improved and he could rather draw some income from the State revenue. No distinction was made at that time between the income of the State and his own private property. In the old days all the Rulers thought that everything that belonged to the State belonged to them: they were the owners of everything. But when I became Ruler, I told my father to keep his own properties and finances separate from those of the State. I then used to take whatever I needed, not much, till 1954 when an agreement was drawn up with the Government of Pakistan, including the fixing of a Privy Purse from the State revenues, which I used to spend on myself and my family.

My father's first concern in consolidating his rule of any new area that acceded to him, or was conquered, was to build roads and forts. It was his theory at the time that he should build a whole grid of forts throughout the country, placed on prominences and hilltops, and spaced so closely that one could see from one fort to the next. He made about 80 such forts; and lots of wood was spent on their construction — and labour too of course, but the labour was provided by the Army, likewise with the roads. My father suggested the idea, and people welcomed it very much. So all the unskilled labour in making the roads was provided by voluntary labour by the public — even the Khans were out there, digging to bring the road to their village. Later it was done by the Army, when there were no more wars with Dir. The Army needed to be put to some task or otherwise they would become soft. It was no hardship on them: they served for two months a year, divided up in shorter stretches of ten days at a time, so that their cultivated fields would not suffer, nor their other work, and their families would not suffer from any long absences on their part. They needed to see their officers, and be under discipline now and again. Someone once asked me, I think it was Field Marshal Ayub Khan: "Why are you keeping an army of six thousand? There is no war you can fight with a foreign country, and no chance of war with Dir any more?" But it was wise to employ those people in the State to give them jobs: they felt honoured, and the State had free labour. And as for commissions, people felt honoured to become a jamadar and subedar; giving them such posts was a way to appease the Khans, and the Sayyeds and Mians. Even in Britain in the nineteenth century, ranks used to be sold for considerable sums of money, to obtain such honours. It is the same idea, basically. And they had their weapons in their official capacity, and were confirmed in positions of authority.

With a land tenure system such as used to be practised among Pakhtuns, it was particularly simple to obtain land for public works.

The forts were mainly built on barren lands on the tops of hillocks, of little productive value, whereas roads in part had to pass over irrigated land. But at that time, the whole village collectively used to redistribute land at ten-year intervals.

The loss of land was divided among the whole village, and no single landowner suffered permanent loss. That way, there was no need to compensate the owners for the land taken for public works.

When my father was chosen as Badshah by the great *jirga* in 1917, there was an agreement between him and the tribes. Every tribe put down in writing how they should be treated, how they should be punished for certain crimes, in short, the main rules of customary law that were honoured in each tribe. There was quite a bit of variation between them — for example, in Nikpi Khel one had to pay 5 Rupees in compensation for a body wound, here in Babuzai it was 25 Rupees and so on. As time passed, we tried to adjust such things, and make the law more uniform by upgrading, reducing and adjusting. But basically we did not change the system; it remained like that till the end of the State. After all, custom depends on the past, and as time passed, the customary law could change slowly too. And for some important things which affected many people, or when we wanted to make some new law or procedure, we used to collect the *jirga* and ask them for their opinion. But we also practised Shariat, and of course you cannot change Shariat. People could choose if they wanted to be judged by Shariat or by customary law; and if the parties agreed about which law they wished to be tried under, then we always abided by that.

One system, which worked very well though it may not sound so good to a Western ear, was that of a collective fine. To punish a whole village for the acts of one person sounds very harsh. But the way we used it, it worked so that justice was done and law and order were maintained. Suppose the enemy of person X burns down his crop, worth ten Rupees. He will claim that it was worth twenty Rupees — and we would decree that the whole village is collectively responsible to collect and compensate the person. They will see that the aggrieved man obtains more than he lost, and so they will never do it again. Towards the end of my rule, I used to refer to this, jokingly, as "self-help, because it means you are

56

1. *Jahan Zeb (left) and Aman Khan: co-winners of the Colonel Keen Tennis Cup, in Peshawar April 1926, with their coach Sandeh Khan.*

2. *Miangul Jahan Zeb as Heir Apparent of Swat, 1932.*

3. *Miangul Abdul Wadud, later Badshah of Swat (centre of picture), flanked by the Chief Commissioner, Sir George Roos-Keppel, and the Political Agent, Col. Keen, at a big **jirga** in 1916.*

4. *British recognition of Badshah Sahib as Ruler of Swat, 3 May 1926. The Wali is seated on the ground beside his father, in front of Col. J.W. Keen, Acting Chief Commissioner of the Frontier Province.*

5. *Badshah Sahib flanked by Sir A. Metcalfe (left) and Sir George Cunningham (right). The Wali directly behind his father.*

6. *Scene from the British conquest of Malakand, 1895. (Watercolour by E. Hobday, 1900).*

7. *Miangul Gulshahzada Sir Abdul Wa-*
dud, K.B.E., Badshah Sahib, the founder
of Swat State, in 1965.

8. *Miangul Jahan Zeb, the Wali of Swat,*
in 1982.

9. *Residential section of Mingora, the largest town in Swat State.*

10. *Followers and clients of a Khan receiving hospitality in his* **hujra** *(men's house).*

11. *Visitors receiving gifts at a village funeral.*

12. *View from the hills above Saidu, overlooking the side valley and a section of the main Swat valley. Ahmed Zeb, the Wali's youngest son, on the left.*

13. H.M. Queen Elizabeth and H.R.H. the Prince Philip visiting Swat.

14. President Ayub Khan (centre) giving his daughter in marriage to the Wali's third son, Amir Zeb (right). The Wali himself, left of centre.

15. *Worshippers congregating in a small mosque, Upper Swat.*

16. *The Wali of Swat receiving the salute of troops of the Swat Army, Saidu 1954.*

17. *The tribal **jirga** of Thana village, outside the borders of Swat State, during meeting. In this form of government, as in Swat before the founding of the state, there is no designated leader and decisions are by consensus in the assembly of Pakthun landowners.*

helping your brother, your fellow villager! You should not call it a fine — it is your contribution to the aggrieved person.'' Or in the case of murder, we imposed a collective fine, and demanded that the *jirga* must produce the culprit or else they would have to pay that fine. A crude procedure, but it worked very well; and by such means peace was maintained.

Nor did the early State have the force and organization to extract fines which my father imposed for criminal and other illegal acts. So, as a first step, my father hit upon the idea of authorizing the Khan of the area to collect such fines — and keep them for himself. That way, the Khans were eager and relentless in collecting the fines, and the population quickly learned to respect law and discipline. Quite soon, he could reduce the Khan's share to one half, receiving the other half into the treasury, and within a few years the Khan's fraction was reduced to one third, while two thirds went to the State, without any expenses to the State or any need to use the forces of the State to enforce the laws and extract obedience.

Another important way my father developed to control and protect the State was through allowances. He paid allowances to persons of influence also outside the State — to some of the Khans of Thana, to the Khan of Khar, to the younger son of the Nawab of Dir — to have some influence with them if need be. But the bulk of allowances were paid to persons of influence within the State.

The sums varied from 20 Rupees up to 4000 Rupees to the most influential Khans and Maliks. All the upper class landowners received it, except for Gujars; they were not treated as upper class even if they were rich. But the others — Mian, Sayyid, Pakhtun — if they had a certain influence, were given State allowances. The Mullahs who were influential were paid in kind, in grain, to keep them pacified. Payment of allowance was a criterion for status within the State, and we would call *jirgas* on that basis: if a small *jirga* was called, we would say that those allowance-holders receiving 100 Rupees or more, should come; and if it was a big *jirga,* the others were also called.

In that way, the old tribal *jirgas* of the Pakhtuns were no longer allowed to dominate, and we enrolled all the influential local persons into the service of the State.

Finally, when he felt strong enough, my father disarmed the tribespeople.

Once, Sir Ralph Griffith, who was Governor of the Frontier Province, asked him how he managed to do this, and how difficult it must have been, since taking the rifle away from a Pakhtun is just like taking away his life. My father said: "I belong to this part of the country, and I know their temper. So I told my favourite *dəlla* that I am going to give concessions to you and license you to keep your arms — but you should declare that you will surrender your rifles." And he called the *jirga* of all the tribesmen, and when the party that was known to be favoured by him immediately agreed to surrender their rifles, then the other *dəlla* thought that the Badshah's own allies would be best informed, and there must be some advantages to be obtained by doing it — so they also dropped their rifles. That way, without forcing them, he disarmed the people.

But only in the sense that he gained control of the arms. They were not unarmed, since most of them were enlisted into the State army. A Khan who possessed 20 rifles previously now would have a son or a nephew who, as subedar major or commanding officer, had 100 or even more armed soldiers under him; and the Khan himself would be given a licence to own modern firearms. Actually, far from disarming them, he armed them better — but in such a way that the weapons could only be used for defence of the State and not for internal strife.

Thus, from its first uncertain basis in 1917, by 1926 my father had transformed Swat into a State with a basic structure that would endure. He was chosen by the *jirga* as Ruler owing to his position, by virtue of his descent from Saidu Baba and his personality and influence. But that mandate rested on a transient constellation of external threats and factional alignments. At first his State had to fight for its survival, using forces of tribal *lashkars* and his own private soldiers; and his rule depended on his intuition and shrewdness, his negotiating ability, and the awe and fear in which he was held. The first positions under him were held by the Wazir brothers: Fateh-ul-Mulk Khan Bahadur Hazrat Ali and his younger brother Ahmed Ali. They were the sons of a Chitrali who had come as a trusted servant with my grandmother when she was given in marriage. Thus the Wazir brothers were very closely tied to my father and, at least initially, had no local bases of authority at all except as his lieutenants. With them and a small handful of others around him at the centre, he quickly built up a structure of administration, establishing Tahsils for each new district incorporated under his rule, and establishing a force of police and gendarmes in strategically located forts. He also transformed the forces of tribal fighting men into a regulated and paid Army, with a hierarchy of officers appointed and promoted by himself. But this whole structure was not an external imposition which had to sustain itself: it rested in an intricately balanced way on the pre-existing society. My father's control was built on that of the Khans, who were already masters of the land, and on balancing the two *dəllas* in which they were aligned so that no party would become absolute in any area. For those Khans and other notables to be entitled to collect *ushur* in an area became a prime sign that they were dominant in that area; and so he harnessed the rivalry between the *dallas* to the task of collecting revenue for the State. In this way, he secured full revenue without exposing villagers to the risk of exploitation and corruption and without any expense to the State. This *ushur,* drawn from local production, was used as pay for an Army composed of local people; and their labour, when there was no war, was used for public works. Khans or their sons, and other local leaders, were the officers of this army, but in command of soldiers aligned in both *dallas* and thus incapable of misusing their command for unauthorized purposes. And finally, through the extensive system of allowances, and the power to give posts in the Army and administration to notables and their sons, every person of influence was himself subject to pervasive influence from the Ruler.

The British watched these developments closely, and were impressed. As my father was also consistently friendly towards the Government of British India, and abided by all agreements he had made with them, they shortly started overcoming their suspicions towards him. In the words of W.R. Hay, who was Political Agent for Dir, Swat and Chitral: "It now became necessary for government to decide to what extent they should recognize (my father) as a ruler of an independent state."

Then, in 1925 Badshah Khan, the Nawab of Dir, died. As told above, my father had been paying an allowance of 4000 Rupees to the second son of the Nawab, Alamzeb Khan; and he had been pressed by the British to relinquish the territory of Adinzai to the State of Dir. The British did not want to see the State of Dir destroyed — they were paying 50 000 Rupees a year in aid and had recognized that State and its Ruler. Now I know it, for certain, that my father had no intention to take back Adinzai at this juncture — but Alamzeb was ambitious to become Nawab. The British put in their hand. The then Political Agent was Col. E.H.S. James, and he told my father: "If you invade Adinzai, the British will invade Swat." Either it was a threat or a fact — but my father said: "O.K. And we will not support Alamzeb if he invades Dir." But my father said that something should be done for Alamzeb's personal safety; and the British told Alamzeb that if he declared his allegiance to his elder brother, they would assure his safety and see that the new Nawab would not interfere in Jandul. So Nawab Shah Jahan was declared Nawab of Dir at Chakdarra by the Government. The Chief Commissioner came for the *durbar.* And because my father honoured the agreement from 1922 and did not start a war with Dir, Col. James wrote a report to the Government of India through the Chief Commissioner that it is time that he should be recognized as Badshah of Swat: "as he has cooperated with us, and for eight years he has consolidated his position of power." Then at the last moment it was decided that the title of "Badshah" was objectionable on the ground that it was enjoyed by no prince in all of India and meant "King", and was applicable to His Majesty the King Emperor, as the British called their King. They suggested that my father call himself "Nawab". But the people used to call him King — Badshah — and they continued to do so till his death. So he said, it is below my dignity to come down from King to Nawab. Finally he compromised on "Wali". Wali means "Ruler", nothing else. In Turkey, Governors were called Vali or Wali, and the province was called Vilayat. The title recognized him as "Ruler". So on the 3rd of May 1926 my father was formally recognized as the Wali of Swat. Col. James had gone by then, and had been succeeded by H.A.F. Metcalfe, so the latter attended the ceremony, with Colonel Keen, the Chief Commissioner of Frontier Province, who installed my father as the first Wali of Swat.

CHAPTER VI:

Apprenticeship and trust: 1926-1935

> "He was always trying to hurry things,
> so I should learn more"

I came back to Swat on the 1st of May 1926, two days before the ceremony when the British recognized my father and the State, having completed my education up to intermediate level and passed my F.A. I did not get a very high education; but my father said: "You must come and learn something here, about the State and its affairs." On the 5th of June 1926 I was 18. For the first year it was an apprenticeship, for my father used to make me sit with him and listen to how he decided cases and how he conferred with his ministers and officials. Then, after a year, he was confident that I could do something myself. I was 19 when a small case was given to me, for decision. From then on, more cases were referred to me, by my father or by the Wazirs. In that way I gained some experience.

Then at the age of 20, my father put me in charge of the treasury — not the revenue side, but to check the registers and books, of income and expenditure. And from that moment I started working hard and regularly, starting early in the morning every day. When I was 22, my father started making me sit beside him — as he always did, even before, if there was a *jirga,* or at his meetings with the Wazirs, what you would call Cabinet Meetings. But before, I used to sit there as an observer and listener. After I became 22 he also asked my opinion — he would speak to the Wazirs, and then turn to me: "What do you think?" and so on. He was always trying to hurry things, so I should learn more quickly, so that he would be able to relinquish his rulership and hand it over to me. That was always in his mind: he was eager to be relieved of his duties and concerns.

Then, on my own initiative, not by instructions from my father, I started asking, enquiring and learning about everything around me. I used to ask the Sipah Salar, that is the Commander-in-Chief, who at the time was the younger Wazir. I used to ask him about every matter: why is this man being promoted, why this and why that? Such inquisitiveness is good for a man — and I felt, inside of me, an urge to know. In that way, after a while, he started consulting me before he went to my father to suggest a promotion. I had no friends around me when I came back from College, no society. I used to invite all these military officers, turn by turn, to have lunch or dinner with me, and we used to go in the car together, two or three of them at a time. My car was a seven-seater, so there was ample room. And of course, those people also wanted to be associated with the future Ruler. It was a privilege for them; and I had the privilege of coming to know them closely. I would also listen to the old Khans. So I always tried to learn something.

And people were learning too — the Swat people, though they were not educated, were more intelligent than in the tribal belt. Even then, they used to travel a lot all over British India, and some as sailors out of Bombay. Whatever you talked to them about, they understood; and they were willing to change. You can see the difference still: in Mardan District and Swabi, local people still wear old-fashioned dress. When I came from College at the age of 18, I brought some few neckties and I told the officers: "You tie it like this," and gradually some of them adopted European dress. After a while all the officials and prominent people used to wear such dress, whether to flatter me, or because they preferred it themselves. I like a man to be well dressed, so people knew that I like good dress, and they would dress well.

British officials also started visiting Swat with increasing frequency — the valley is so beautiful, and they enjoyed the shooting and sight-seeing. In this way, I came to know them also, and I continued to improve my English and enjoy their company also.

In forming our administration, we copied the British administration to the extent that our finances allowed. Of course they had so much greater resources, and their officials were highly qualified — our people were not much qualified, nor could they claim comparable salaries. But their pay was raised gradually, as their competence increased.

The control of the revenue, the auditing of books, and so on, was in my personal hands. The revenue was collected by the *Wazir-i-Mal,* or *Mushir-i-Mal* if he was less senior. But payments and books were under the *Mohtamim,* whom one might call the Treasury Officer. He was directly under me — though he was in fact lower in status than the

Wazir, but he could require information from the Wazir on where certain moneys came from, and when payments would be coming, and so on.

My father preferred to work through others — through the two Wazir brothers, and later on through me. And after those first few years when he went around to the Khans and *jirgas* in Upper Swat he preferred not to travel around too much. He used to go for shooting to Buner; or for a funeral of a prominent Khan. He never went for marriages.

For contact with his people, he used the telephone most often. He started building the telephone system in 1926. He could have started before that too, but the British would not allow it, since he was not a recognized Ruler. Every evening, he telephoned most of the people and asked them how things were, what was happening, and so on.

In that way, he kept in close contact with everyone and knew what was up all over the State.

A new challenge to the State, though not a very serious one, arose only three months after my father had been recognized by British India — indeed, that recognition was the immediate cause of the trouble.

My father had allowed the Government of India to send in a land-surveying team to Kana, on the border of Indus Kohistan. Beyond Kana are the villages of Bisham, inhabited by Mians, and Lahor inhabited by Kohistanis; and they were still independent. They were uneducated people, and the mullahs excited them and said my father had been installed by the British so we were all infidels and so on. Their leader was a Kohistani mullah, called Mazoob Mullah. So he made *jehad,* holy war, against my father. Those Kohistani people are very brave and fierce, and the country is very mountainous, so the fighting was severe. The war went on for two months, and then the Kohistanis were thoroughly defeated — so they had a real taste of our power. Mazoob Mullah was killed in that fighting. After a year or two, gradually their *jirgas* came in and accepted my father's rule. And it is a striking thing, my father used to say, that if you conquer by force, the people will submit, but if you take an area by peaceful means, the local people will usually attempt to rise against a new Ruler, to test how strong he is. Thus, for example, we took Buner by peaceful means, as described above. But after six or eight months, the Nawab of Amb came and started fighting again. My father sent his troops to the front line in Chamla valley, whereupon those

63

Bunerwals fell on the soldiers, in Salarzai, where they wanted to spend the night. The reason was, these people had been conquered without a fight and so they made a rebellion. They killed about 60 of those soldiers — and my father had to send a thousand troops and punish them, killing some, while others fled to Mardan as refugees. That was the reason: these people had not been conquered by the sword, so they rebelled. But the Kohistanis, who tasted the sword when they were conquered, never rebelled, and they are loyal to me even now, after merger.

When I returned from College, my father gave me a separate house — it has been rebuilt now, and is occupied by my son Aurangzeb. He drew me increasingly into all aspects of his administration, and delegated ever more responsibility to me; but of course the crucial political decisions remained with him — I had to work inside the system, the way it was set up. But I could make small suggestions, and I could also discuss the possibilities of major changes with him. I did not believe in feudalism at all — in his manner of ruling and controlling the country through the big Khans and the two-dalla system. Yet that was the political foundation of the State. At the time he had his own *dalla;* but he also sought the help of the other *dalla,* and sometimes he had a finger in the decisions on both sides.

As told above (pp. 27 f.), my father and my uncle Shirin Sahib had been leaders of opposite *dallas,* and the Khans of the Babuzai, in this part of the valley adjoining Saidu Sharif, were divided between the two *dallas.* After the death of Shirin Sahib, Jamroz Khan became the head of that *dalla.* His half brother, from another wife of Malak Baba, was Mir Abdullah Khan, and he belonged to my father's *dalla,* as did the only son from the third wife of Malak Baba, who was in fact the eldest of Malak Baba's nine sons and whose name was Janas Khan (Fig. A).

When Mir Abdullah Khan died, his son, Nowsherawan Khan, was very young, and then these other Khans, his uncles, wanted to redistribute Mir Abdullah's widows and land and influence. But my father went to the assembly for Mir Abdullah's funeral, and he said: "Whoever harms young Nowsherawan Khan, I shall see that and prevent it." So he made Nowsherawan Khan prominent, inside his own *dalla.* Though he was the grandson of Malak Baba, it was my father's support that was decisive. Later, he became the local leader of my father's *dalla* — he was a party man. And Janas Khan joined the party of Nowsherawan Khan, remaining with the party of my father.

Then Jamroz Khan, leader of the other *dalla,* died around 1930-31.

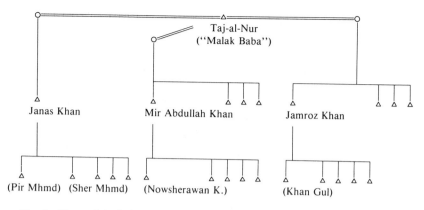

Fig. A. Khans of the Babuzai in the late 1920's

Jamroz Khan was not killed by the initiative of my father. It came about like this: Khan Gul, the eldest son of Jamroz Khan, had some controversy with his uncle Janas Khan; and he got a stick and attacked Janas Khan, and broke his head in three or four places. Now Janas Khan's son, Pir Mohammed Khan, wished to take revenge. But he knew that Jamroz Khan always kept a small pistol with him, in his pocket or in his hand. So he thought: "I cannot take my revenge like that, attacking him with a stick — so I shall have to kill him." And when Jamroz Khan was on his way to the mosque, he shot him. But he was not punished. My father did not like Jamroz Khan, whereas personally, I liked him. It tended to be like that, more and more through those years: whoever was aggrieved or disgruntled with my father, they would come to me. Anyway, in those days a Khan could not be punished by shooting as *qissas*. This was a matter of politics, not law, in those days. Instead his father Janas Khan was taken out of Nowsherawan Khan's *dalla* and made head of the other *della*, in the place of Jamroz Khan! My father gave that *della* to Janas Khan, so as to reduce Jamroz Khan's family. And that position was later taken over by Janas Khan's sons.

How could my father do that, not only in his own *dalla* but also in the other *dalla*? Because my uncle Shirin Sahib was dead, so they had no leadership there, and they were undecided as to how to replace Jamroz Khan suddenly. And my father did not try to make any Tom Dick or Harry head of the *dalla*. But as the eldest son of Malak Baba, Janas Khan was a strong candidate, so by persuasion and tactics, and having

65

him defect from the stronger party with his following, my father managed it, while he himself was above these *dəlla* divisions, since the State was strongly established then.

From then on, my father treated Nowsherawan Khan and Janas Khan on the same level, as leaders of opposite *dəllas*. But gradually Nowsherawan Khan became less important, for he was not a pushing man; and Janas Khan had many sons, and as time passed they all came into State service. Especially his second son, Sher Mohammed Khan, had the real Pukhtunwali, Khan-like qualities. He became a Subedar in 1922. Then he became tahsildar in Charbagh for ten years, and then he was posted to Nikpi Khel for a year. But he refused to serve there longer, he said: "Those people are so head-strong I cannot punish them, and they take their cases to Saidu instead of coming to me. I get so tired of that so I resign — or else transfer me." He was transferred to Barikot for three or four years, after that he became Hakim of Totalai, in the south of Buner, and then Hakim in Daggar, the main centre in Buner. After that he was made Mushir-i-Mal, and then promoted to Wazir-i-Mal, all with my support. Although he was a favourite of my father's, still someone had to suggest his promotions. And the Wazirs did not like him.

His eldest brother Pir Mohammed Khan became subedar when my father eliminated the *lashkar* system and expanded the Army by one thousand men. Then he was made Subedar Major and then Captain, eventually he became Commander and then he retired. And I made him *munsif* that is special judge, along with Abdul Khaliq Khan of Kambar, and Shirin, a retired Captain. These people never took bribes, and people trusted them.

Sher Mohammed Khan, the Wazir-i-Mal, I finally retired because of age in 1967 — he is 8 years older than I am. Secretly, he intrigued against me and the State; and when the State was merged, he came out in the open with his enmity to me. He joined the National Awami Party, the Red Shirts. He thought they would make his son a Senator. And when they made Kamran their candidate instead, he changed to the People's Party. When my son Amirzeb also joined the People's Party, they got along very well and became very friendly. But still the Wazir-i-Mal will not come to me, nor will his son. He seems to be embarrassed to come back, or something. He is shy, after having come out against me. He was bitter because I retired him — he thought he should continue till his death! But it was difficult for me.

In some few parts of the State, my father's policy of balancing the two *dəllas* failed. One was in the valley of Kana, as I mentioned above; but that has not created any problems for the State. Another, more difficult case was that of Sebujni and Shamizai.

Long ago, long before the State, there was a balance between the two parties there. One *dəlla* was led by the Khan of Jura village in Sebujni, the other by the Darməi Khans of Shamizai: the brothers Masam Khan and Habib Khan. Masam Khan was the elder and the power lay in his hand — he was very powerful. But Habib Khan used to go for *jirgas* and negotiations: he was very intelligent and could foresee things. A very exceptional man. Masam Kahn was without issue, and when he died — a natural death — Habib Khan carried on. They were of my father's *dəlla*.

The Khan of Jura was also a very prominent man. This was at the time when the Nawab of Dir exercised much power on that side, the West bank of Swat, and used to come out of Dir, and rule for a while, and then go back, as told above (p. 29). The son of the Khan of Jura died in this fighting, he was only 18 or 19 years old, and his son Khan Bahadur — some say he was born two months after his father's death, some say he was very young — in any case he was less than a year old. His grandfather the Khan of Jura married to have new sons, but they were also very young when the Khan died, so their distant cousin Taj Mohammed Khan of Arkot became the leader of the family. He used to be very friendly with the Nawabs of Dir, while the Darməi Khan was for us. My father was all for Darməi Khan, because he was of his own *dəlla* and the richest and most powerful man of the area.

When Khan Bahadur grew up, before the State, he also fought a little bit for the Nawab. But then my father wanted to defeat Taj Mohammed Khan, and he offered to give the power to the true heir of Jura Khan; and thereby he became a very close friend with Khan Bahadur, who was about 25 years old then and a very intelligent person. My father liked him very much. So Darməi Khan got annoyed with that, that my father should boost Khan Bahadur so. My father's purpose was to boost him to take over from Taj Mohammed Khan, not *against* Darməi Khan. But from then on, the suspicion grew.

In 1927 Darməi Khan went for Haj pilgrimage. While he was away, his son Mohammed Rasool Khan and all his party, without any reason, attacked Jura village and burned it, and chased Khan Bahadur into exile. This happened after the State was created, without regard for the rule of my father. My father became very annoyed. When Darməi Khan returned home, he said: "My son was a fool, he made a mistake in taking the law into his own hand." Yet the suspicion grew even more. Shortly afterwards, my father and Darməi Khan went out together to shoot the wild sheep, which the English call *gurul*. A stone slipped from under his foot, it was a very steep place, and Darməi Khan fell down. He fell on his head and died. Just like these skiers, who come under an avalanche. My father has told me, in confidence, that he did *not* kill him — he has sworn to it. But these people said that he had been killed by my father, and they spread that story. Yet my father tried to assure them, and he gave the sons, led by Rasool Khan, the same facilities as the father had enjoyed.

This was in October 1927, and soon after the road up along the river to Madyan was completed. My father decided that he should inspect the road, whether it was good or not. The sons of Darməi Khan heard about this, and they conspired also with Habibullah Khan of Miandam (cf. p. 48) and laid an ambush near Fatehpur bridge. My father went in one car, with his secretary Ataullah and a big mullah with whom he kept company, and one or two orderlies. There was no other protection. And I followed in my car with my brother, my cousin, one driver and one bodyguard in that car. There were five hundred men of Darməi Khan's party; and when they saw my father cross that bridge, they were certain they would get him. But I had a new car, bought only a month ago, and the road was quite rough. I decided I did not want to spoil my car, so I turned back before reaching that bridge. I was not in my father's retinue, my father had told me not to go, and I had said I would go by myself. And it is strange that my father should start wondering: "Where is his car, what has happened?" — anyway, he quickly turned around and came back. And when he came home, he was a little annoyed with me, and said: "You are a very good companion, leaving us alone halfway and just going back!" That is all he said.

Next day the Political Agent — M.C. Lattimore, who had succeeded Metcalfe — was scheduled to come to see the road. For the Political Agent's protection we would always station soldiers every 50 metres or so along his route when he visited. The very same evening, therefore, my father ordered soldiers to be sent and posted along the way. And when those Khans saw the Army coming, about 500 of them, they thought that my father had come to know about their plans, and that was why he had turned back and now sent soldiers to arrest the plotters. So they all fled to Dir. That is the only attempt that was made on my father's life while he was a Ruler, and we were all miraculously saved. As for my own life, I have never known of any such attempt. Maybe some people have conspired — not putting it into practice, but just talking about bumping me off. But as far as I know, no one has ever attempted to put such a scheme into effect.

Some months after the Darməi Khan party fled, a few other minor Khans also defected to Dir, as did the sons of Mian Hamzullah of Sardari (cf. p. 46). As a result, by 1930, there were about 25 important Khans and Mians and nearly 500 of their servants and retainers residing in different places in Dir State. They were given subsistence by the Nawab, but no land and no positions. So in June that year, these refugees, with the assistance of the Painda Khel, collected a *lashkar* and advanced to the watershed between Dir and the Sebujni-Shamizai valley. My father sent the army under the younger Wazir, as Commander-in-Chief to oppose them. But when he had taken up positions facing them, my father learned that there was treachery planned by friends of the refugees' *dəlla* in the valley, in the army's rear. So the younger Wazir was ordered to withdraw and use the army to disarm that *dəlla* throughout the valley, and this he did. Meanwhile the refugees' *lashkar* dispersed, whether because their plans had been unsuccessful, or as a result of orders from the Nawab, who was under pressure from the British. But as a result of this, one of the *dəllas* in the Sebujni-Shamizai area was completely crushed, and Khan Bahadur of Jura became absolute in his area, with no opposition to counterbalance his *dəlla*.

As for the organization of society in Swat, the big thing that happened around this time, about 1930—31, was the permanent settlement of the Pakhtun landowners. As I have mentioned (cf. p. 24), there used to be *wesh*, whereby the landowners redistributed the land between them, and moved, every ten years. My father decided to end that system — but to do so was very complicated.

Because in the old times, when they changed their villages and lands after ten years, there was enough trouble, with some landowners gaining a little and some losing a little by the new redistribution. Yet people did not need to care about small differences, for they knew that after another ten years, it would change again. But when it was going to be a permanent thing, then everyone was up in arms about his rights and his share, and my father had to take a personal hand in it and put great effort into supervising every detail.

To explain it all, I first need to explain the land tenure system in some detail. The total landed property of each branch of the Yusufzai tribe — i.e. the land of each side valley leading down to the Swat river, or a certain stretch of the main valley along the river — was divided into a number of equal shares, or fractions.

And each landowner in the tribe owned, not a certain set of plots of land, but a certain percentage of the whole, expressed as a number of such standard shares or fractions of shares. At each *wesh* distribution, he would be allotted land corresponding to the number of shares he owned, which would be his for the next ten-year period, till the plots were again redistributed.

The "share" which formed the unit or measure of land in a tribal district was variously called a *Rupei* or a *Brakha* — the former being the same name as the monetary unit, the latter meaning simply "share".

Each such share was subdivided into parts, generally called Paisa. In the Babuzai area each *Brakha* was composed of 48 Paisa. And one Paisa, again, would not be the equivalent of one field: it was composed of a specific combination of *so* much irrigated land, so much unirrigated land, so many village houses, and undivided rights in the hillside pastures and forests. If you put together the unirrigated land and irrigated land that made up a Paisa in Babuzai, it would be approximately half an acre. In Nikpi Khel, they call the big shares Rupei, and each Rupei was divided into only 12 Paisa. While lower down the valley, each Paisa is only about one fourth of the Babuzai Paisa, or one third. Even further down the valley, in Thana outside the State, they call their Paisa a "Putcha". And in Adinzai, they call it "Sarei", that is, "man". Thus every tribe varied both in the names of their units, and the sizes of these units. I think some of these variations came about with growth of population, or with losses of land because of war: some just subdivided the shares they were left with; others started reducing the land equivalent of the Paisa measure — like a kind of devaluation of the unit.

The hill area was not allotted to shareholders, but was held jointly. So there was no value put on the forest — every man could go and cut a tree in his own tribe's forest. Then there were also settlements in those hills and forests, called Banda, inhabited by Gujars and other hill tenants. They did not work in fields allotted to particular landowners, as did the tenants in the valley floor, on the irrigated or unirrigated land there. They paid *kalang,* that is rent; it was collected by the Malik or Khan and divided among the landowners, in proportion to their shares. But the Malik had the right to fix the price of the *kalang.* Some did it honestly, and some took a little bribe from the Gujars, saying pay me this and I will give you a little bit of good land. In some parts, there were large populations of *kalang*-paying tenants under the Pakhtuns; other tribal sections had little such land.

Most of the land called *daftar* and owned in this way by the Yusufzai

Pakhtuns was either allocated according to the amount of Paisas each man owned or held collectively for its *kalang* income. But over the years, certain lands had also been given and set aside for Saintly people, Mians and such families as were not Pakhtuns. And those lands were fixed, they were called *siri* and were not redistributed, and they had no share in the forest or any such things. My father's landed properties were of this *siri* kind.

And when the Pakhtun landowners made *wesh,* they would, before they allotted the land, set aside certain fields for the carpenter, the blacksmith, and the *darogha* — the village crier and messenger. And also for the mullah. They would have the use of those lands in return for their services to the whole community of landowners; and if they left their service or were removed, then they had to part with that land. So it was not *siri* land — it was called the land of the *karigər* — those performing services. Once this was set aside, then the landowners would divide the rest, according to their shares.

If you try to measure the Paisa in terms of production, each Paisa in Babuzai would give an annual crop of about 8–10 maunds (a maund is about the equivalent of a hundredweight) of maize. Wheat would not be grown every year, for it is grown on dry land, and so they would alternate, and get about 2 or 3 hundredweight of wheat. Of rice they would get about 4 or 5 hundredweight. These proportions would likewise vary between different tribal branches and areas, because the proportion of dry land to irrigated land would vary owing to geographical differences.

Finally, the Pakhtuns would own houses in the villages in the same proportions as they owned land, and at each *wesh* they also had to divide and allocate those houses. And here in Babuzai, there would be big differences, because there was the big village of Mingora, with so many shops, some big and some small, and good houses and bad houses. So they would divide the shops roughly according to their value, and classify the houses into good areas and bad areas and allocate each owner a share of both — not scattered houses all over but in two places, one good and one bad. The people living in those houses had no say in the matter — the poor people that is, the tenants whom we call *faqir.* They used to pay a small rent. When a Pakhtun was allotted houses, then he was responsible for those faqirs living in those houses; they were sort of his subjects and he had to protect them, from the aggression of other people: that was a matter of *nang,* or honour. By the code of *nangwali,* he was responsible for them. In return, they had to sit in their house-owner's *hujra*, his men's house, and fight for him against his enemies. But they were free to work on the land of another landowner — wherever they could obtain a tenancy contract.

In the very old days, more than 90 years ago, these Yusufzai tribes had really big *wesh*, where large branches of the tribe would change areas every ten years. The two branches that are now in Upper Swat, across the river — Sebujni and Shamizai — used to alternate with Nikpi Khel and Adinzai respectively. Down the valley from Saidu, the Aba Khel had *wesh* with Khan Khel of Thana, and Musa Khel had *wesh* with Maturizai, up the valley around Charbagh. And of the uppermost two branches on this side of the river, the Azi Khel had *wesh* with Chakesar, across the mountains near the Indus; and Jinki Khel had *wesh* with Kana. Babuzai had *wesh* with Puran; and Ghorband belonged to nobody — it was just a forest. Anybody could come and make a house there, if they could defend themselves and live on their own. So the people who settled there do not belong to any particular tribe, but are of different *khels*.

These different areas that were linked in *wesh* are very unequal — especially the Babuzai: *this* area is large and good, while the Puran land is less than half of this. After a while, when one branch of the Babuzai became more powerful, they said we will settle here, you can settle over in Puran, we will have no further *wesh* with you. Likewise, the Khan Khel who are now in Thana, they were powerful, so they settled in Thana and did not allow another *wesh* with the Aba Khel. So these big *weshes* ended in an arbitrary way, with the more powerful group permanently annexing the area they preferred.

The other *wesh*, inside each area, continued as I have recounted (p. 24). One consequence of this *wesh* was that the tribes in Swat were more independent, and more rebellious, than the Dir and Jandul people. There, they learned to be obedient to their Khans, because from time immemorial, they were under the same Khans. Whereas here — every ten years, when the Pakhtuns moved with the *wesh*, they would re-allot the lands and relocate themselves and their alliances and select a new Khan of the ward and the village if the old fellow was not behaving properly. It was like a sort of election every ten years.

In other ways, it was a pernicious system. No one was interested in maintaining houses or building better houses — even the big Khans lived in mud houses, for they would be leaving them after ten years. No one planted fruit trees — for the

72

next fellow to harvest; no one was interested in making permanent improvements on the land.

So my father made speeches to the *jirgas* explaining the benefits of permanent settlement, and supervised every settlement personally, by negotiating the agreements. And by these means, it was all achieved peacefully, thank God, from 1928 to 1932. In Upper Swat, he travelled and did it himself; in Nikpi Khel he did it through his Sipah Salar, the younger Wazir brother, and he used to visit him often and give him instructions before the Wazir called the *jirga* and made the settlements. As for the Babuzai, that was done here, in Saidu, because the *jirga* would meet here, where the college now stands. The Babuzai have four branches: one is Aka-Maruf, one is Bami Khel, one Aba Khel, and one Barat Khel. Even before the State, I don't remember when, they had divided into two parts; Aka-Maruf and Bami exchanged between themselves, and Barat and Aba exchanged among themselves. As for the first pair, when one was around Mingora the other would be in Manglawar. By 1930 Mingora had developed into the central trading bazar and a big town in Swat, so the land there was more valuable. What my father did was divide Mingora in half, and likewise divide Manglawar in half, and both branches of the tribe got land in both places; whereas the rest of the villages went by lot as usual. Finally, everything was distributed, except the strip along the river bank. It is exposed to floods, and when the strong floods come, land is washed away, while in other places new silt may be deposited. So that strip remained for redistribution — even now, I think.

My father says: "Altogether, it took me five long years to complete the settlement work. Without exaggeration, it proved a more formidable and laborious affair than the military exploits, because it involved displeasure and vexation for others. Paying no heed to the obstacles in the way, I undertook to deliver my compatriots from the necessity of leading nomadic lives and put them on the road to progress and prosperity." (Story of Swat pp. 91f.)

The development of education in the State — a matter that was to become a major interest of mine when I became Ruler — started from the very beginning of the State, but did not proceed so quickly in the beginning.

I think the first primary school was established in 1925. The first initiative in the field of religious education, in 1943, was mine. I suggested to my father that the State establish a Dar-ul-Ulum in Mingora for the study of Islamic subjects. We were able to find the necessary teachers and scholars here, in Swat: persons who had studied in Deoband in India, and in madrasas in Delhi, Fatehpur Sikri and such places, and from Lucknow there were quite a few who were well versed in several fields. Though it was my initiative, my father actually took more interest in that kind of education; and there were one or two Molvis who came from Chakesar and such distant places whom he invited and had living with him.

Later, with the establishment of Pakistan and the increasing emphasis on Pakistan as an Islamic state, I made the same suggestion to President Ayub, and even before that to Iskander Mirza: Pakistan needs formal institutions for religious education which give degrees like other universities. In European countries they have such educational institutions where the clergy get degrees, like Doctor of Divinity and so on. Such people only should be entitled to interpret the religion, not everybody who comes out and says he is a mullah, and gives his verdict that this man is an infidel and this act is forbidden. That is why I started the Dar-ul-Ulum in Swat — and that is what I told them too. But in Pakistan it was started only very late, in the last days of Ayub's presidency or even afterwards. Now they have a religious university in Bahawalpur. But it should have come first, and framing an Islamic constitution come afterwards.

Another thing we did was to change the *ushur* — that was also done in the early 1930s. In the first years of the State, people had to produce *lashkar* to fight the wars with Dir and Amb, besides paying the *ushur* to support the State and its militia. For every two *brakha* of land they had to provide one armed man to serve under the command of his Khan.[17] When he went to serve in the *lashkar* the man would have his own food, his own cartridges, everything. And when the *lashkar* was not mobilized, he would serve as a retainer of the Khan or Malik. So my father decided to increase the militia and do away with the *lashkar* system: it was like *begar,* or forced labour; as people became softer, they did not want to serve in the *lashkar;* and the authority over the men was with the Maliks, not directly with the State. So my father started collecting both contributions directly: one tenth he took on the threshing ground, when the crop was ready, and then, when the grain had been brought to the houses, he took a tithe as an extra tax, to cover the *lashkar.* For this reason, grumbling continued. So I calculated the whole thing, how much the *ushur* comes to and how much this tithe adds to it, and I found that the sum came to the equivalent of taking one part to seven-and-a-half, or two parts in fifteen, and not one part in ten. We said: Let us not have this double taxation, one lot in the field and one after you get the grain to your house. What is more, by the old system, the *siri* land was exempt from the *lashkar* tithe — only Pakhtuns used to have to provide men to the *lashkar*. When we imposed the one part to seven-and-a-half rate, then everyone was made to pay equally for an enlarged State Militia. During the last six months of my rule, more than 35 years later, this was one of the complaints that arose! And I thought: "Since in any case the State is going, I can say All Right." Hence the *ushur* was again set at one tenth. When the Government took over, it was collected for another year or two. After a while, Mr. Bhutto decided to waive it.

In 1931 there was a certain mullah in Chakesar, who was known as Sundia Baba. He apparently wanted to wield some influence without my father knowing about it. Nobody reported on it to my father; they thought this man was just a Pir, and that people were coming to pay homage to him. But privately, he was agitating in the whole Indus watershed area: Chakesar, Puran, Kana, Ghorband, and Bisham. He planned to launch a rebellion against my father. But the Hakim of Chakesar reported to my father, through the Wazir, what was going on. My father took his precautions: he sent two columns of armed forces, one from the north side and one from the south, and they surrounded Sundia Baba's place and arrested him. About four thousand soldiers of the militia were sent in. He was arrested and brought here, and he was put in a fort in Sher Atrap, up in the mountains above Murghzar. These Pir people used to eat very little food — they would say "Let me starve" and so on. The man was very weak, and owing to that weakness, not to our treatment of him, he died there. He was just a local mullah, unknown. And he died unknown because he had no wife, and no children. He was a very old man — above eighty. I have a rather different opinion of him; as I think, the man was a simpleton. I doubt very much that he himself initiated these things — rather, other people took advantage of him, and used his sainthood and his person for their own purposes. My father in fact knew of these other people who were involved, and who may have been the originators even. But he chose not to act against them. As everything was finished so quickly and easily — it was not a campaign, just a matter of arresting this man and bringing him here. Everybody else said: "I was not in it, I was not in it" and so on. My father did not want to push matters further and make enemies — the important thing was to show that it had no effect, that such attempts could not succeed.

In some British accounts, this incident of Sundia Baba has been linked as part of a larger plot directed by the Red Shirt Movement — Abdul Ghaffar Khan's wing of the Congress Party. This is entirely wrong. It just happened to coincide in time with troubles which the British Indian Government had with the Red Shirt Movement in Peshawar — and this was on their mind, so they saw Bolsheviks and Red Shirts everywhere, rather as the Americans today see "communism" in any and every kind of subversion. One reason may also be that there was a Political Agent, W.R. Hay, a couple of years later, who wrote a small pamphlet on Swat. And he asked my father about what happened to Sundia Mullah, and got only a short reply: "It is none of your business, where he is and where he was; but you should appreciate how I keep the peace!" He did not even say whether the mullah was dead or alive, and so Hay never heard a true account of the matter.

In fact, there was never any direct involvement of the Red Shirt movement in the State. They always thought, during British rule, that my father was loyal to the British, and so they concluded that they could not achieve anything there. But they had Swat on their mind, and I know that they had decided, if they got into power, that they would absorb the State of Swat and make their summer headquarters on Mount Ilam, between Saidu and Buner. Later, when independence was approaching, relations between them and the Muslim League became very strained, and they knew that we were for the Muslim League. So they stayed away and never contacted my father or me for any support or requests. But finally in the last two or three years of my rule in the late 1960s, I allowed them to come: Wali Khan (the son of Abdul Ghaffar Khan) and his friends, and let them build houses up near Madyan. But they had secret meetings with the people.

During the early 1930s, there were some small final adjustments made in our boundaries in the South, between Buner and Mardan, which was then part of Peshawar District. One concerned a ridge of hills between Ambela and Rustam. Usually, the boundaries between the areas of different tribes would follow the watershed. But the Bunerwals, on our side of the border, had been more powerful than the tribes in the settled districts, so they had grabbed their lands along the hill on the *other* side of the watershed. When the Revenue Settlement Officer came, he reimposed the watershed as the boundary; but they recognized also that my father had been receiving *ushur* from these lands, and so they fixed the revenue at 500 Rupees a year, corresponding to the value of the *ushur*. But the Bunerwals would not give up possession, and finally a *jirga* was appointed composed of prominent Maliks from Dera Ismail Khan, Bannu and Kohat. The *jirga* said: "Let the Bunerwals have that land, for they have been cultivating it for fifty or a hundred years". Sir Olaf Caroe, who was Assistant Commissioner in Mardan at the time, was very angry. He told me that if he ever got a chance, he would reverse this decision. Later he became Deputy Commissioner in Peshawar, then Chief Secretary, and finally Governor — but he never brought up the matter with me. Passions cool with time.

At another place on the southern boundary, closer to the Indus, my father had extended his administration over some small tribal groups of Mian villages that had been independent, including some land which the Hassanzai — who were protected by the British — had recently conquered from those other tribes. The Hassanzai counter-attacked, but my father retained possession of a small strip of land up to the watershed which the Hassanzai claimed. The Hassanzai appealed to the British, who appointed a *jirga* to visit the spot and fix the boundary. This *jirga* made a divided finding, but the majority opinion favoured my father, and that was eventually accepted by the Chief Commissioner. But then a survey party was sent in by the British, and they came back with a report that the settlement inflicted injustice on the Hassanzai. In February 1932, the decision was reversed.

My father got angry and stubborn, and would not give in. The dispute continued through the summer — May, June, July, August — four full months. The Chief Secretary in Peshawar went on leave, and Hay went there to act as Chief Secretary, and a young man, Ambrose Dundas (who eventually became governor) took temporary charge as Political Agent in Malakand. He became very friendly, most friendly with me and remained so till his death in 1973, and his wife Lady Dundas continued the friendship till *her* death only very recently. He never allowed me to stay anywhere in Peshawar but with them, as long as they were in Peshawar. But during this dispute, my father would go to Malakand and bang the table and say he was not going to sign an agreement reversing that decision. "I know that the British government has overwhelming power. They can do anything they like. But *I* am *not* going to sign. I will make this compromise only: I will abdicate in favour of my son, and even tell him to sign, but *I will not* sign!'' And as Dundas was a young fellow at the time, he became frightened. So he reported to his government that this is the attitude of the Badshah. And then, the British appointed another commission to inquire, and finally backed out! It was Dundas who told me this story, not my father.

It was a very small area of land, I don't think it would have been more than five or six square miles. But to him it was a matter of principle. And it was not an empty threat, that he would abdicate. He meant it. Firstly, there was the principle of following the watershed. Secondly, in those days he liked me very much, and he meant to give me the State very soon anyway. He was very satisfied with how I was managing things.

On the 14th of April 1930, Lord Irwin, Viceroy and Governor-General of India came to Saidu, and in a formal durbar decorated my father with the Order of Knight of the British Empire, in recognition of his management of affairs and his maintenance of law and order in his State. Ten years after my father had proclaimed me his heir-apparent, on 15th May 1933 the Government of British India also recognized me, again in my personal capacity only, as Waliahad or heir-apparent in a durbar in Saidu. With this, my father's consistent policy to achieve friendly relations and full recognition by the British in India was brought to a completely successful conclusion.

CHAPTER VII:
Downfall: 1935

"It was the Wazirs and I who became
tarburs"

Before the State was created, the elder Wazir, Hazrat Ali, was my father's scribe, and his younger brother, Ahmed Ali, looked after my father's lands. When my father became Ruler, Hazrat Ali was made Chief Minister and Ahmed Ali became Tahsildar; later he became Commander-in-Chief. My half-sister was married to the elder Wazir; and the Wazir brothers married their daughters to powerful Khans, who gave their daughters in marriage to the Wazirs' sons. Thus, step by step, they came to wield great influence.

The elder Wazir was a very intelligent man: a good administrator and very quick to give decisions, both a capable and a wise man. His younger brother also had good qualities, and was a man of principle — though he could not read or write. When I came home from College, I was very young and inexperienced, and they were already in charge.

Now I had about five maternal uncles, my mother's brothers, and because they were brothers-in-law of my father he gave them important positions in the Army. They were uneducated and not very clever. Without consulting me, they were always praising me and telling people to be loyal to me — and in their heart, they were telling people to be loyal to me against the Wazirs. But later, those people were sent by the Wazirs to my father, to report what they had been told as if it were directed against *him!* I was young, and eager to learn, and I mixed with all the people; and as I said above, came to have the privilege of knowing closely many of the young officers and many others. And when I heard people talking about the Wazirs and their influence, I would talk to convince them that my *father* is the Ruler, and these people are his servants. My tussle was with the Wazirs, not with my father. I used to convince everybody that whatever position they had was owing to my father, not owing to the Wazirs. But they would always tell people: "It was we who recommended you." Such were our respective games and rivalry.

As time went on, I was given more and more cases to decide, and also more and more people came to me. But the big Khans, like Khan Bahadur of Jura and Darmai Khan did not bring their cases to me. They went direct to my father — not even to the Wazirs. Their cases were political: feudalist politics. But by 1934, there were so many cases that I felt very tired, because nobody went to the Wazirs, they all came to me. And my father never took the ordinary cases himself, unless they were referred to him or he was interested in them. I did not tell people to come to me; but there was no distribution of power, people were free to go to the Wazirs, or to me. And they believed in my justice, because I had no axe to grind. I am quite sure that at that time, and also when I became Ruler, I never did *dalla* business when parties came to me: I decided according to the merits of the case. Nobody was aggrieved. But Swat was divided into two *dallas,* and some would come to me, some to the Wazirs. Not necessarily in accordance with the over-all alignment of *dallas,* but locally: if a Khan was the Wazir's relation or favourite, the other side naturally went to me: *Da dushmand dushmand dost ye* — your enemy's enemy is your friend.

Through the cases, I handled and controlled the Tahsildars. But I felt very alone some times. I could not change the system, and I was so tired when I finished, at 2 p.m. Then I used to go swimming or riding or playing tennis.

The Wazirs started "whispering in my father's ear" — through the Khans, not by themselves — that I was going to rebel against him. My father's suspicions took root at the end of April 1934. Whenever we met, his attitude was cold. In fact he thought that I had become too powerful. It was not fear, rather a sort of jealousy. So in the summer of 1934, it was the beginning of May, I went to Peshawar because I used to have an occasional fever, and I did not know what to do about it. There was Col. Diamond, another good Irishman who had succeeded my old friend Col. Charles Brierly as chief medical officer. He said I should take a holiday, that might cure me. So I took the younger Wazir, who was Sipah Salar (Commander-in-Chief) at the time, and another fellow who was a Captain, and my own personal servant, and we went in two cars to Kashmir for two weeks. I sent a telegram to my father that the doctor had recommended that I go to Kashmir.

When I came back my father had already shifted to Murghzar for the summer, and we went to pay our respects. But all the time he kept talking to the younger Wazir about whether he had enjoyed the trip and so on — not asking me about the trip. It was a very cold attitude. Then I realized: "My father thinks he has got no power, that *I* have *all* the power!" So I asked him if I could be permitted to shift to Miandam, up the valley at 6000 ft. altitude, for the summer. In that way, he could feel secure, and I would be out of his way for two months — though I used to come for a weekly salaam, to pay my respects, have lunch with him, and go back. And the younger Wazir was to come with me, and I thought that he being with me, my father would not suspect me so much, for he trusted the Wazir brothers. Yet when I came back, relations still did not seem improved.

In the autumn I went to Peshawar again to check my health, and the doctor told me I had tuberculosis. I excused myself, and went to Captain Coldstream (who was later killed by one of the chaprasis) and took that report to him. He assured me it was wrong, that I was well — but mentally, I did not feel well. Therefore, again I made a trip, this time to Calcutta, Lahore, Delhi, Lucknow — and I took the son of the younger Wazir, whom I appointed as my private secretary, though there was no work for him to do! I just wished to say that he should be with me, so my father would have no unfounded suspicions. In Lahore, I was examined by a few specialists, and they advised me that I had a bad case of tonsilitis, and that my tonsils should be removed: it was giving me temperatures of 99 and 99.2 in the evening, and I had no tuberculosis or any other disease.

I spent Christmas in Calcutta, and came back home to take my father's permission before the operation. And he said: "I don't believe in this chloroform business. Usually people die on the operating table. You should have local anaesthetic!" That showed that he had affection for me. When the doctor, Colonel Dick, asked me, I said: "Local anaesthetic if you can." Though I would never advise anybody in my life to do it: all the time you are conscious, with those scissors in your mouth! And it was not a simple operation then as it is now — there was no penicillin or such products, I was kept for 8 days in hospital and then spent 2 or 3 days in the hotel before I could travel home.

My father told me to have a rest. And I wanted particularly that he should be convinced that he was the Ruler, so whenever a chance arose, I stepped back. And in this desultory fashion, things moved on.

There used to be an investiture ceremony in Peshawar every spring. The titles and awards were announced in June, on the birthday of the King Emperor, and then on the 1st of January again — but the investiture was held on the 1st of March at Government House and at the Vice-regal Lodge in Delhi. My father was always invited for these functions, but he never attended. He used to say: "I am a simple man"; and I was next in line, to represent him.[18] The elder Wazir was being invested as Khan Bahadur at the time. So he said: "We will go together". All right. He stayed in the Government guest-house in Peshawar; and Sir George Cunningham, who was No. 2 after the Governor as a senior executive, invited me to stay with him for the night. I dined with them, and he showed me the procedure for next day. We had to take our places at a quarter to ten, as we were to sit on the stage. Exactly five minutes before, we left, and we arrived on the stage — there were very few places there: the Governor, Sir Ralph Griffith, and his wife; Sir George Cunningham and his wife; the Minister for transferred subjects, Nawab Sir Abdul Qayyum; the Speaker; Khan Bahadur Abdul Ghaffar Khan; and the Major-General in command of Peshawar. Lined up in front were the Chief Secretary and the Revenue Commissioner, and some other officials and notable people. It was a unique honour they showed me in giving me a place on the stage.

I was in my tailcoat, with a white tie as was everyone else. There were many people whispering and asking: "Who is this new Sahib?" Because my colour was fair. "It must be the new revenue commissioner, or this, or that" — they were guessing. But after the investiture, there was a reception, and all my old class fellows came crowding up: "Jahanzeb, how are you?" "We are so happy to meet you!"

My program was to have lunch with Col. Brierly, and then shift to Ambrose Dundas, who had become Deputy Commissioner, and stay the night in his house. I was just finishing my lunch when I saw my treasury officer waiting on the lawn; I was shocked, because I knew something was up. So I rushed outside: "What is the message?" And it was an order for me to send all the officials back who had come with me, and that I would not be allowed to return to Swat. "And what more news?" I asked. "All your maternal uncles along with many officials have been dismissed."

It was a great shock. So I went to the Wazir in the Government Guest House. He pretended: "Oh! has Badshah Sahib gone mad? What has happened? Why?" and so on. After that I went to Sir George Cunningham — I wanted to get in touch with the Political Agent Malakand who was with him for lunch. His name was L.W.H.D. Best: Leslie William Hazlet Duncan Best — and the English people used to call him Archie.

Why Archie? Because he had so many names, he needed one more! So to friends, he was Archie Best. He was lunching with Sir George; they were eating late. I had lunched early with Brierly, so they were still sitting at the table. Showing no courtesy I just took him by the hand, and I said: "Sir George, please excuse us, I want to talk to him!" He said: "All right". Best was another good fellow, and in this crisis he was very sympathetic to me. He told me that in the morning, the Wazir had gone to the Governor, and Best was there, and the Wazir said that he had brought a letter from my father saying that I was planning to rebel against him, and that I was ordered to remain in Peshawar till my father felt secure enough to call me back. I exclaimed: "The Wazir? But I have just met the Wazir, and he knows nothing!" "Ah", said Best, "you don't know that man!"

I stayed the night with the Dundases. They had planned for me to go to the cinema after dinner, but I said: "I am not in the mood". Next morning they were going on tour to Mardan — which was then part of Peshawar district — and he told me to remain in his house for the six days till they came back: "That is your room and this is for your servant, and the cook is here and you can order anything!" But as soon as they left, I shifted to Dean's Hotel — because I did not know what I would do, and how long I would be staying.

I had taken 1000 Rupees and a dinner jacket, tails, and two other suits, and other things for two days only. So I told one of my companions to go and request my father to allow me some clothes and other things I needed. Out of my 1000 Rupees I had already spent Rs. 300/-; there was Rs. 700 left, which was still quite enough in those days, when a room in Dean's Hotel cost 12 Rupees a night, all meals included. Soon my companion came back with 3000 Rupees from my father, and that made me happy. It meant I could pull through for quite some time, a month or two. Meanwhile the Political Agent, Best, was telling my father: "You have done a wrong thing!" and so on. Best would not visit Saidu; he called my father to meet him in Barikot, and said: "I will not visit Saidu till Jahanzeb is back." And after 10 days my father said: "He can come back, but you will bring him!" But the day I was coming back, the program was like this: that we should have lunch together, and Best would come with me. But there was trouble with the Faqir of Alinghar and there was a battle going on, across Dargai. So he had to excuse himself and his wife entertained me. She was the only child of Sir Norman Bolton, the Chief Commissioner in 1925. Finally Best sent his

Assistant Political Officer with me. And ten days later Mr. Best was killed accidentally in battle: some say he went forward and the Gurkhas, not knowing who he was, shot him with machine guns; some say he was killed by enemy fire. In any case, the poor fellow died in that battle.

When I met my father, he told me that nobody would be allowed to see me; I must remain in my house, but that I would enjoy unaltered privileges, pay, servants and everything. I said: "All right". He repeated it again. I said: "I shall obey you. You will see, the time will come when you will realize that I was *not* a rebel. But I have one request to you". And he said: "What is that?" — politely, as always. I said: "That I shall have lunch with you every day". Oh — he did not hesitate: "That's no problem! Great pleasure!" And in that way, I did well, for whenever people were lunching there, they saw me, that I was sitting next to my father, eating together and having *"gupshup"*, chatting with him. So the Wazirs were not at ease. My father never talked with me alone — because he thought that the Wazirs might get suspicious.

From what I have been able to ascertain, my father's decision to dismiss me like that was made only two or three days before the act. Khan Bahadur Sahib of Jura village has told me something about it. He was related to the Wazirs — the younger Wazir's daughter is married to his eldest son. So they all had the same purpose: to deprive me of power so they could have a free hand. For even in those days I did not allow Khans and other notables to use their power to dominate or threaten others and grab their lands; so they were afraid of me. Khan Bahadur of Jura — he was not yet Khan Bahadur then, he was just called Jura Khan — was actually consulted by my father. He said: "Within a few days, I am going to take power from Jahanzeb, and also those officials who are loyal to him" — without naming the officials. Then Khan Bahadur told him: "You know, Sir, he is going on the first of March to Peshawar, and will be there for some days". My father became very happy and said: "All right, when he goes, we will do it!" But he must have been thinking for a long time about what he should do, and how he should do it: should he take drastic action, or be lenient.

After my uncle, Shirin Sahib, was killed in battle with Dir, there was no other figure to oppose my father. As regards me, to set my cousins against me, did not arise. Because Shirin Sahib died when I was 10 years old, and he had one son and two daughters. The son was of my age, so he became the ward of my father; and his sister was married to me and became my children's mother, while the other sister was married to my half-brother Sultan-i-Room, who was only thirteen months older than my eldest son Aurangzeb. My eldest half-brother was only four years younger than me, and he was a very capable boy. If he had lived, there might have been great difficulties; because he was intelligent, and ambitious. He always stood first in his class, and if he had been misled by people intriguing against me, it would have been very difficult. His and Sultan-i-Room's sister was given in marriage to the elder Wazir; and I know that the Wazir brothers, with some Khans who were their relations, had some plans to persuade my father to make *him* the heir apparent. But he died while still in College (p. 39). It was fortunate that my father was there, at his death-bed — otherwise some people would have suspected something else.

After some time, it was the Wazirs who became my *tarburs* (patrilateral cousins/enemies). They thought that when my father died, they might succeed him. I don't think people in Swat would have accepted them, or that the British Indian Government would. But everyone has some plans.

My father dismissed about 20 officers that he thought were directly loyal to me. There were more people who were close to me; but he thought it was wise to divide them between themselves and from me — as the higher-ups were dismissed, the others were promoted to gain their loyalty. Somebody put the idea to him that I had some kind of union with my cousin Bahramand, my wife's brother. My wife wanted him to marry Sultan-i-Room's sister, so that he could remain in Swat. But my father said: "All right, he can marry her, but he will not remain here: both will go out from Swat!" He was given his share of the family property below Malakand, and he was told to go there and live outside the State.

The Wazirs favoured Sultan-i-Room for three reasons. The elder Wazir's wife was his full sister. Secondly, he was a small boy, and they thought that if he became the Ruler, they would have all the power. And thirdly, he was afraid of me: that if I came into power, I might remove them. Sultan-i-Room's mother very much wanted to promote her son's candidature too. And she was the favourite wife of my father, being the youngest. But my father always said: "If you interfere in Jahanzeb's work or make any intrigues, it will not be good for you". She was warned, many times, in spite of the love he felt for her. My father was a man of strong principles, and he was a realist.

Fate was very much in my favour — fate and luck. We believe that if

God destines a person to do some good work, then He protects him — until his utility is finished. That was why, in the time of the crisis and the following years, I had great faith in God — as I have now also, even more. I thought that I was destined to become Ruler some day, and that God would take care of me. So I never lost hope. If I did not have that confidence, I would have become very pessimistic and might even have committed suicide; for there were moments when everything looked very bleak.

People make up so many stories afterwards — it has even been said that my father and I only pretended to fall out, so as to tempt the opposition to come out into the open. But it was not a scheme, it did happen; he was not utilizing it for any covert purpose. He was annoyed with me. But my own idea is: he never believed that I would rebel against him. He said to people that I might be plotting a revolution against him, but in his heart he did not believe it. What he really thought was that he had lost his power — as in those days he had given me everything. He thought that he was losing the power to rule; so I think he became a bit jealous. Therefore he dismissed my maternal uncles, and those other officials, and told me not to meet them.

CHAPTER VIII:

Years of waiting: 1935-1940

"In your downfall, you can learn more"

For six months I was not allowed to meet anyone. It was not fixed for that duration, it just took that long. By then, I think my father had repented of his acts; but he did not want to reverse his decision so soon, nor annoy people by accepting me back. So one day, I asked him: "Sir, can I beg you to tell me one thing?" He said: "What is that?" "Did you really believe that I was going to rebel against you?" He said: "No." — Later, he told me: "You should try to gain my confidence." Trust or confidence, those were his words. But trust is not an article, something that you can give to somebody and then you will be trusted. You have to prove that you can be trusted. That proof took another three years.

I had no one to speak to or confide in; no one who could console me. Not even my grandmother, who used to love me so. Talking to her about it would be like grumbling, and I did not want to grumble. Deep inside, I knew what would happen; and I told Ataullah, my father's chief secretary (cf. pp. 41 f.): "My father will change some day; let us wait". Because the affection and love of a father was always there.

Ataullah was on my side, at heart. But he was very cautious, and he did not want to annoy the Wazirs — though they never trusted him. He knew that my father was not going to deprive me for the rest of his life; he would eventually give me power again. So Ataullah could understand that his future lay with me, and covertly he backed me, very cautiously, while being very obedient to them and doing whatever they said. No one dared back me openly; but I knew there were many people on my side: many officials, and some of the Khans who were of the opposite *dalla* from the Wazirs. Sometimes the aggrieved party would come to me and say: "Sahib, if you become Ruler, I hope you will restore our position!"

I kept thinking of the future, when the chance would come for me to become Ruler; so I took an interest in everything. After six months my father relaxed the restriction on people meeting me. The officials were allowed to come, collectively, for dinners and lunches. He thought that if they came here individually, I might intrigue with them; that was his concern. The rest of the time, I used to read books, in the mornings; and in the evenings I used to play tennis, or go riding; but generally I kept myself busy. I had more time for thinking, and planning how I should manage this State, and what I should do. When I was going along the road, I thought how I would straighten this curve, and rebuild this bridge, and things like that. I tried thinking about the future, always, so as not to become pessimistic.

It was the second hard period in my life. The first was from the age of five to thirteen years, when I lived with the Mullah and suffered there. Yet I feel that it was good training for the future. Then the second period came in 1935; though I had all the comforts a person needs — I mean servants, food, clothing, a nice house, and the opportunity to meet foreigners — but I was undeniably depressed, though I was not without hope. Sometimes it would almost overwhelm me: How long will it take, and so on. Yet when I look back at that part of my life, I acknowledge that it had a good effect. Had I been let loose at that time to do anything I liked, I might have failed in life. Instead there was a bridle on me, and that gave me some perspective on myself, some insight. I had time to spare, and I read most of the books in my small library. It gave me time to advance my knowledge, and it gave me time to think: if I became Ruler, what would I do, in the way of making roads, schools, and hospitals. But sometimes, when I thought of why it had happened, as I had done no wrong, I felt depressed, overwhelmed for ten or fifteen minutes — and then I shook my head and pulled myself together.

I had my own opinions, and I expressed them to my father. It was mainly about his State policy, the issue of feudalism, that I differed with him and held a different opinion. He was a very strong-minded person, and a very kind father. Even in those five years, he had great affection for me; he loved me immensely, and always prayed to God for me. I think that, when God has destined something for you, then that is good for you. Personally I think that those five years have done much for me, and given me a richer experience. In your downfall, you can learn more than when you are in power — so it was a blessing in disguise. And my father's intention was to teach me a lesson, otherwise he could have exiled me, removing me from here; but he never wanted that.

I learned from the British too, from British officials and visitors:

about etiquette and all such things. The Political Agents became my close friends, and I was never shy of asking: "How does one do this and that?" They would tell me, very politely: "If I were you I would have done it this way; if I were you, I would have done something like this...". The local people here are very intelligent people, even though they were not educated — neither was my father — but they had tremendous knowledge. From *Molanas* I would learn religious things. I was never shy, and did not pretend I knew everything, and I would ask my father "What was this story, and how was that story?" He used to relate to me all the stories of tribal warfare, and the traditions of the people. And there was one Khan of Kana, Pir Dad Khan, and Khan Bahadur Sahib of Jura, they were really wise people. I would bring them here and entertain them, and we exchanged ideas. From them I learned a great deal; and also from the elder Wazir.

Objectively, though, my position was precarious. One day, Sir Ralph Griffith came here on a visit — he was Governor of the Province, the last Chief Commissioner and the first Governor. He came for shooting, it was in 1936. At that time, the custom was for everyone to disperse an hour before dinner, to change into evening dress. Usually, the guest of honour would propose that we disperse; when there was no distinguished visitor, I would propose it. That evening, Sir Ralph Griffith proposed that we go to dress for dinner. I remember it very vividly: we sat down together and he said he had a few things to ask me. "If your father were to die suddenly, can you sustain life for three days — in such a case would you be able to mobilize some support so you could hold out?" I said: "I cannot". "Why?" "I have no power. The Army will do as the Wazirs say. The finance is with them. The Khans are their relations — they are with them. I have no power". Then he said: "Not even twenty-four hours?" I said: "No." He told me: "I have made my arrangements; but I wanted to confirm it. I have instructed our brigade in Nowshera, that the moment they hear that Badshah Sahib is dead, they immediately move to Saidu." This gave me great pleasure and confidence, at the time.

Later, after partition, I had a visit by a British officer — I do not recollect his name, he was a colonel. Just conversationally, he suddenly asked me: "What was the matter in 1936, was there a battle here or something?" I said: "No, there was no battle..." Then he said: "We were told to be on the alert!" Then I remembered the words of Sir Ralph. The colonel must have been a junior officer at that time — he had not known what it was about; but they were in readiness should the crisis arise.

As I see it, this was done in sympathy for me as Jahanzeb, as a person. Though I was in contact with them as the Badshah's elder son, the Heir Apparent, that was a sort of introduction. But then the mutual affection was created by our contact and the circumstances, and for *that* reason they wanted to help me. Later also, it was not interference in State affairs that they practised, it was persuasion they used: request and persuasion. Not from the Goverment's side, not officially, but in personal capacities, as Sir George Cunningham, as Sir Ralph Griffith. There was no interference from the Government's side at all.

Later, in 1937–38, the elder Wazir approached me. He also had his fears; he was not a strong man. He may have been brave in the wars, brave in battle, but politically he was not very brave. He suggested that we swear to each other: he would swear his loyalty to me for ever; and I was supposed to swear that I would never harm him and his brother. I said I could not enter into such a bargain. He asked: "Why not?" I explained: "I cannot make such a promise, for though you may swear, I will not believe it. Because it will all depend on circumstances. Suppose my father were to die — may God forbid. If you prove your loyalty to me at that time — how could I wish to harm you? And if you clash with me, either you or I succeed, and how could I promise not to harm you in any way?" He tried many times, but I always gave him the same answer.

To this extent, we could speak openly to one another, and we had relations in other respects. He used to come once a week, and his younger brother, Wazir Ahmed Ali, came every second day — if I wanted him, he would come every day. We went by car together, and we went riding together. We never acted as though we were enemies — all those things were done underhand. Face-to-face, they were very obedient — especially the younger one, he was *most* obedient.

I also had time to observe the British, at some distance — both to get to know them and to reflect on them and their society.

W.R. Hay, who was Political Agent in Malakand for two-and-a-half to three years, even stayed for a month with us in Murghzar. He brought his family, and he used to go to Malakand to work in the morning and come back at night to be with his children. In brief meetings with my father, he used to ask questions and thus collect the material for his brief pamphlet on Swat.

He was a very shrewd person. He was a Roman Catholic, that is why he had four daughters. Just after the First World War, he was in Kurdistan, then here. His last job was as British Resident in the Persian Gulf. They had much influence there, through an administration which was under the Government of India. But though Hay was an intelligent man, the British people never liked him much — being clumsy, lower class. That was his handicap — otherwise he would have become Governor or something like that.

They were very snobbish in those days. For example, there was a very good man, and a very able Political Agent, shortly after Hay, in 1935–36 — his name was Harry Hall Johnson. He had served in the ranks during the First World War. Therefore, the other British never associated with him — they used to keep to themselves. He was a first class gentleman, a first class administrator, and a practical man. He did some good for the Agency, whatever was in his power. He was also very sympathetic to me, even in my position. But he never rose in the service, as his work and ability qualified him to. He finally became Resident, in Waziristan. He died in England in 1967 — I happened to learn this because I was in England then, and read his obituary in the paper. He was like a Pathan: brought his wife only once here for lunch, to show her the place — otherwise she was kept inside the compound. I do not think that he imposed this on her, it was by mutual understanding. Either she did not like to go out, or the other garrison people in Malakand did not wish to associate with them.

In such ways, they were very snobbish. And whenever there was a lieutenant or a captain even — they sometimes came with their wives, to make a "reccy" as they said, meaning reconnaissance — if there was a major there, he would not have his meals with the others, only one rank below.

One man who rose from the ranks was Field Marshal Lord Robertson, after the First World War. But that was exceptional, very rare. Only the best people came to the frontier, in the political service. As I remember, one third came from the Army, and two thirds came from the Indian Civil Service. Being in the I.C.S. they were already highly qualified. They used to select people from good families, and people whose fathers had also served in India. After obtaining high education, they had to enter into competition to enter the I.C.S. in England, and then they were trained further. So there were only a few who passed and got these jobs. Even our own people, those who entered the I.C.S. and are now Pakistanis, have those special qualities. They were chosen there in England, while they were getting their education there.

Of all the British administrators I have known, I judge Sir George Cunningham to be the most outstanding. He had exceptional inner qualities, no one could have such command of people as he had — from his ability to earn their respect. He was also very generous in hospitality. One of the reasons was that he had a large personal income. At the time, I think it was around ten thousand pounds a year — an enormous income in those days. He was also the first to break the barrier and start mixing more freely with his staff, and with the Frontier people. Sir George Cunningham gradually started inviting people in the province for dinners, for more informal meals, for playing tennis, and playing bridge even. He became close to Dr. Khan Sahib, the brother of Abdul Ghaffar Khan, and Dr. Khan Sahib's second wife was British — anyway, he took their son Jan as his honorary A.D.C. and let him live with them. Khan Sahib used to go there a lot and play bridge in the evenings.

Sir George Cunningham and his wife had no children — they married late. He was Private Secretary to the Viceroy Lord Irwin before he married; and she was past forty when they married. And they were very devoted to each other. When he died, she could not bear the loss. She survived him by only a month, then she jumped from a cliff into the sea near St. Andrews in Scotland.

During these years of waiting, I also experienced a painful personal and domestic sorrow. As told above, I married my cousin in 1925, and in 1928 we had our first son Aurangzeb. Then after two years, we had our second son. He was a very lovely child. But after a year — we did not know what it indicated — he started having fits. The best doctor we could get was a civil surgeon from Malakand, an Englishman. He came and felt him along the sutures of his head, and said that he had hydrocephalus. The doctors in those days, even now, don't know the cause of it. I asked about the fits, and the doctor said he would do a lumbar puncture to take away the extra fluid and relieve the pressure on the brain.

They told me to go out, and tell someone to come and hold the child. But I said: "I cannot trust anyone here to hold him firmly and safely, I must do it myself." And so, while I held him, he had a lumbar puncture, and the drops were coming from that syringe — I don't remember how many drops per minute, but at least, the excess was drained off. With that, the fits disappeared — but he was not normal, and it affected his eyes. I showed him to many doctors, and they all said: "He will die". There was even a Director of Public Health, who said: "It is no use, no use. I will give him morphine, and let him pass away." But of course, I answered: "It can't be done".

In 1936 my father developed cataract, and H.H. Johnson, the Political Agent, advised him to bring Sir Henry Holland, the famous missionary doctor and eye specialist from Quetta. He operated on my father's eye; and I also showed him Alamzeb, who was six years old at the time. "He will not live beyond 17," said Dr. Holland, "I can bet he will not — and if he lives, he will be mad, stark mad." But he is still living, and he has fathered nice children: five of them, two girls and three boys, all brilliant. The sisters are married to very good and cultured men. The first grandson Akbarzeb is now in the Pakistan Foreign Service after getting a B.A. degree at Cambridge. Aslamzeb, the second, is in the Pakistan Army, and the third, Anwarzeb is a doctor. So Alamzeb has very brilliant children and descendants. But he himself is so intransigent that he will not visit me. When his monthly payday comes, he sends someone else to collect the money. Usually, I send it to him beforehand. And he is in the hands of his servants, we cannot do anything. He gives all his money to the servants. If they had looked after him well, I would have been happy, I would have increased the subsidy. But they don't do very well for him. And he has no feelings for his children — if they go there, he says: "How are you?", that is all. He won't meet his wife; for eight years he did not go to his mother. Now he goes sometimes, but he does not come to me. One can still say that he is intelligent. But he has a one-track mind.

I have two more sons: Amir Zeb and Ahmed Zeb. They are well educated — but throughout the existence of the State I kept them entirely away from all State matters, training my son and heir Aurangzeb for the State, and them for a private life. This was what my father did with me — even in those difficult years, he never allowed any doubt as to my position as Heir Apparent.

During the five years while I did not take part in the administration of the State, my father also extended our territory to include all of Indus Kohistan. First one of the *dallas* in the border areas of Duber, Ranolia, and Bankad invited us in to support them, and they were put under administration. But the more distant, and largest, village of Patan, deep in a bend of the Indus gorge, was the main stronghold of the Kohistanis. From there, they continued to resist and intrigue against us. So the Army mounted a campaign across the high mountains and passes, and seized Patan. After that, the *jirga* came in from Kandia, the largest and northernmost of the tributaries to the Indus in Indus Kohistan; and they asked to join the State. My father answered: "First, I want a telephone line in there so I can talk to you!" So he kept the *jirga* waiting in Saidu for two months while the telephone line was laid, and only then did he accept their accession to the State. It must have been the only time in history that a telephone line was sent in first, and troops and administration only afterwards, to incorporate a new area into a State!

CHAPTER IX:

The road to kingship: 1940-1949

"The happiest day in my life."

Time passed, and I continued to wait and seek to build up my father's trust in me. By 1939, Sir George Cunningham was very keen that the process should go one step further, and that I should be given some recognition and responsibility by my father. The Political Agent in Malakand by then was Sahibzada Khurshid, who later became the first Pakistani Governor of the Province — and he was Governor at the time of my installation as Wali. Towards the end of 1939, Sir George Cunningham was going on four months' leave, and he told Khurshid that he should try to persuade Badshah Sahib to give me some work, some duties in the State. But my father said: "No, I cannot. He must first re-create my trust in him!" Sardar Khurshid contacted me, and said I must speak to my father myself about it. "But you are not to show that you know that I have spoken to him about it, and that Sir George Cunningham has suggested it". "But", I said, "how can I bring up the subject, and not show that I know something about it?" So he answered that I could say that the Political Agent had seen me, and told me how he had brought up the matter, and how my father had refused. With this plan, I went to my father. The procedure worked. And I said to my father: "Apparently, you feel that my so-called sins are unforgivable. But you feel you cannot destroy your own son. So the policy you have been pursuing is that I should wait — and after your death, I should be destroyed. If this is correct, then as you are determined, I shall abdicate from my position as Heir Apparent; and you can give it to Sultan-i-Room! But *not* to the Wazirs!" And my father flared up: "If you cannot wrench the power from those people, how can a 13-year-old boy like him do it? Go to the Political Agent tomorrow; tell him that I will do something!" There was much love between me and my father.

After that I met Khurshid. He was about to be transferred; but he was very happy to get this message. Later, my father said: "You must write two or three statements which will be witnessed by the Governor. Then,

I will give you some power. One is that you will not harm Sultan-i-Room, and that half of my property will go to him, and half to you. This I want guaranteed by the Government. Secondly, as for the two Wazirs, you will not harm their body, or their property. It is for you to decide, after my death or after I have handed over to you, whether you wish to keep them in service or not. That is your free choice. But their property and their lives must be safe; and if they are retired, they will be given a pension of 400 Rupees each per month."

So I went to the acting Governor, Sir Arthur Parsons, but he said: "I am incapable of signing and guaranteeing this on behalf of the Government, because I am only a temporary man here. You must wait for Sir George Cunningham; when he comes back he will sign it." I had to go back and tell my father: "And I am sorry to see that you are a little suspicious that I am hesitating and producing excuses. But this is not so. And I can wait — he will come, and he will sign it." In due course, Sir George Cunningham came, and he did sign it — and my father asked me: "Do you mean it?" And I said: "Yes, I mean it."

My father then gave me the choice of three ministries: one was Finance, the other was Justice, the third was the Army. "Whichever you want, I will give you". I answered: "This must depend on you, how far you trust me." He said: "No, you must choose..." I said: "No, Sir" and so on — but in my mind, it was the Army. At last I said: "Any one of those I ask for, you will give me?" "Yes, yes" he said, he was sure about that. So I said I wanted the Army. He just sprang up, and embraced me! "That's the thing! If you want to win the power from them, it is best to take the Army! Otherwise, they have the force, they can intrigue against both you and me!" Khurshid had been succeeded by Major Mallam as Political Agent. He was a very noble person. My father informed him of the decision, that by the beginning of January 1940 he was going to hand over the Command of the Swat Army to me. The Wazirs were reconfirmed as ministers. The younger Wazir, formerly Commander-in-Chief, was made "Minister"; the elder Wazir was made "Chief Minister". Kicked upstairs, so to speak. But after that, the Wazirs could not trust my father. The suspicion dividing them became wider and wider — but it took another three years before it broke.

It was the happiest day in my life, the day my father gave me the Army, and trusted me. And when the Wazirs left in October 1943, my father gave me full power. One thing he never told me till afterwards: he thought that I would not do the work myself, but do it through somebody else, as he himself had done through the Wazirs. But I was very enthusiastic, and started working immediately: case-work, roads, building, checking the treasury every morning. Every morning up till the end, the treasury officer would come to me at breakfast and I would check the previous day's accounts. That way, it became very easy after the first month, because I would remember what I had ordered the previous day. When the State was merged, I gave those books and records to the Government, so they could see what had gone on in the State. They could not find anything wrong.

My father was very happy: "I never thought you would do the work yourself, I thought you would give it to someone else. Otherwise, I would have given it to you long ago!"

I liked the work. Even now, I don't have a secretary. I do my writing myself, and my own accounts — not through my sons here, or anyone else. I don't believe there is a single bridge built in Swat that I have not examined, from underneath as well as on top. Whenever a bridge was made, I went there. I went down to that place because the local labour was there, and I inspected the foundations to see how strong they were. The near places I used to inspect on my evening drives, when I went out now this way, now that way for 15 miles or so. In Buner, I did it when I went for shooting, in the winter. The most distant places, I went to when the shooting season was finished, usually in April. Then I examined what had been done, and gave orders for further work, and by autumn I went there again, to see how much progress had been made.

I never spent the night away from home: I would go early in the morning, and come home here late in the evening. I would go in one station-wagon, with some people, my associates, then one open jeep with the bodyguard, followed by another jeep with the people from the Public Works Department.

The first thing I did when I took over the Army was to put them in uniform. Till then, there had been no restriction on their dress; they could wear any clothes they liked, and so nobody could recognize them as Army. I introduced khaki uniforms, but in native style. Later, I changed to the grey-blue cloth. I put badges on the officers; and gradually I started with training for parades, etc. Just for prestige; but it created a greater *esprit-de-corps*. And our Army proved its strength and usefulness in Kashmir in 1947 — they distinguished themselves, and some of them also fell there. Among them was one of our best men, his name was Fakir Mohammed; he was killed in Omtitwal in Kashmir, fighting the Indians. I later had four or five people sent to the military training school in Kohat, where they had a few places for admission without commitment to enter the Pakistan Army. They came back, and could train others again. Not with the rigour that a modern army is trained, but so they would have a basic discipline, with parades and saluting and such things.

I set about reinstating those people who had been dismissed in 1935. Some of them were called back immediately, and given the same jobs — with the permission of my father. Others he did not want — so they had to wait until I became Ruler. I also had to dismiss people who claimed they had been loyal, and wanted too much. It is just like dacoits: looting some people, and then while they are distributing the booty, they kill each other. If you try to please everyone, you end up with none. The Wazirs likewise wanted to strengthen their *dalla* for the future, and protect their friends. But now I was the stronger party, being Waliahad, and so the general public looked to me. Knowing that I was going to be the future Ruler, they were more inclined to me than to them. The Army was under my command, and the Civil Administration was under the Wazirs. Secretly we intrigued against each other. If they did not like somebody, I liked them, and made them Jamadar or Subedar, with the approval of my father. Sometimes, with some persons, he would not agree; but 98% he accepted. Then on the other hand, if there was a friend of mine who was accused of a crime or misdemeanour, the Wazirs usually punished him very hard. It was a kind of diarchy, and it was difficult for people.

My father stayed out of it. Either he was ignorant, or he thought that he should let things run their course and settle in my favour. I don't know; we never discussed it. Neither side sought his partisan support. Perhaps he just pretended ignorance, and did not want to do anything to patch up the relationship between the Wazirs and myself — another case of divide and rule! For *he* had a problem too, in retaining authority for himself. It was an intricate game, with many players. But as he was a strong man, the Wazirs feared him. It never came out into the open — they never dared; and in their relations to me they showed respect when they came here, and always behaved very nicely and properly. The only way they could have achieved something was by finding a candidate whom they could control, and then waiting. My father's position was unshaken. And he had great confidence in himself — very great confidence.

On the 18th of June 1943, my father made me Chief Minister also. Shortly after, in September, the elder Wazir made some excuse, and went to Kashmir. I think he was afraid that he might be killed by my father — he stayed away. In October, my father went to Peshawar to see the Governor, just on a courtesy call. The elder Wazir came to him, they were both staying at Dean's Hotel, and put in his resignation there to my father, saying that he did not wish to return to Swat. Then he telephoned his younger brother here — while my father was still there in Peshawar — and told him: "You must pack up and come!" People came and asked me whether the Wazirs were being dismissed, I said: "I am sorry, but he was instructed and he had to go". So I gave them vans and some lorries for their luggage, and on the 18th October 1943 they left peacefully, with their families. They had already made their houses in Wazirabad, near Dargai, so there were no problems for their accommodation.

Since that day, I only once met the elder Wazir, in Karachi, and the younger one I met by chance once in Dean's Hotel in Peshawar. We spoke briefly together — I smiled, and he said: "We were loyal to you, and you did not trust us." I said: "I have not removed you, my father has removed you. I never removed you."

When they resigned and departed, my father disregarded the points in the document that I had signed: that I should not confiscate their property, and that they should be given a pension of 400 Rupees/month each. Four hundred Rupees meant something at that time. Then later, the elder Wazir went to Sir George Cunningham and said: "What about my pension? And what about my lands — they have all been confiscated!" They were not confiscated by my father for himself, they were made State property; and even now, after merger, they are State property. He appealed many times to the Governor, but nothing happened. Then once when I happened to be there, at Sir George Cunningham's invitation, he told me about it — how the elder Wazir came pleading. I said: "You know English much better than I, and you have signed the document yourself. You can see what it says." He understood, but said nothing; so I continued: "My father said 'after my death or my handing over the State in my lifetime', then these conditions must be fulfilled. But he has not handed over to me, he has done it himself! So that document is null and void now." Sir George Cunningham had a nice smile — and now he smiled: "It must be up to Badshah Sahib, whatever he thinks." And nothing more happened.

From 1940, and even more from 1943, the relation between me and the Government of British India became more and more intimate. They started talking, thinking of giving me some title. There was a Political Agent, his name was Nawab Shaikh Mahbub Ali, who had been Oriental Secretary to Sir Frances Humphrey at the time when King Amanullah of Afghanistan was deposed. This Shaikh Mahbub wrote and recommended that I should be given the C.I.E. — Companion of the Indian Empire. They answered that an Heir Apparent was not usually given any award or decoration, because on becoming Ruler he would automatically receive big honours. But Shaikh Mahbub wrote back and said: "He is not only Heir Apparent — he is de facto Ruler! He is Chief Minister, Commander-in-Chief, and Heir Apparent. His father has given him all responsibility, and is consulted only on high policy!" — So the Government awarded me the order of C.I.E.

I have always made a point of going very punctually to my office, because others would then also have to be punctual. If I did not go there, then others would be late, and discipline would suffer. Exercising discipline over others must start with self-discipline. The people in Swat had to learn to keep time; and it greatly increased my own capacity for work, because I never had to waste time waiting.

In many ways, I was now in a position to start changing things — changing the system a little. Some of those changes, my father was enthusiastic about.

He liked the new discipline in the Army, the uniforms and such things. But sometimes I felt he put his foot down, because he did not want me to decide everything. When that happened, then for two or three months whatever he said I obeyed, and never mentioned anything that was against his will. Then, after three months or so, he felt convinced again that he was still the Ruler. Suddenly, when I spoke to him and consulted him, he would say: "Oh — this is your problem. You can do anything, as you like. I have given you the power!" But after a year or two, again it might come back, that feeling of his that he needed to reassert the fact of his ultimate control.

Likewise, with his own private lands. He made a will in 1939, as noted above, that my brother and I should share equally; but he did not specify which land I should get and which my brother would get. He thought that if he allotted the land that way we might not contribute the income from the land to him. Rather he wanted to have some leverage on us, that we should look forward to his charity. Only this did he specify: that

Saidu, Murghzar, Guligram and Salampur should go to me, and Sultan-i-Room would be given the villages of Sheratrap, Spal Bandei, Kukrei and Chitor. He did not want to give any share of the Saidu area to my brother, for we needed that land for the development of the capital of the State.

Mostly, it was I who dealt with the officials of the British Indian Administration; but the most distinguished visitors, would of course pay their respects to him, as Ruler of the State. On such occasions, I would act as interpreter, since Badshah Sahib spoke no English.

Even during those five years when we were somewhat estranged, I would be his interpreter — because he always trusted me, and there would be no political questions discussed at such times. The Political Agents, who did most of the detailed political consultations, all spoke Pashto, up to the level of Governor. They were made to learn Pashto, and only after that were they sent here. But with the guests from England, or some-where else in India, then I would be there to interpret.

The last Viceroy was Lord Wavell — that is, he was the last Viceroy before Mountbatten was brought in to oversee partition — and he was the last Viceroy to visit Swat. The Governor, Sir Olaf Caroe, accom-panied him. Caroe was sitting outside — I don't know why, except that he was so scared of Lord Wavell — and my father and I were sitting in-side, with Lord Wavell. He told me to tell my father that he would pro-bably be the last British Viceroy, that the British would be leaving India very shortly... "And is there anything I can do for the State, or for Bad-shah Sahib personally?" I translated this to my father, and he answered: "A moment ago he told me that he is the last Viceroy and the British are leaving — then how could *he* do anything for *me?*" Politely, I interpret-ed to Lord Wavell: "My father is very thankful and grateful to Your Excellency, but there is no problem for the present."

The last expansion of the State took place at this time — into Kalam or Swat Kohistan. The people of Kalam are different Kohistanis from those in Indus Kohistan, and speak separate languages.

Three states made some sort of claim to the area: the Mehtar of Chitral claimed it for himself, the Nawab of Dir claimed it, and my father claimed it. The claim of Chitral was that whenever any Ruler from Chitral was exiled, he used to come and take refuge in Kalam; and there are still about 400 houses there who speak Khowari, the language of Chitral. They also used to take some ponies from there annually, as tribute. The claim of the Nawab of Dir was that the Dir Kohistani people and the Kalami people have the same language. Our claim was that geographically, it is a part of the Swat valley; and they cannot take out their timber, which was their only product of potential value, except through Swat, nor can they bring anything to Kalam, of merchandise and other imports, except through Swat.

In 1926, when my father was recognized as Ruler by the British, all these three States were told not to interfere in Kalam, that it should be a buffer area. Later, when the *jirgas* came in from there in 1937 and wanted to join the State, we were stopped from incorporating that territory. The British never established a local administration there either; every Political Agent had his own idea about it. There was one, his name was William Thomson Glover, who wanted to establish government rule there, in some way or other. So he went to Kalam and hoisted the Union Jack on a post, put a Tahsildar there and some levies. Local people would not cooperate with them, except to the extent they were forced by the levies. When he was transferred, the next Political Agent did not care, and so it was *status quo ante* again.

Then, in 1947, some British official hinted to me that by midnight of August 14th there would be no British rule, so we could occupy it. So I did it, though against the will of my father. He said that the new government would be very angry. I answered that all they can do is take it back — so let them take it back! The matter rested till 1954, when I signed the first constitution of Swat with the Government of Pakistan. I tried to have our possession of Kalam recognized; but they said that it belongs to Pakistan, and Pakistan cannot transfer its sovereignty to another party. "But", I said, "is Swat not part of Pakistan? If one part wants to join another, what is the harm?" But they never agreed, and the compromise they found amounted to the same, or was even better: to leave the area in my hands and give me absolute powers there as I had in Swat, but that I would be called "Administrator for Kalam". I was even given a yearly allowance for doing the job!

By 1947, Swat State had completed its expansion in all directions as far as it was possible: down the valley to the Malakand Agency, in the west up to the borders of Dir, in the south down to the borders of the administered area of Mardan District, in the east to the banks of the Indus river, and in the north up to the borders of Chitral State and Gilgit Agency. These were all limits set up against us by the Government of British India, whether consisting of areas they administered, States they recognized, or unadministered, chaotic areas which they merely chose to declare out of bounds.

With the creation of Pakistan in 1947 we immediately joined the new state. We were very patriotic, both my father and I. We had also contributed before partition, supporting the Muslim League and the struggle for independence. Though one will notice that Pakistanis generally refer to it as "partition" rather than "independence" — the separation from the Hindus was much more important to us than the eviction of the British. We had supported the Muslim League with money, and by influencing our *murids,* the followers of Saidu Baba, all along the Frontier, from here to Bannu. So we wished to join as quickly as possible. And after partition we sent our Army to Kashmir — one thousand men at a time, relieved by a fresh contingent of one thousand every second month. We contributed to the refugee fund and to all Pakistani funds for defence. My father bought a "Fury" fighter aircraft for Pakistan — it was named after me.

The Political Agent at the time was from this country, but he was an exceptionally experienced person — the Nawab Shaikh Mahbub Ali, whom I have mentioned before (p. 100). In Kabul, at the time of King Amanullah's fall, he and the British Ambassador, Sir Francis Humphrey, had to be flown out. But some people say that this Shaikh Mahbub Ali was behind the trouble, that he had fomented the opposition to Amir Amanullah Khan. For his services he was made a Nawab and awarded the O.B.E., and from the Provincial Civil Service he was elevated to the Political Service. He took over in Malakand from Col. E.H. Cobb, who had advised us to take Kalam, after the creation of Pakistan. I talked to him over the telephone, and told him we were going to sign the Instrument of Accession. He answered: "I know you are a sensible person, that there would be no difficulties with you and that in any case you would do it. So I must clear these other matters, with the other States first." He went directly to Chitral and made the Mehtar sign the Instrument of Accession; then he brought it, on the way back, to Dir, and showed the Nawab that Chitral had signed and told him that Swat is going to sign. "Please sign this, here!" So the Nawab signed it. That is how Swat came third.

In that Instrument of Accession, we formally surrendered defence, foreign affairs, communication, and monetary standard to Pakistan. It did not change very much, because with British India we were limited in the same ways, and Pakistan did not move in to take over everything. Even with the British, there was a similar written agreement. It specified that we would be friendly to the government, and that we would surrender all the outlaws, and that we would not seek to extend our borders beyond the agreed limits. There was one point which my father and I did not register at the time: about not harbouring absconders from the settled areas. But afterwards, he put his foot down, and he never surrendered an absconder. He said this is *melmastia* (lit.: hospitality), a sort of refuge they have sought here. We will extract an undertaking from them that they will not raid the settled area from here, or misbehave. But as regards surrendering them, that is against *Pukhtunwali,* the Pathan code of honour. We never did that.

Never in my time either, with Pakistan. President Ayub Khan said to me: "This is not good, with these absconders and so on coming here." I countered: "It is very simple: we will make a reciprocal agreement that if *our* absconders go to you, you will surrender them to us, then we will do the same to you." He said: "Our laws are different, and your law is different. You may mistreat them." I said: "All right: when you surrender absconders to us, we will make a joint commission of myself and the Political Agent to see that nothing wrong is done to such a person. After all — if a Swati Pakistani kills a Swati Pakistani in Swat, is it right that he can take refuge in Pakistan?" By arguments like that, nothing more came of it!

We had no difficulties and riots against Hindus and Sikhs at partition. Here they were safe; nobody would wish to harm them, and nobody would dare to harm them. But when things settled, after the first war in Kashmir, some of them went away — saying goodbye to me before they left. When they got better jobs in India, or good business, they invited their family members to join them. But we still have Hindus and Sikhs here: in Mingora, in Chakesar, and many Sikhs in Buner. Even before the State, under lawless conditions, Pathans said: "They are innocent people, why should we harm them?" The Hindus were obedient to a Khan or a Malik, and even to a Mullah. If they became very rich, they might be looted and exploited — but not differently from Muslim merchants in those times. Likewise in the whole tribal belt: the Sikhs are still there, and they are protected by the tribesmen.

As I see it, the intensity of communal conflict depends very much on the proportions between the populations. If they are approximately equal in population, there is conflict; but if the minority is only 5% or 10%, people don't have any quarrel. At partition, Muslims were about 7% in Madras — and there were no riots at all. Here in the tribal belt, nobody molested Hindus or Sikhs. But in Panjab where the numbers were almost equal, there was conflict. Secondly, it is a question of economic competition. If economic conflict developed and there was little difference in the size of population, then the killing started. One may ask why there was killing in Bombay and U.P.? The reason was that Muslims in those areas made great efforts to create Pakistan. Panjab, Frontier and Sindh people, they got it ready made; it was Bombay and U.P. people who were the activists, and who suffered; and to take revenge against those people, the Hindus rioted and still kill them sometimes. After all, Qaid-i-Azim (i.e. Jinnah) came from Bombay, and Liaqat Ali Khan (Pakistan's first Prime Minister) came from near Delhi.

CHAPTER X:

Rule: 1949-1969

"I was the pivot of it all."

On the 12th December 1949 my father abdicated in my favour, and I was confirmed as Wali of Swat. The Prime Minister of Pakistan, Liaqat Ali Khan, came for the ceremony. Qaid-i-Azam was dead by then, and Khwaja Nazim-ud-Din had succeeded him as Governor General. He was a highly respected person, but he did not wield the power that Qaid-i-Azam had done. The actual power of the people on top depends on their personality, and whereas formerly Qaid-i-Azam as Governor General had been the leader of the nation, now it was Liaqat Ali Khan, as Prime Minister, who became the leader. And it was he who came for my inauguration and recognized me as Wali. In his speech, he praised me very much, and promised me every moral support for the State, "for it is one of the shining States of Islam!"

Why did my father choose to abdicate? He had great affection for me and wanted to give me the chance to prove my worth. He also told me once that, when he became Ruler, he looked forward to the time when I would grow up so he could hand over to me. "I was going to hand over to you in 1935, but then these unfortunate things happened, and that was why it was delayed". The thought of being no longer a Ruler was not a cause of regret to him — just as I now, after the merger of my State, do not regret the government taking away the State. That was the main point. There was a further point, though it was secondary to this main point, but it expressed a feeling which every human being must harbour. He felt — and I know because he told me — that he created the State, and if it were to disappear, be merged, in his time, then he would have what we call a "bad name" — he would be remembered for losing it as well as for creating it. He would rather pass it on to his descendant intact, so his name would be wholly and purely that of the founder and maker of the State.

In most respects, the change on becoming Ruler was not so great for me: I had already for some years been de-facto ruler, Chief Minister and Commander-in-Chief. But from now on, I no longer had to work inside my father's system — I could change it, taking the changing circumstances into account. So I started, in 1950, to break this feudal system.

Some of the Khans realized that they would lose their power, and rebelled against me. It was the only case, till the end of the State; and my father told me not to mind it, he said it happens to everybody — *any* Ruler, after a year or so, local people will make some attempt to test how strong he is.

It was a fairly big and powerful group — not so much in the amount of land and villages that they controlled personally, as in the influence they wielded. There was Afzal Khan and brothers, the sons of Darməi Khan; there were several of the big khans from Nikpi Khel — Bahram Khan; Qalandar Malik Aligrama; Sherzada Khan; Abdur Rashid Khan of Odigram; Abdur Rashid Khan of Derei — and so on. I was getting rumours that they were intending to do something, but that they judged that they would still have to wait for some time and collect more people, for I was still too strong for them. Some of them had old grievances, like the sons of the Darməi Khan; some had more recent grievances, like Rashid Khan of Odigram, whom I had retired early from his position as Captain in the Army, after he returned from Kashmir. All of them knew of my views on the system whereby these feudal leaders controlled the villagers and exploited them. At the same time, there were developments in Pakistani politics, so they thought they could get support from there. Khan Abdul Qayyum Khan had taken an active part in the creation of Pakistan and had been close to Qaid-i-Azam; but when he became Chief Minister in the North-West Frontier, that made him very pompous. Power went to his head, and he wanted to enlarge his province by incorporating Swat, Dir and Chitral into it, while acting like an absolute dictator. So those Khans thought that they could also get some support from him.

In December 1950 I went to Peshawar for an appendicitis. My minister informed me on my return of how the Khans' plot was developing; and I went and consulted my father. I said: "Do you know that such intrigues have been going on?" He smiled, and said: "Oh yes, I know everything — but you don't consult me." So I said: *"Now* I ask you, what to do?" And he said: "Yes, what do you intend to do?" Then I told him that I would make the opposing *dəlla* strong and at the same time allow the followers in *their dəlla* to become *Maliks,* so that their power would disperse. He said: "That is good."

By coincidence, my half-brother, Sultan-i-Room, was getting married at that time. So my father said: "This is a very good occasion!" I could not move freely, because it was only ten days after my operation for appendicitis, so I had to stay in Saidu. He said: "I will invite all these Khans, and take them to Peshawar for the marriage!" So in the morning they left, and by that very evening, I had recognized their opposition, and elevated those smaller khans and landowners to become Maliks. When they came back, they discovered that they had no more power — so they ran away. They left separately, but gathered in Malakand and went in a group there to the Political Agent, Col. Mufti Mohammed Yusuf, and said they had been expelled. He said no, they had not been expelled, and they were free to go back.

They were also disappointed in their attempt to obtain support from Abdul Qayyum Khan. The Central Government got annoyed with his headstrongness in the Province, so they moved him to the Centre and made him minister there, where he was more or less rendered harmless. And it was not the Central Government's policy at the time to assimilate the States; it had been a scheme of Abdul Qayyum Khan's only; so when he left, there was no further danger.

After three or four months, the Political Agent contacted me and said the Khans wanted to come back. I decided it was better to forgive, so I assented; but I set one condition: that they should not return together, in one group, but had to come in smaller batches as they had left. At first they did not agree, so a couple of months passed; then they started trickling in, one after another. They would come to me, and apologize for what they had done, and I said: "Well, your property and everything is safe and I have not touched it." Altogether, I think there were about fifty of them — for they had not taken their servants and wives and children, they had remained here, and only the Khans themselves had gone.

Some of them I even raised up again, after a short while, like Rashid Khan of Odigram. When he rebelled, I gave jobs in the army to his cousins: they were of the same *dəlla,* but at heart they did not like each other, so it was easy to entice them away from him by giving them these jobs, and letting them take over his position in the village. When Rashid Khan returned, he sat very quietly and was repentant, and so in 1954 I restored his *dəlla.* My maternal uncle's daughter was married to him;

and his father and grandfather had been most loyal to my father. What is more, we always liked to keep both *dallas* in position, so that if one made some mischief, the other would be on our side and counterbalance them.

In 1953 I was approached by the Pakistan Government, that I must sign some sort of constitution, so that other people wouldn't object, i.e. other States, and people of Pakistan. It was formulated as a "Supplementary Instrument of Accession" — but in practice it restated things as they already were, in most important respects.

The Governor of the Frontier was shy about telling me to do this, so he made an excuse that we would hold consultations in Saidu. I said: "No. Kalam has a very pleasant atmosphere, there is the background roar of the river, and no humidity, and it is a neutral ground, so let us negotiate it there!" Finally, he accepted the site, and the delegation came up: Shahab-ud-Din, the Governor, his Chief Secretary, Political Secretary, and the Political Agent Malakand. From our side, I came alone. I took no one along for consultations even, because they would not be of any help: they might well be flatterers, or choose to say: "No Sir, you should not sign away your sovereignty like that!" They would be of no use, because in any case I would have to sign. I had read the original Instrument of Accession, and already we had surrendered our autonomy.

We sat down around the table — it was August 1953 — and the Governor wanted to speak first. I said: "No, I will speak first." He said: "No, I will speak!" Then his Chief Secretary and the others told me please to let His Excellency speak first — at the time he used to be called His Excellency; after 1956 this Excellency business was abolished. I said: *"No.* Let me speak. If I can say it all, why have two speeches?" So he agreed and said: "Oh, all right, you have your say." I said: "It is quite simple. You want to convince me. I am already convinced. And now you want to make a big story of it, how in Kalam after intricate negotiations we did this and we did that. If I wanted to refuse, I have in fact some very good arguments. Number one: Ask the people of Swat." — At that time, in 1953, my people were *so* devoted to me, because of the development I was making. — "But I am not going to say that you must ask the people. Number two: I can make another excuse — that if the Nawab of Dir signs it, *then* I will sign it." — "No, no" they said, "if you sign it then Dir will sign it!" — Though he never signed. — "But I am already convinced. I am a loyal Pakistani, a patriot, I am going to sign it. But show me what you have brought, and allow me half an hour to go to my tent and read it first, before signing.'' So they gave me the document they had already drawn up, in writing, and I read it, and I said: "O.K., finished". And I signed on the 12th February 1954, in the Governor's House, Peshawar.

I did not even consult my father. When I signed this second Instrument of Accession, some critics said I had sold the State or given away the State. But I told them, even by the first Instrument of Accession everything already belonged to the Government. If you voluntarily surrender defence, then tomorrow if the Government does not look favourably on you any more — what can you do? As regards communication: if they take control over the communications — telephones and everything — what can you do? So I signed, as it was already surrendered.

When I read the document there in my tent, I did not study these main items closely, because I recognized them; they were already in the first Instrument of Accession. So I skipped over them. In other States — Bhawalpur, Khairpur, and the Baluchistan States — the Ruler was made a constitutional head and all the power was put into the hands of a Chief Minister. Whereas they did not impose any Chief Minister on me: I was President of the Council, Chief Minister, *and* Ruler. I think their idea was merely to bind me legally, for the future.

In fact, the formal system they created made no difference. They stipulated that there should be a State Council, with 15 elected members and 10 members nominated by me, and that I would be the President of the Council. And then the Government fixed my Privy Purse — from the revenue of my own State. It was ample, and provided what I needed to spend on myself and my family.

The Council had no real power. I collected them twice a year, and always told them what to do. Some people would make suggestions that were important for their village. So I generally said I would do it, but that they must always look to the State's overall priorities and needs. Other people just praised me and said: "You are doing everything, so what can we suggest?" Then in June I presented the budget of the State, and discussed it with them.

In some ways, this Supplementary Instrument of Accession strengthened me, in some ways it limited my power. Now suppose I had changed the constitution of the State without the permission of the Government, giving people more rights and so on, then the Government would have thought that I was encouraging an idea among my people of indepen-

110

dence from Pakistan. So I could not dare to do that. From the point of view of Pakistan, I became a sort of caretaker administrator. Though they did not interfere in my internal affairs, everybody knew that I *could* be removed and the State could be merged. Politicians might also start their agitation here — a few of the parties did. My own idea was to train the Swat people into a constitutional form of government. If you educate the people, and then you don't consult them and don't give them the right to speak and such things, then people get agitated. Being a state with small resources, I had to develop education, to give people something so they could compete in the larger Pakistan. But that again had consequences for what took place *inside* Swat. If you give people education, how can they obey an uneducated Khan?

Once my father said, a long time ago, at least 40 years ago, that the best form of government is dictatorship — provided the man does not get swollen-headed. This view he also practised. And I practised it too, but I knew the time would come when I would not be able to practise it any more. I had to go with the times. I had to foresee. And I had been reading: the books on Communism and all this social upheaval. Even in England, they are reviewing the powers of the Lords and Barons, and by high taxation and death duties they are eliminating their privileged class. So, when I became Ruler, then gradually, very slowly, I started changing this feudalism.

I started with the small Maliks, bribing them with small offers of service in the State, or small allowances, to waive their rights over the people. The big guns were more hard to break. And at that time, even, my father used to say: "Well, it is your State, and now you rule it and it is for you to decide. But I don't agree, *I do not agree at all.* One big stick is better than four or five small sticks to beat a man!"

It was not my personal idea, or even my preference, but times were changing. People came from outside and criticized the State, and said there is still feudalism. So I thought: it is time to start to change. So I created more Maliks who were under the Khans, and in area after area I made everybody Malik of his own land — free to run his own land. That was a sort of liberation from the Khans. And those people, they were with me. When I started, around 1954, people did not understand the implications of it. Some Khans laughed at it — but most who owned land wanted to be "Maliks of their own land". And very gradually, by the last five or ten years of my rule, from 1964 and onwards, the Khans had no power.

My main interest was to speed up the development of this State. I have three very close friends, from school, and they would come and visit me occasionally. We would go shooting, these friends and myself, and every time they came, there was another new school, another new hospital, or something else; and they would tell me always: these are your monuments, to your work and to the future.

As I have said, when my father started his career he could not find a single literate person to employ as his scribe in all of Swat. And our first primary school was opened in 1925. At the end of my rule, the literacy rate in Swat State was about 20%. From zero to twenty percent in about forty years, and all by our own efforts. According to our registers, there were 40,000 pupils in our schools in 1969, from primary class to higher. That is a good number, for a total population of three quarters of a million. All levels and groups of society were eager for education: all they could obtain here within the State, and even outside at State expense or at their own expense.

In the late 1950s, I also encouraged a Christian mission school to come to Swat. I did not invite them, but the Bishop came and offered to establish one. However, they had no finance. Our people were already going from here to the mission schools outside, and they used to spend a lot of money on this. I thought it would be a good idea to have one here — it would be cheaper for my people; and the children from the surrounding villages could also be enrolled as day scholars, so they would not incur the expenses for hostels. There were a few fanatics against it who said these mission people would come and convert Muslims and so on. I said: "No. They will not be allowed to convert people. If you like, instead of mission school I shall call it Public School. Or if people will promise me that they will not send their children to mission schools outside Swat, then I will promise not to start one inside Swat." They wanted to send their children because the education these schools give is good, and discipline is good. But it is expensive, compared to other education.

So I bought land for the site — unused land, for 50,000 Rupees, and I financed the construction of buildings according to their specifications, but paid for by the State. It was cheap, for the amount of knowledge Swat has obtained in that way. And I also had one thing in mind, that if they don't agree, we can tell them to leave, as the buildings are ours. Now they have become so popular: there are 500 candidates waiting for admission for the next two or three years!

In every way, I have sought to promote education. I also used it as an excuse to get rid of what we felt was an embarrassment: the annual allowance paid to the State. In 1926, Swat was granted a subsidy of 10,000 Rupees by the British, when they recognized us. But Dir was receiving 50,000 Rupees, so my father objected, and many times he refused to take it — compared to what Dir was given, it was degrading. But the British said: "Oh yes, you must take it, otherwise it would mean you were no longer friendly!" When I was made Ruler, I surrendered this to the Government. But even then, when the Government was Pakistan, they said: "We cannot just strike it out — you must specify it for something!" So I said: "For education. Make it an educational stipend." They would not stop it; it is still there in my name, and given away as stipends.

Started in 1952, Jahanzeb College was made a graduate college in 1954 — and so many of our young people have now gone through it and received their higher education there. It brought in many new social and political ideas, and with unrest in the universities all over the world in the late 1960s even that was felt here. But it was never a serious problem, because they were disciplined boys, and the standard of the education was also very good. The Education Department of the Frontier was responsible for exams in our schools and college; and I made special arrangements to encourage sound work and high standards. At the annual examinations, if the pupils of a certain teacher averaged 90% or above, then he was given one month's extra salary; whereas whoever had an average of 30% or a poorer result in his class, then one of his normal salary increments would be stopped. In that way, I ensured that there was always a little reward, and a little punishment, for all the teachers in the system. As a result, they all worked to the best of their ability.

In the very end, when I was obliged to loosen my grip a little, there was some unrest. All over Pakistan, the students were agitating against President Ayub Khan, and people came and spread their poison here too, and started agitating against me. I called the students together and asked: "What is your demand?" "To remove the Principal". "All right." "And we should have this and that". I said: "But there is no fee charged you!" And they said: "The hostel fee should also be waived!" I said: "These are personal matters connected with your education. We will solve them." But when they started saying: "And you should increase the pay of the Police, and you should discontinue this tax and that tax..." I said: "These are political questions, I am not willing that you should put pressure on me for that." So I closed the College, for two months. But now after the merger, whenever agitation starts in Peshawar University, it spreads here also.

In 1965, on the 24th of December at the fifteenth convocation of the University of Peshawar, I was given an honorary Degree of Doctor of Law (L.L.D.) from the University for my services to education. I was the first Pakistani ever to receive this honorary degree. The Vice Chancellor, in his speech conferring the degree, said:

"Major-General Miangul Jahanzeb H.PK. HQA CIE the Ruler of Swat is an old student of the Islamia Collegiate School and Islamia College University of Peshawar. The educational development of the Swat State is mainly due to his efforts. Since 1949, when he became the Ruler, he has established 300 educational institutions, including a graduate college, and many high, middle, and primary schools for boys and girls.

Not only has he spread a network of educational institutions in the State, but he has made education free at all levels, which is a unique feature. Besides this, large numbers of scholarships are granted by him to deserving candidates. He has been the cause of the immense progress of his State in every field and is always in the forefront to serve the Nation. The syndicate of the University of Peshawar has considered that Major-General Miangul Jahanzeb, Ruler of Swat, is by virtue of his service to the country and humanity in general, a fit person to receive the degree of Doctor of Law (Honoris Causa)."

This recognition was also in part due to the importance my educational developments had for our native language, Pashto. My father, at the very beginning, introduced Pashto as his court language: that was unique for its time — in Afghanistan they used only Persian, and in Dir they continued to use Persian in correspondance till the end of the State. Since very few people knew Urdu at the time, it was easy to change to Pashto, and thereby to promote our language. My father also had some religious books translated into Pashto — because very few people here can understand Arabic. He encouraged Pashto language, and I continued that. It is a problem, though, with so many languages: our pupils start with their mother tongue, but then they also have to learn Urdu, and English; and after the 9th class they must have an optional subject too — either Persian or Arabic.

I think, personally, that after English, Pashto is the most expressive language. And it is rich — I always take care not to use *any* English words when I speak Pashto; people say: "You don't show that you are educated, because when you speak Pashto you use only Pashto words!"

Now, in Urdu, when one listens to radio or TV, they speak in Urdu but they have to use English words all the time, here and there, to express themselves. And Urdu is a mixture to begin with, of Hindi and Persian, developed by the Moghul emperors. While I sat as a member of Parliament in the middle fifties, the Bengalis brought up the language issue — it was a way to criticize West Pakistan. What they said was: if you go by Islam, you should make Arabic the state language; but if you go by the majority, then you should adopt Bengali. And Urdu is no tongue of West Pakistan at all, except of the Muhajirs, the refugees. There was no argument they could make against that, except they said that Qaid-i-Azam decided that Urdu should be the state language. Being the founder of Pakistan, people could not dare to criticize him at that time. But I think it is at least important that English should remain — not as the state language, but on a par with the state language. Because all education is in English — you cannot translate all the books into Urdu, and for further education you need to go to America or England, so you have to use English then. It should never be eliminated.

The economy of the State has steadily expanded: To give a full account of it, one would have to add together the major sector, which remained in kind and paid for basic services like police and army, and on the other hand the monetary sector. The total production of grain increased steadily, so our income from *ushur* likewise increased; and we were able to sell grain too. Exports from Swat rose during most of the period of the State. In the early 1930s Swat exported about 30,000 maunds of rice, 60,000 maunds of maize, and 25,000 maunds of barley. By 1949 that had increased to about 100,000, 200,000, and 50,000 maunds respectively.

But with a steadily increasing population, after a while we had to start *im*porting wheat. Then came the new, high-yielding varieties of wheat and rice, which we obtained and introduced; but that was only in the last few years of my rule, so the full effects of the "Green revolution" were not felt till after the State was merged. And in fact, our agriculture here in Swat has always been very intensive, and has given big yields. The monetized income of the State rose very satisfactorily. When I became Ruler after my father, the total monetary income was 5 million Rupees per annum. It ended up at 20 million — with no extra taxes, and no income tax. The *octroi* duty alone, which in the early days started at 14,000 Rupees, had risen to 2 million Rupees when my State ended.

Very helpful to the State's economy was also the emerald mine: it gave

115

us another million Rupees a year. It started in a very small way — some Hindus were digging a bit, on the surface, and they used to find some small stones and then take them to Rawalpindi and sell them. Then an entrepreneur became interested; he asked for a lease, on an agreement that whatever he found, half would go to the State, half to himself, and he would pay for the labour. He pretended that it was exploratory, to see if he could find anything — in fact, he knew very well. He started digging, and he worked for a year. But I found that many people — our own people also, who were involved in supervising — were stealing stones, and so we were losing possible profits. So I told him, after a year, that it was better that he did it on contract, pay a lump sum, and then anything he extracted would be his. The first year, the operation had given only 150,000 Rupees' worth, which we divided half and half. But he would not bid for a contract. I told him in that case, he could wind up and leave. So he thought better of it, and made me an offer of 500,000 Rupees lump sum to the State, and whatever he got would be his. But then, to raise the money, he started selling shares to other individuals here, without my permission. Suddenly a man from Karachi, Haji Ibrahim, turned up and made me an offer of one million. And luckily I had the excuse to tell the first man that he was selling shares without my permission, and I could dismiss him. Haji Ibrahim was afraid of how he would handle local people here and protect his production. So he made a private partnership with my son Aurangzeb to ensure local protection. I said: "All right, you give the one million to the State. Carry on!" And just before the merger, he again bid for 1½ million. But then the Government of Pakistan moved in and took over. They have still to make a net profit on it — they are spending every year more than what they are able to extract. So contract business is a far better way of administering these things, because the big difficulty is supervision: everybody involved steals some stones. By my method, the State obtained some income from that mine too. And when I handed over the State treasury to the Government, after the State was merged, it contained 15 million Rupees in deposits and shares.

The main effort of the State in economic development was building the infrastructure, especially the roads and bridges.

Much of it could be done with Army labour, but to make bridges needs money. That again, we had to manage largely on our own resources.

116

The British, in all their time here, made us only two development grants of any magnitude. One was the road at Faza ghat, two miles from Mingora, where the rock is steep. It was a difficult stretch, and formed a bottleneck for all traffic up the main valley. When the Viceroy, Lord Irwin, came for the durbar on the 14th April 1930 to decorate my father with the Order of Knight of the British Empire, as a gesture of good will he said: "We will make that road." They spent 30,000 Rupees on that. Afterwards, when I became Ruler, I widened it.

Secondly, when we were making the road to Buner over the Karakar pass, a Captain Jeffrys came here. Later, when Pakistan came into existence, he was the first engineering chief of the Pakistan army. At the time, he was Captain. And he made a very wrong estimate of 45,000 Rupees, with bridges and all. — So it was left unfinished. With my father's blessing I pursued the matter, with every new Political Agent: "You are committed, because you sent your own engineer for this estimate!" In the end, they spent 200,000 Rupees to make that road. Afterwards, I widened it; and later I metalled it.

Then, when Pakistan was established, they started this Development Grant system and the government used to give us up to one million, not more; and that did not go very far, because we made all these bridges, which was expensive, but useful. Now if we had been independent, then all the customs that our people paid directly or indirectly on the excise duty on salt, sugar, cloth, and all other imports, would have come to the State. It would have doubled or trebled the income. We were actually taxed — as was all of Pakistan. But we did not get anything in return from them, apart from these very minor development grants.

We tried to encourage the development of new crops in agriculture, as well as new seeds and methods. There used to be very few orchards, and we brought in plants from outside, from Quetta and Parachinar: apple trees, which we distributed to whoever cared to take them. Then people saw that there was profit in the crop, and they made more orchards. Now, there are many apple orchards, and the price is naturally reduced. People look for a good cash crop. For example, they are cultivating opium poppies. In my time, there was very little production of opium; I would put it at 5% of what it had become in 1979. And that was also sold for medicine. Then strict control came four or five years ago, because America was giving money to the Government to discourage opium-growing and develop other agricultural products that are equally profitable for the cultivators. But people don't care, and I wonder how

117

and where this very big crop will be disposed of — because there are very strict laws now, it cannot be bought, sold, or used legally.

. All the irrigation system as it is now in Swat is very ancient; it was all here when the Yusufzai conquered Swat. We made plans to create a new irrigation canal, in the Nikpi Khel area. The plans were ready, everything was prepared in 1940. Then the war came, and after the war Pakistan came — and the arrangements could never be settled. Because we could not make it entirely ourselves — we needed technical help, as well as monetary support. So it was never launched, till now recently, years after the merger of the State.

As for industries, the only possibilities here have been cottage industries. I have encouraged outsiders, mostly they were people from Panjab, to come and install small weaving factories. But that also has declined after the State ended — when the Bhutto regime came, there were quarrels between the labour and the owners. Most of them wound up their businesses and went away.

I had some very clear principles regarding social policy which I upheld. There were some harmful old Pathan customs, for example, in regard to circumcision. People made big celebrations. But we said nobody was allowed to have music or entertainment at *sunnat,* i.e. circumcision, except privately for the ladies of the house. My father introduced this, and I continued it. But now, after merger, big celebrations are again made for *sunnat,* according to the status of the parents, but the minimum is not less than 2000 Rupees. Because now there is no effective authority to stop it. Likewise, I never allowed fireworks at Shab Qadar, the annual ceremony. They used to have it; it is a custom that came from Persia, what is now called Iran. Before they were conquered by the Muslims they were fire-worshippers — and after they became Muslims they still used to perform their old ceremony, once a year. So that tradition came to India and Pakistan. But it is not Islamic, and I never allowed it.

People also enjoyed music and dancing. In the old times, there was no music in the sense that there is today, with radio and records — there was *surna,* flute, and *domb,* drum. Dancing is not Islamic. But people do it. Adultery is bad, but people do it. Some things one can stop more effectively than others. At weddings, I disapprove of big celebrations. In our family, we just had very simple wedding, no *tamasha* — no show. Pathan custom was to spend much money at weddings. My father controlled it to some extent, and I also put some restrictions on it; but sometimes it was very difficult. If a man was of some importance, like a big Khan, and he did it — how could we punish him? Put him in jail, and make him our enemy forever? But we always tried to reduce it; and other people, ordinary people, were fined if they celebrated to excess; the big Khans were warned by the local magistrate that they had done wrong. This was the reason I never attended any marriage myself. I knew they would make elaborate arrangements for me. That would also have served as a precedent for the other Khans. Besides, I had no time to waste on such things. And I never performed the following two ceremonies: laying a foundation stone for a building, or conducting an opening ceremony. Never in my life! Whenever something was completed, ready, I simply said: "O.K.!" Ceremonies like that waste time and money; people use them for propaganda only.

Only once have I been inadvertently involved in that kind of propaganda. In 1954 I went on my first visit to Europe; and on my return I was met — after a long and strenuous journey — with great welcoming demonstrations, and honorific gateways along the road from Landakai, where I entered the State, and up to Saidu. It took me three hours to drive those few miles. Afterwards, I issued instructions that anyone who ever erected such gates again would be fined!

The big marriages, likewise, are a waste of resources, and their purpose is competition. That form of competition has also started up again, after the State was merged. Now people entertain 2000 or 3000 people at weddings, although there is a law against it. The Government is unable to put authority behind that law.

I have always realized that my period has been difficult, because it has been a transition period; and I was in the middle of it. I had to satisfy and pacify the educated class, and also the Khans. I had to deal with modern society, outside the State, and with traditional society inside the State. My lunch was served on the carpet, and Khans and other notables and people from the villages came here for their cases, others just paid their respects — 20 people or more every day for lunch. When I came from the office at twelve o'clock, I brought them with me and we would converse and be free with each other. At night, I dined at the table and had English food. Always with a few associates — I hesitate to call them friends, for it is difficult for a Ruler to have that kind of relations with his subjects — or with visiting officials from outside the State. God gave me this ability: that I could be at rest, and feel happy, talking with British officials or talking with an ordinary villager. I think it was inborn.

And if the highest people came: Monarchs, Viceroys, and Governors, I have entertained them too, and felt happy with them. Always confident.

In 1961, Queen Elizabeth and Prince Philip visited Swat. It happened like this. In February 1959, Prince Philip was touring Pakistan and India, and he decided he would see Swat. He had a *chakor* shoot in the morning and a duck shoot in the evening — and the next day he left, after spending two nights. He liked the place very much, and enjoyed the shooting. And I was very impressed by him; he is a highly intelligent person.

The President, Field Marshal Ayub, went on an unofficial visit to England in 1960. While dining at Windsor — the story was told to me by my son Aurangzeb, who was there — Ayub suggested that the Queen make an official visit to Pakistan. So suddenly Prince Philip jumped in and said: "Provided you take us to Swat!" That was the reason they came here, on the 7th of February 1961. As I saw them, during that visit, I think the Queen loves the Prince immensely. And he behaves in a very manly way. In no way subdued by her position — he has his say. But both are very devoted to each other, which is good. May God bless them! He has such an active, original, and observant mind; and they show the greatest respect for each other's judgement. They left on the 10th of February, having spent three days with me.

From my schooldays I also have a network of acquaintances — many of them have become prominent: there was Aslam Khan Khattak, who became Ambassador and then Governor, and General Sardar Abdul Rashid. They and others have been part of my circle of acquaintances, and even now they visit me. For me personally they have been important; but for the relations of my State to the Government of Pakistan these pre-established personal connections have meant little — there, I have had to deal with whoever was in the official positions.

Inside the State, I was the pivot of it all — and thereby I also secured the efficiency and economy of my administration, and above all, the authority of my Rule. Basically, it was by mutual affection with the people, and mutual trust. The poor classes all trusted me, that I would protect them and help them. They could not find another job outside the State, in Pakistan, if they went; and then they would also have to leave their family behind. So whatever I could give them, they were grateful for that. And the lower middle class was also loyal: they needed my protection and received justice. The Khans, many of them were loyal to me and they needed my support against the other *dəlla*. It was the upper middle class, who in many ways were most favoured, who grumbled most (cf. pp. 131 f.).

Then there were a few Khans, and a few of my own senior officials, whom I had to watch. There are always some people of influence who want more power for themselves, and seek to intrigue. I had to be always well informed. As my father never kept any Secret Service, or Intelligence staff, I also had none. He told me: "There is no *need* to keep an intelligence service, because everybody in Swat is an intelligence man with respect to all other persons!" And it was true. Nobody was paid by me, to come and bring news — people came of their own accord, and they always said something about other people, told news — and so I could judge and guess. The secret was to have the broadest contact with my people. And *anybody* could come to me. Anybody. If someone said "I have something private to tell", then we met privately in the office — I told the others to get out.

I had to keep it all in my head, and all the background information, and guess. But it was a small State — it was manageable. Half a million when I started, about one million now by the 1982 census. But more than half of them are children. Troublesome people who want to make intrigues, are few. Dealing with people all the time, I learned to understand things from small hints and signs — that was why it was necessary for me to come home when I was 18, rather than proceeding to UK for higher education — I needed to learn the local politics. Now, the moment I see a person, I know what he will say, what he will want, what I can do. I had to learn to do it accurately and very swiftly — how else could I decide 20–30 cases a day, while also attending to all the other aspects of my administration? The other essential thing is knowing all the facts about people. I had a Deputy Secretary in my office, Mahmud Khan, who had a B.A. degree; after merger he was taken into Government Service and was made D.C. in Bannu. He went to Harvard also, to get an M.Sc. He is one of the sons of the big Khan in Kana. I told him that a certain Abdul Ghafoor was his uncle. "Really?" he said. So I knew his family better than he did. In general, I know the families better than their own youngsters do. Even outside the State — all the Charsadda Khans, and those in Bajaur and Mardan.

In so many cases, these details matter a great deal. For example, take my relations to the Khans of lower Nikpi Khel, just across the river. The Khans on that side used to be quite powerful: there was Zarin Khan, the elder brother, and Amir Khan, the younger. Zarin Khan got his daughter

121

engaged to the Nawab of Dir, just before the State came into being. Then that marriage did not take place, because those Khans feared that my father would be angry (though my father never minded it), and so she remained a spinster all her life. Her brother is Jamshed Khan of Kuza Bandei, who was close to me. Amir Khan's son from his favourite wife, Parvez Khan, married the elder Wazir's daughter from his first wife. While Zerin and Amir Khans were together they were very powerful. But when the Wazirs left Swat in 1943, my father distributed the power of Amir Khan as leader of the *dalla* into three parts. One third was given to Jamshed Khan, one third to the sons of Amir Khan, and one third to Taj Mohammed Khan, who was a distant cousin. The sons of Amir Khan turned against the State because they had lost prominence. I supported Taj Mohammed Khan, who was very loyal to me, and I made him Mushir of Lower Swat. In 1954, while I was away on my first long journey abroad, my son Aurangzeb, who was acting as Wali in my place while I was away, dismissed Taj Mohammed Khan. And I did not wish to reduce my son's authority by reversing the dismissal when I came home. But I compensated Taj Mohammed Khan in other ways. He remained my best friend till his death at the age of 82 in 1982.

In such matters, I had to rely on myself. I rarely sought advice from my father — frankly, I never encouraged him to advise me. In some very grave matters — like when those Khans rebelled in 1951 (cf. p. 107) — I discussed with him how I thought about it, that was all. If I had sought his advice, he would have got used to that, and then if I had acted differently from what he said, it would have been as if I had disobeyed him, and our relationship would have suffered. I avoided it, as far as possible. Sometimes he would say something, and then I would try to agree, in general. But mostly he himself held back, too; and he never tried to impose his will. He would recommend his friends, this or that Khan, and suggest that I should avoid annoying them, that was all. Mostly, he never interfered in State matters.

There was respect from both sides. He knew my views and he did not want to impose his will. We had a very good mutual understanding. And on the basis of my intimate knowledge of him, I could also avoid annoying him. If there was a man I wanted to promote, and I thought he might not like it — then I never talked to him about it. But if I knew that he liked a person, and I had decided to promote him, then I took the opportunity to go to my father in the morning and remark that I was

thinking on this matter and would be promoting so-and-so today —
then my father would be very pleased!

From the beginning, he trained me to become strong and self-reliant;
when I grew up he treated me like a friend or brother. He was very happy
when I was with him, and he showed his great affection. If he was angry
with me, he told someone else, but never showed his anger to my face.
Sometimes he would speak about it to his close associates — so that it
would be conveyed to me. Then I would tell him my reasons.

But gradually, during my rule, he developed a little complex. Too
many people would go to him, and praise me, for my ways of handling
problems where he might have done it differently. He was proud that I
was doing well, but felt a little left out.

He had some favourites, whom he always protected and remained
friendly towards: the strong Khans in his own *dalla*. And for that reason
he was sometimes annoyed with me, because I was doing away with
feudalism. He did not want his friends to suffer from that: Pir Dad
Khan of Kana, Kamran Malik of Shamozai, Shakirullah Khan of Gali-
gai, the Sipah Salar and the Wazir-i-Mal — the malik families, because
they had been his supporters under his rule. But among all of them, he
was very fond of Khan Bahadur of Jura, and remained so till he died.
The reason was that he was very respectful to my father — and to no
one else. Although he had been with the Nawab of Dir in the beginning.
He supported the Nawab, but out of duress. He was young, and an
orphan, and Darməi Khan was determined to expel him from Jura.
Darməi Khan supported his enemies in Jura and Shangwatei. Khan
Bahadur came to my father and asked him to give him asylum. My
father answered: "I cannot compel Darməi Khan — he will be annoyed." "Then protect me from him in Upper Swat and guarantee my
life!" He answered: "I cannot do that even." Then, as a third way out,
he asked my father to allow him to go to Dir. He always justified himself that when he went to Dir, he did so with the approval of my father.
But my father said in his presence: "No, I did not tell you to go there;
but I could not defend you. So instead of going to Dir, you should have
gone to Thana!" Eventually he attached his men to the *lashkar* of the
Nawab of Dir, but during the battle, he defected from the Nawab. Because my father offered him protection. He always liked him. Rather,
he was my father's creation. And he was his friend and companion, to
whom he could tell anything — any story about personal matters also.

My father sometimes said that he would *leave Swat* if I did anything that annoyed Khan Bahadur Sahib.

He was my father's closest personal friend. But my father had other friends, and mixed with them very freely. In his retirement he kept himself very busy by reading the Holy Koran, or playing chess with his Subedar Major, or playing cards with his staff. He had his exercise, and prayed regularly. He was very fond of shooting. For some years, he used to go out at night in the car and shoot jackals in the beam of a searchlight. Always very active.

When I became Ruler at the end of 1949, it meant that from then on I had the ultimate responsibility for the life and death of the people of Swat. We had capital punishment, in accordance with Shariat, if murder was proved — beyond all doubt. I did not take any chances. If the relative of the murdered person, like his father, son or brother, did not want to take the life of the culprit, he could compromise with blood money. But that would rarely happen. Otherwise, in the presence of a police officer, a doctor, and the local magistrate, the relative would be given a rifle, and he would shoot the murderer.

There used to be, on an average, 22 murders a year in Swat State — and half of those were in Indus Kohistan. In Indus Kohistan, we always had difficulties collecting full evidence and judging the evidence: they would generally try to embroil many people, in the hope that they would be dismissed from service and the aggrieved party could obtain their posts in the Army; and for that reason I never punished a man with a death sentence in Indus Kohistan — not a single person. Elsewhere, I used to allow a maximum of two or three murderers to be shot in a year. I wanted to be absolutely sure; and — where there was full evidence and they had nothing to hide — if out of 22 murders 3 were punished, that was enough. The rest of them were put in prison for 7 years, 10 years, or were fined heavily. And I am very proud of two things: no innocent person has been shot; and nobody has been tortured in jails during my 20 years' rule.

In those cases of the death penalty, I felt it personally. For two or three hours, when the death sentence was passed and till the man was shot, I could not work. We let it be finished quickly; we usually did not inform the murderer till one hour before, so that he should not be kept in suspense for long; we just gave him a short time to adjust himself. But when I was informed that: "It is finished", then I was satisfied.

The only prominent person to be executed in my time — not *very* prominent, but of some prominence — was Zarin Khan of Manglawar: he was responsible for killing Doste Khan, of the same village. They had some dispute and rivalry. One day, as Doste Khan was passing, there was rapid fire from the *hujra* of his *tarbur* Zarin Khan. Now this was the only case that was very difficult for me to decide: extremely difficult. Because according to Shariat there should be eye-witnesses who can certify who killed the victim. So when there was rapid fire from the *hujra* — by whose bullet was he killed? In any case, the man behind it was Zarin Khan, so we put him in prison. If I had saved Zarin Khan, then many local prominent people would have said it was *I* who had told him to kill. The rumours had already started going, to that effect. Doste Khan's relatives, prominent and good people, came to me and pleaded that the murderer must be given to them, for revenge. Then I consulted all the ministers in my State, and my Commander-in-Chief — which I otherwise never did. Speaking to them alone, they said yes — but when they were together, they hesitated because each was uneasy that the others would tell Zarin Khan's relatives. Eventually, I went to my father. I said: "What do you think, what is your opinion of this bad thing that has happened?" For half an hour I consulted him — but he would not commit himself. So finally I asked him: "If he is given *qiṣṣas* (the Koranic procedure of letting the aggrieved party execute the murderer) — will you mind?" As he was interested in both parties. He said: "No." "And if I don't?" He said: "No." "So if I use my free choice, you will not blame me afterwards?" He said: "No." — The next day, he was handed over near the jail, to Professor Shah Dauran, Doste Khan's son, who shot him. That settled it, and with that feud was also finished. If we had not let him be killed, Doste Khan's people would have killed those people, back and forth, and the problem would have continued for years. Now instead, both parties have left it at that. That is the *only* case that did not go to the Shariat bench or the regular court, before coming to me. I had to handle it directly because it was a dilemma, and political in its implications.

I always had to acknowledge the existence of local custom, and take it into account in judging the consequences of decisions. There were old disputes coming from previous generations; if one person killed another person, then the latter's relatives later used to kill a close relative of the killer. And this same thing would go on for a long time. So I could not give a death sentence for that, as it was a kind of revenge. But we could fine them, and imprison them, or both. As time passed, I usually referred them to some *jirga* court, to try by compromise to reach some settlement. One custom was for the aggrieved person to receive a daughter from the other feuding family, to be married to his son. By the end of my rule, there were only between 20 and 30 such feuds left, which had not been settled and finished by compromise. They still carry on.

The last five years, I felt that the load of work on me was too great, especially the judicial work. Not just the serious cases, but all manner of big and small disputes. I used to say that if I were just meant for development work, I could have achieved much more. But this case-work took much of my time. The population grew, there were more conflicts, and they also learned to go to law to find some excuse and restart the case.

Another thing was foreign tourists: they were a great problem. They used to come to the office, and take photographs and ask questions, and each group might take a full half hour. Then I used to entertain people, Pakistani officials who came here; some stayed in the Hotel and I had to invite them for lunch or dinner. It was a great strain, during the last four years. We wanted Swat to be open to tourists; my father and I both welcomed them. In his time, there was no hotel here, so whenever a European came, he used to stay with me. Luckily they were few. My house became home-cum-guest-house. When the Wazirs left Swat and I became Ruler, I took the house that had been occupied by the elder Wazir and made it into the Swat hotel — it has been expanded several times since then. From then on, we put most of our guests there — they were not charged of course — in that way I could be free to do my State work.

Later, a suggestion was put to me that there should be an airstrip here. I said categorically no. Not because I did not want to open up the country: anybody could come by car and stay wherever he liked, in Madyan or Bahrein; I made inexpensive resthouses. But I was against the airstrip because I thought: then all these officials and self-important people would come. We would have to send our cars and meet them. I can't tell them to go and stay in the hotel when I send my car there for them. Then they would say they wanted to see Kohistan, or some other place. Then they would use the state cars — and all the time I would be busy entertaining them. So I did not encourage it. Later, I *asked* Mr. Bhutto to make an airport here, after the State was merged; it would be convenient for people to use the plane some times. "But you refused!" he said. I answered: "That was a different time, and this is a different time. At that time, I wanted my own convenience, and now I also want my own convenience — as the guests will not come to me, except personal friends!''

In 1958 I married my present wife. Ever since, she has been my constant companion whenever I go outside Pakistan. I do not find any difficulties without my servants, or other arrangements, when we travel together: she is so attentive, so intelligent. Here, we observe purdah, but not outside Pakistan. If I cannot see my servant's wife, how should I allow them to see mine? So it is only when we are outside Swat that we can be free and have meals together!

She is of a poor family from Mingora. It is better that way — no big family, with ambitions, intriguing and interfering in my affairs. And by mutual consent, from her I have no children. There is just the close relationship between us, which I value very highly.

My eldest son's marriage, on the other hand, *did* have political consequences.

My son Aurangzeb was in the Pakistan Army, and at the end of 1952 or beginning of 1953 he was made A.D.C. to then General Ayub Khan. I had known Mohammed Ayub Khan for a number of years, but not very closely. Aurangzeb and he developed a very good relationship, and on 17th February 1954 Aurangzeb became engaged to his eldest daughter. The marriage took place on the 10th of April 1955. Up to the 8th of October 1958 General Ayub was Commander-in-Chief of the Pakistan Army. Then President Iskander Mirza abrogated the constitution, and made Ayub Khan ''Chief Martial Law Administrator''. After 10 days or so he was removed and Ayub Khan became president. A year later the Cabinet proposed that he should be made a Field Marshal. He ruled by martial law until 1962, then the elections were held and he became an elected President. He then handed over to General Yahya Khan in March 1969. After that, Swat State was merged on the 28th of July 1969, along with the other Frontier States. And as we were close to Ayub Khan, so by his end our end came.

I ruled as the Wali of Swat for nearly twenty years. In that time, I would say I achieved about 80% of what I wished. I could profitably have gone on for another year or two, if circumstances had not changed so soon.

CHAPTER XI:

Merger and its aftermath: 1969–1979

When Pakistan and India were separated at Partition, the Home Minister in India, Mr. Patel, started merging the States. There were about 562 States in British India, and 552 went to the other side; only 10 States came to Pakistan. So whatever they did, it was easy to foresee that Pakistan would do the same. The phase would come to us as well. I could foresee it, and, as described above, I hurried up with development in Swat so that, when the time came, my people would not be dominated by the other people from the Frontier, but would produce their own cadre of leaders and have their own say. I am glad that I had my police officers trained in the Government Police Training School in Sihala, near Rawalpindi — so that they had a recognized competence, and most of them now hold good jobs as superintendents of police, deputy superintendents, and police inspectors. The Inspector General of Police, who is my friend, only just recently told me: "Swat dominates the whole province! Everywhere I go, when I ask my officers where they come from, the answer is Swat!"

One may ask: why did it take so long, twenty-two years, before Swat was merged with Pakistan? There were a number of reasons, some of them just chance events. In the beginning of Pakistan, Qaid-i-Azam had no thought or policy of merging the States. After Liaqat Ali Khan became Prime Minister, he recognized me as Wali of Swat. But Iskander Mirza — he was then Defence Secretary in the Government of Pakistan and a great friend of mine, who eventually became President of Pakistan — told me that before Liaqat Ali Khan embarked on the 'plane that took him to Rawalpindi for the big meeting at which he was assassinated on 16th October 1951, he told Iskander Mirza that the time has come for us to merge these States. But he had not yet acted on this decision; and with his death, the Government was involved in its own politics.

I would say that Swat was lucky to have a long spell of self-rule with peace and development. The internal strife in Pakistan in regard to who was to be Prime Minister, and who was to have which authority, was subsequently very disturbing, and policy and planning suffered, and Swat would also have suffered had the State been in the larger Pakistan.

So it was my policy to be vigilant, and try to maintain our separate identity.

Then the question of One Unit for West Pakistan came up, in 1955: abolishing the provinces and uniting all of West Pakistan into one unit, with parity with East Pakistan.

I was a member of Parliament then, and I supported the One Unit scheme wholeheartedly. Many people came to me and said: "Oh, we are Pakhtuns, and we must have our own province — why are you not supporting it?" I said: "I am supporting One Unit for my personal interests. As a big unit, they will be involved in their own affairs rather than merging the States. Whereas a small unit like the Frontier Province, would wish to expand as Qayyum was doing (cf. pp. 107 f.).

But in the interest of Pakistan, I still believe in one unit: for the integrity and survival of Pakistan. Now they want provincial autonomy, and they want separate control of every subject except defence, foreign affairs, currency and communication. What has happened in Baluchistan confirms my judgement — this small province with hardly 3 million people, torn by personal enemies and tribal interests. They can do what they like: harm their enemies, crush their opposition. For the sake of Pakistan, as a patriotic Pakistani, I still think there should be *one* central government and a unity of policy. There *should* be provinces, but with governors and advisers; not separate elected bodies who think they have independent power.

Later when the idea of one unit for West Pakistan was rejected by Yahya, then the parity was lost between East Pakistan and West Pakistan — and that was one of the causes of the separation. It created a one-man-one-vote situation, and with the population of East Pakistan exceeding that of West Pakistan, they had the edge. And they were bitter, because before the partition of British India, Muslims in that part were given third class treatment and were dominated by Hindus. So it had to take time, after the creation of Pakistan, for them to reach maturity. They spent their time instead complaining that they were dominated by West Pakistan, and that they earned more foreign exchange from their jute. Now the jute is still there — but look how much better off we are than Bangla Desh! Yet, it was the greatest mistake, thus to destroy the unity of West and East Pakistan; and it was General Yahya who did it. Why? From self interest. He thought: "I need not pacify these people, I can manage West Pakistan somehow. But by pacifying Mujib in East Pakistan, I can become permanent President."

Another question affecting the possibility of these States being merged was the conflict with Afghanistan over "Pakhtunistan". It did not affect Swat directly, but indirectly through the position of Dir.

They never tried to spread their propaganda here — in my time. But they were active in Bajaur and the Tribal Belt. The reason was, there was no democracy in Afghanistan, so they wanted to divert the attention of their people by claiming that the Pakhtun land belonged to them. And I told both Iskander Mirza, and Ayub Khan: if there was a referendum, "Pakhtunistan" would never win. Internationally, it would be very difficult, since it would seem as if Pakistan were willing to give away sovereignty — but *if* there was a plebicite, in Afghanistan and in the Frontier Province, we would never join them, though they might vote to join us! Iskander Mirza and Ayub said: "We cannot offer that, because it would be like recognizing their claim." But if he had to vote, I don't think even Wali Khan would have chosen Afghan rule.

Now of course, all that is past history, with the tragic development in Afghanistan. But at the time, the merging of these border States was linked with problems in Pakistan's relations with Afghanistan, and the "Pakhtunistan" issue.

A third factor of a very different kind was our relationship with President Ayub.

I was very close to him — rather, I started out being very close to Iskander Mirza, because from 1927 up to 1958 our friendship grew. He was in Abbottabad as Assistant Commissioner. From then on, I knew him very well. I did not come to know Ayub Khan till 1944. One of my close friends, Said Khan, brought him here to introduce him; he was only a major then. After that we did not meet, because he was posted elsewhere, as Brigadier in Waziristan, and went as Major-General to East Pakistan, from there he was promoted as a First Commander-in-Chief. Then he used to come here for shooting, and we became very close. My son Aurangzeb was in the Army, and General Ayub proposed that he would take him as his A.D.C. I said: "I will consult him." My son said that this was a great honour, and accepted it. After 3 years,

Ayub's daughter was married to Aurangzeb, on 10th April 1955. I gave a reception in Rawalpindi, for the guests whom I invited. Then we went in a procession to the Commander-in-Chief's house, and he gave us lunch. Then we came back to Saidu, and I gave lunch here to the officials of the State.

Seven years later, my third son Amir Zeb also married one of Ayub's daughters. That was arranged by my daughter-in-law, Mrs. Aurangzeb. When they had made the arrangement, they came for my blessing.

Throughout those years, I would say we had very good relations. He was very kind to me. But in one way or another he did not want anything that could be understood as criticism. If I suggested something to him, he would not like it.

Internally, Swat was very secure and peaceful, after the affair with the Khans in 1951 had been solved. One reason why Pakistan was in no hurry to merge the State may have been the peacefulness — to most people's minds, Swat was a show place for foreign visitors. But being linked with Ayub Khan as we were, people were also thinking, and accusing him of keeping the State for his own benefit, for his daughter and his son-in-law who would inherit it. So they also thought that, when he goes, then the State will go too. And I always had to have the question in the back of my mind: When is this State going to be merged? For that reason, I could not make long-term plans, or concrete commitments that would last more than two or three years. All the time I was feeling: one day, maybe tomorrow, maybe the day after, maybe after one year... Even the safety deriving from President Ayub was equivocal: there was little danger from him; but yet, under the pressure of the public opinion against him because of his connection with us, he might also have felt he had to do this merging — but in a dignified manner.

During the last four or five years of the State, there were also internal changes that had some effect. The Khans had become soft and lost their power; but a new upper class was emerging.

In the old days, the Paracha families of shopkeepers could never become rich. Before the State, whenever a shopkeeper accumulated some money, the Khan or Malik used to accuse him of some misdemeanour — that he had gone into somebody's house and committed some mischief, any fabrication would do as an excuse — and then the Khan would loot the whole property or fine the shopkeeper so heavily that he never got a chance to become rich. When peace came, my father would not allow those Khans to fine them or to raid them. If they were guilty, they were fined by the State according to the rule of law. In that way they got a chance to create more wealth — and after 1960 they became very important. Money became the main source of prestige, and they no longer cared about the Khans, and the Khans did not like that. As I have explained above (pp. 53, 120), in a way we also favoured this class a little, because we preferred them for all our contracts: a man without means cannot pay back, and we needed them to carry on the business. But the effect was, that whoever had money, he could make more money.

Now these people became very proud — haughty, I would say. There are people whose fathers were not worth a thousand Rupees, or at most two thousand Rupees, and now they themselves are millionaires, *nouveau riche,* and it has gone to their heads. They don't care about anyone. These people, together with some disgruntled Khans who wanted their old powers back, started agitating against me. Secretly, not openly: by giving money to people to write articles against me in newspapers in the rest of Pakistan. Those who were in effect most favoured by me and who had increased their wealth thought perhaps they would now have more advantage from Pakistan. Ungratefulness. It shows that a Ruler can never expect to create loyalty from gratitude: people look for their own advantage. Having the money, they thus had the means to make propaganda against me in the newspapers, and also to bribe some officials.

Strong agitation against Field Marshal Ayub started in October 1968 and gained momentum quickly. By the middle of January 1969, people were sure he would abdicate, or be thrown out. As we were linked with him by marriage, people started thinking that when he goes, they will go. This feeling spread, even through my own administration. If I ordered something, they just did not care very much; they said: "Yes Sir, yes Sir", but they did not act on it. So I was losing my grip on the officials — not the people, but the officials. And those officials were smiling, thinking there were only a few days left, and so on.

Under those circumstances I approached the then Political Agent, and also General Akbar Khan, who was Intelligence Officer in the Army — and later became Ambassador in the U.K., where he died. I also consulted a few other friends. I said to them: "You should tell Yahya Khan (who took over from Ayub Khan as President of Pakistan in March 1969) to take over the State." If one cannot rule properly, it is better to retire honourably. The Political Agent, Doctor Humayun Khan (who is now ambassador in Bangla Desh), was very friendly to me. And when I told him to try to have the State merged, he said: "No Sir, no Sir — not in my time!" I said: "If it is going to be merged, then it is better that it should be in your time, because you are my friend and it would be a peaceful transfer of power." If I had to deal with someone else who was not friendly, he might think and report to the Government that I was obstructing their action. One must always seek to judge the actual circumstances, and then find the best way under those circumstances.

Before going on, I must explain the situation in Dir and the changes that had taken place there. Economically, culturally, educationally — in every way, Dir had remained undeveloped, and the people were not given the facilities for development which were their right.

The Nawab of Dir never cooperated with the Government on development — though he was loyal to the Government. But he wanted his separate identity to remain a Ruler. President Ayub used to tell me: "I would merge Dir *today*. But that would affect you and that is why I am not doing it!" I said: "Please, don't think of merger. You can *order* the Nawab to make a certain number of schools. And if he does not make the schools, the Government can go ahead and make schools, without taking a penny from his State revenues. But you should insist that there should be schools and hospitals for the people!" "No, I can't do that, for if he refuses, as I have committed myself it would be necessary to take strong action."

Then this incident happened, I think in 1960 or 1961. The Heir Apparent in Dir was the present Nawab, Khusro; and the second son was made a sort of Governor of Jandul — they called him Khan of Jandul. Then the second son thought that Pakistan would never support him, since they had already recognized the elder son as Heir Apparent. He pretended he had gone to a place in the hills, because he was ill and he wanted to go to a healthy climate. Secretly he went to Kabul, and the C.I.A. was very quick. He grew a beard there, and negotiated with them — I don't know about what. But the Government came to know about it. I still think that his father, Nawab Shah Jahan Khan, was innocent of the whole business. But troops were sent and a helicopter was sent in and the Nawab of Dir was taken away, and so was the Khan of Jandul; and Khusro was installed in his father's place, with a Political Agent in Dir at his side.

That meant that all the power was wielded by the Political Agent.

Without any written agreement and formal change, the Nawab was in effect transformed into a constitutional ruler. Sometimes, he interfered in State matters, but that was not on the basis of any powers he had — it was owing to his good relations with some of the Political Agents. They were constantly changing, and with some he had very friendly relations, so that he could request them, please do this or that.

When the decision was made that the State was going to be merged, Aurangzeb and the Nawab of Dir were called to Rawalpindi, and the message of merger was announced to them. Out of respect the government called my son instead of me. The Mehtar of Chitral did not matter, because Chitral had already been taken over by the Political Agent, and the Mehtar was only a small boy, attending school in Lahore. It was on Friday morning, and the State was merged the following Monday, on the 28th of July 1969. When he was informed on the 25th, the Nawab of Dir was quite unconcerned — he said to me, subsequently: "My State has in effect already been merged. It is your State that is going now!" The Chief of Staff to General Yahya, General Pirzada, informed us that they would announce it on the 28th. Aurangzeb told him that the State should be merged peacefully and gradually: officials of the government should come and take charge. The answer was: "Don't you bother — it is our affair!" Aurangzeb and Pirzada did not have good relations; the latter used to be Military Secretary to Field Marshal Ayub Khan so they were personally acquainted.

The merger was announced, and I told the Political Agent Malakand to come here and take over. He said: "I have no orders, how can I take over?" I said: "There is a vacuum! People know that the State has been merged, so I have no authority!" Some people told me to go to the office anyway — I said: "No. Nothing doing. I will not go. If there is some work that you deem it necessary for me to do, you can bring it here to me in my house. As regards cases, let the Mushirs decide them, or the Ministers." After three days, Humayun Khan was given the rank of District Commissioner: Political Agent Malakand plus D.C. Swat. He came here to Saidu, and he stayed with me, since he was my distant relation and very great friend. After two or three days of his staying here, opposition people protested. "How can we approach the D.C.? He is living with the Wali, the Wali is instructing him!" and so on. So he shifted to the Hotel.

There was still no special order that I had lost my power, or that the Government had taken over the powers of the Ruler — not till the Commissioner was appointed and arrived on the 17th of August. So up to the 17th of August I was checking the treasury as usual every morning and the D.C. was consulting me: "What is your opinion about this and that?" When finally the Commissioner came, he took over the power. Humayun did not want to live here, and people kept grumbling that he was my relation, so he went back as Political Agent Malakand, and they appointed another D.C.

All that while, I refused to go to the office. Because I thought that if I showed myself there, then some people would come weeping, and some would be saying they were very sorry and show their pathetic faces, and some people would think that this is a time of transition and we can take advantage and gain something. And also if I had decided any case in those few days, then those who lost the case would surely have re-opened it immediately afterwards saying "he was no longer the Ruler and had no authority to decide the case!" So to avoid all those complications — they brought me the applications to my house, and I signed them.

To hand over the State took about 20 days; and I cooperated with them and told them what to do and how to do it. I have no regrets, because it was a great responsibility, and to shirk one's responsibility is very bad. So I did my utmost till the end. There were pitfalls and possible misjudgement I might have made. Some people even said we should resist. If I had made a wrong judgement it could all have ended differently: people might have been killed, and I would have been taken away from the State forever, not allowed to come back, just as Nawab Shah Jahan was not allowed to come back to Dir till his death in Lahore. I knew my own future, and the welfare of my people, depended on my judgement.

Flatterers came running to me: "We want to fight, we want to fight!" Consider the facts of the case. The *ghazis* of Ambela, during the *jehad* of 1862, had swords and hatchets, the British had the muzzle-loader. So when they had fired and were busy reloading — these people rushed up and cut off their heads. There was no great difference in armaments. Then in Malakand, in 1895, the British had their Martini-Henry rifles — but the Ghazis had their quite accurate matchlocks. There was again little difference in arms. But how can we fight Pakistan or some other modern power? They can send aircraft — they need not send a single tank, or a single soldier. Just one bomb in Saidu, and another in Mingora — what would be our position? I told General Yahya in May 1969, beforehand, that whenever they thought the time had come to merge the

State, I would offer it to them. "No Sir, no Sir," he said, "we are in no hurry!". I answered: "Whether you are in a hurry or not, my offer stands." Then when the day suddenly came, it was announced on the radio, and it came out in the papers. No agreement, and we had only three days' warning. But it passed off peacefully. And I am very glad that the people did not revolt against me, that Dir never conquered my State; today, anyone can see for himself that people still respect me; they come to my house and seek my advice. So I am grateful to them, and they are grateful to me — 95% of them.

Even those who were against me in those last months also come now, most of them. I used to tell them then too: "I will be in the same position, it is you who will suffer!" I had seen how other States had been merged before: Bahawalpur, Khairpur, the Baluchistan States. When they were merged, their Rulers were left with all their dignity and titles and privy purse intact. Now it happened with me. I was made an Honorary Major-General in 1955, given titles, declared loyal to Pakistan. The privy purse was left intact, the bodyguards — all with no change.

General Yahya himself did not last very long. Elections were held in November 1970, and Zulfikar Ali Bhutto won the majority in West Pakistan, while Shaikh Mujib-ur-Rahman had the majority in the whole of Pakistan, with 95% of the votes in East Pakistan. So he would not come here and Bhutto would not go there; and Yahya sought to go there to make a compromise, but ended up trying to subdue the rebellion. After East Pakistan became separated, Bhutto took over as President from General Yahya on the 20th December 1971.

On the 22nd of December, just two days afterwards, he took away *all* the privileges of *all* the ex-Rulers, including our Privy Purses. Nineteen days later, we were all called to go there, to Rawalpindi, on the 10th of January 1972. The evening before, on the 9th, the Nawab of Dir came to my hotel room. He was always very friendly to me. His father was not friendly, his grandfather fought against us; but even then, in his father's time, when we met in Government House Peshawar, he was always very respectful. He is younger than me, by about ten years. So he came to my room and said: "I told all my servants to leave. I kept only nine. What have you done?" I said: "I have not yet done that." He said: "What will you do?" I answered: "I have about four million Rupees; if I divide that by as many years as I can expect to live, I can still live comfortably. And God knows what will happen next. Why should I tell them to go away?" I had not reduced my staff by one single man. And then, when we went for that meeting next morning, he said: "What will Bhutto say, what is he going to do?" I said: "He cannot harm us any more; for we have lost everything. So when he calls us to a meeting, it must be because he is going to give us some favour!" At the time, I thought he would compensate us somewhat and might offer us half of the maintenance allowance.

Bhutto opened the meeting by saying that nobody any more would agree to these titles and pompous statuses. "And our party, the Peoples' Party, put pressure on me, and that is why I took away all these privileges." Nobody said anything, except the Khan of Kalat, of Baluchistan; he was very angry: "We served Pakistan, we did this, we did that..." and he banged the table many times. Bhutto left the room, and he called in the ex-Rulers one by one, in *reverse* order of precedence. And he told each of us: "I restore your allowance, and it will be known as 'maintenance allowance'. It is for your lifetime only — your heirs will not have it." So nobody lost a penny even, not even during those 19 days, because it had been due on the 1st of January and it was paid.

But to the newspapers, Bhutto announced that we, the ex-Rulers, had brought documents signed by Qaid-i-Azam guaranteeing the allowances, and that we had come weeping to him and pleaded with him, "What will we do without our allowance?", and so on. It was all fabrication: nobody had pleaded or wept, there was no agreement with Qaid-i-Azam or any other document. But we could not object to the story he put out. I am sorry for him now he is dead.

I do not know what struck him in the first place, and why he changed his mind. Perhaps it was just to show his Party that he had committed himself to his high command, because India had already taken away these privileges, and so he had to do something. In India, of course, they are no longer given any allowances. But most of those rulers had collected lots of jewels, over the generations, so they are well off. And most of the Indian states were just relics of the past, not recent creations like Swat.

Throughout my period as Ruler, I kept very strict rules to prevent graft and corruption in my administration. I succeeded quite well — I think very well compared to Pakistan — but it is difficult to prevent it completely.

Some of my administrators were very honest, and there was not a single case or accusation of bribery among them, but they were what we call *dəlla-baz* — they would favour their own party a little. They did not

137

take money, but when conflicts and cases came before them, they would be partial to the side that was of their own *dalla*.

Then there were one or two of the Mushirs, and some few of my Hakims: during my time they never put money in the bank, they never bought land, and there were no serious complaints against them that came to my notice. But after merger, they suddenly bought land and started building nice houses. Probably, they were in collusion with contractors, secretly. In the forest, for example, contractors might cut more trees than their allotment, and give something to the Hakim or Mushir. Over the last four or five years of my rule, they must have amassed some wealth in that way. They *may* have taken bribes too; I don't say that all of them were clean. It cannot be entirely avoided — for example, someone has a case, a man owes him a thousand Rupees. So if the Hakim or Tahsildar handles that case quickly and gets back the full sum for him, he might give him 50 or 60 Rupees.

Even giving someone a false recommendation is a kind of corruption. People come *all* the time to me and want me to ask favours for their son, their brother, themselves. It is wrong, because if you recommend a person you are trespassing on the rights of those other people who are also competing for that place or that job, and who are more capable. After merger I once did contact Jamshed Barki; he was Commissioner here and he was always very nice to me, respectful and friendly. He was interviewing boys for admission to medical college. And my chauffeur wanted his son to get into that college. So I telephoned Jamshed, and said I had this small recommendation. "No Sir, no Sir, they will go by merit! And merit only!" I liked that very much — he being devoted to me, yet saying: By merit. Because when I was Ruler, and people were making recommendations, I felt it very much. My father found a good solution, at that time. When there were some vacancies, he would send ten or twelve people, and recommend them all! In that way, I had a big choice, and if I chose one of those twelve, he was happy!

People still think I can do anything, and ask me to tell the D.C. or the Commissioner to favour this man or that. Of all the people who come here, every day, to my house, most do it merely to pay their respects, but many come for some purpose. But I don't want to interfere. Unless a man is very much aggrieved, and I know that he is not getting full justice. I have some influence still.

Working towards merger, preparing the way for it, I had not planned to take part in political life after the end of my Rule. But then, in the last three months, when they saw merger approaching, some people came out against me and had those articles written against "the dictatorship of the Wali". After the merger, there were others whom I discovered had been dishonest, behind my back, during the last years of my rule. At the same time, people from outside put pressure on me — thinking they could use me to serve their interests. And, finally, after merger my eldest son Aurangzeb thought that he was now free to pursue his own politics for the future.

So I wanted to show them that I am still here, I have still some influence. That is why, when Khan Abdul Qayyum came here and asked me to nominate candidates for the Muslim League for the 1970 election, I cooperated with him. There were two national seats — now there are three — and six seats on the Provincial level. I put the proposal to Qayyum, who would be the Muslim League candidates, and we agreed. Then after agreeing with me, he changed two of those persons. I would not accept that, I stuck to my original candidates and supported them. But then my own sons, Aurangzeb and Amir Zeb, supported Qayyum. It was a rather minor matter. Aurangzeb had suggested that he stand from this constituency; and from the Buner-Malakand constituency, there was my first cousin from my mother's side, my maternal uncle's son Rahim Shah. I said O.K. For the Provincial Assembly, Aurangzeb said we should support this man and that man and so on. I said: "All right." And Ziaullah, Ataullah's son, was among them. But then he broke with Qayyum; and on the initiative of Amir Zeb, he and Aurangzeb went to Qayyum and put a Paracha from there by the name of Mohammed Rahman on the Muslim League ticket against Ziaullah. I said: "You have promised you will support Zia, now you support this fellow!" They answered: "It is not in our power, it is Qayyum's own choice!" So I said, in any case I would support Ziaullah.

Now everybody says, probably correctly, that the 1970 election was the most fair election Pakistan has ever seen. Yet even then, there was a little pressure. Yahya Khan wanted to support the Muslim League, and he used to consult Qayyum often. So Qayyum told him, that if the Wali is in Swat, then Qayyum's protegées might lose the election. And because I supported Ataullah's son instead of the Muslim League candidate, I was exiled. General Yahya put me outside Swat and the Province, across the Attock Bridge. I spent 34 days in Flashman's Hotel in Rawalpindi, living there. But even there, people used to come to consult me; they came in batches of 20 and 30 to ask me; there was no ban on that.

And having ruled the country, I wanted to impose my idea; I wanted to prove that people look to *me* for guidance, nobody else. Even though I had been sent out of the State.

There was an interval of a week between the elections: the National Assembly election was held on the 10th December 1970, followed by the Provincial election on the 17th December. For the National elections, I was in a fix. The National Awami Party put up my former Sipah Salar, a Sar Mian by the name of Badshah Gul. I could not support him. I did not want to support Aurangzeb, because of this conflict over Ziaullah. I did not want to support the Jama'at Islamic people, or the People's Party. Those were the candidates. So I could do nothing. However, Aurangzeb won it: he got elected, and the Sipah Salar came second, number three was a candidate from Madyan, number four was People's Party, and number five was Jama'at Islami.

When he got elected, Aurangzeb went to Mingora village to electioneer for the Provincial candidates, and he said: "You have given me one leg, but I am lame on the other leg. Please support my candidate." And so on. He went to every house and to every man. In the end, they got more votes than Kamran, who was an opposing candidate, and Ziaullah came third only — because I was in 'Pindi, and besides, he was an alien, since his father came from Panjab and he does not belong to this part. I guess I should say it was a blessing in disguise. If Ziaullah had been elected, he would have become minister and got very pompous. The other fellow, Mohammed Rahman, was very obedient to me, even after getting elected. I did not meet him for six or seven months. He came here to the gate — I sent him away. He may have been elected, but not by me!

So through the latter part of the campaigning, and the days of voting, I was kept away. I wanted to meet President Yahya but somehow I could not succeed. I had two friends in his Cabinet: Finance Minister Nawab Sir Muzaffar Ali Khan Qizilbash and Major-General (retired) Nawabzada Sher Ali Khan. I approached them, and they gave me a chance to explain my position, why I had been exiled. But the matter was delayed, for 34 days till the election was over. On the 17th it was finished, so Qizilbash telephoned to me and said: "You can go tomorrow." I said: "I know I will go tomorrow. Because the election is over and the purpose of this exile had been served. So whether the President says he allows me or not — I am going on the 18th."

When I came back to Saidu on the 18th of December 1970 I never allowed Aurangzeb and Amir Zeb to come to me. Not till my father's death on the 1st October 1971. I had to take my revenge! I stopped their allowances too. Then, when my father died, someone friendly to both sides intervened, saying that your sons will come and say they are sorry. Which they did.

Only two of our candidates got elected, and that was owing to our differences — my differences with Aurangzeb and Rahim Shah, my maternal uncle's son. Rahim Shah got elected to the National Assembly. His younger brother Mohammed Ali Shah stood for the Provincial Assembly. I told Mohammed Ali Shah: "If you support Ziaullah then Ziaullah and I will support you." He would easily have got elected. But he did not agree, he said: "I am going by party rules, I have to support Mohammed Rahman." Ataullah put up another son in the Upper Swat constituency against Mohammed Ali Shah; and then there was Afzal Khan, Darmai Khan's son, put up by the National Awami Party. So when people asked me, I said, "I support the son of Ataullah, Sanaullah", though I knew he could not succeed. Mohammed Ali Shah got 8000 votes — he would not have got that even, except that people said he is my cousin. And 4000 went to Sanaullah. But 8800 went to Afzal, so he was elected. He was the only Congress man[19] elected from Swat, and that was only because my supporters were split, 4000 for Sanaullah and 8000 for Mohammed Ali Shah. Another non-Muslim Leaguer belonged to Kohistan; the constituency there stretched along the Indus from Kohistan to Chakesar. Our agreement was to support Sultan Mahmood Khan of Chakesar. But Qayyum subsequently gave the ticket to one of the grandsons of the Kana Khan. In that way, the Pathan vote was split on two candidates, while the Kohistanis gave their solid vote to one man, Molana Abdul Bagi, and he was elected. He ultimately became a minister and Afzal Khan also became a minister. Because these parties made a coalition, and formed a majority in the Provincial Assembly, against Qayyum's 12. If there had not been this disunity, we would have got the Upper Swat seat also, and have been equal to that coalition.

In the next election, in 1974, Amir Zeb joined Bhutto's People's Party and stood as their candidate, against Aurangzeb. He won by many thousand votes; Karim Bux, a Paracha, came second, and Aurangzeb third. It was a shock for Aurangzeb. One easily takes for granted the importance and attention one receives by virtue of one's position: as Waliahad, my Heir Apparent, he found all the Khans and Mians so respectful to us, and he had much contact with them. But the poor people being in the majority belonged to the People's Party and gave their vote to Amir Zeb. Aurangzeb reproached me for his loss, saying that I had supported Amir Zeb. I actually stayed out of it; I could not canvass for him, nor did I canvass for Amir Zeb. Some people came and asked me whom they should vote for. I said: "Vote for that Paracha fellow!" They jumped and revealed their surprise, and so I said: "If you have already made up your mind, why do you ask me?"

With his electoral success, Amir Zeb became a member of Parliament, and has now patched it up with me, and we have good relations. Owing to these various circumstances, relations with Aurangzeb were not as good as I had hoped, as I had expected. Aurangzeb is now looking to his own future, and he wants to make himself prominent in the new set-up. I think he is playing an influential role there, in Islamabad, and is very popular.

People may have known, without my ever saying so, that I favoured Amir Zeb in 1977, and that maybe is why he did so well. For the next three years or more, I am still popular and people listen to me — but then it will fade away. Young people grow up; they know little about me and are little influenced by the old times. Older people, on the other hand, may speak even more highly of me now than they did before. Because before, there were demands: give me this service, give me this contract, give me this and that. Whatever someone got, other people felt aggrieved. Now, there is nothing to give — so they remember the old days. And my achievement was in the field of development in Swat. Even the Pakistani officials, the Commissioner, D.C., higher up and lower down, have great regard for me. Everybody respects me.

CHAPTER XII:

Reflections

We created something new, my father and I: a State that was different from any other state in the region. From its inception, when the tribes selected him as their Ruler, and through the swift development that it underwent, we had no precedent; we could not copy from other established states, from what they had done. We had to understand the circumstances, the facts of the case, and act in terms of them. We had to anticipate the changes, and be mentally prepared for them.

Dir and Chitral, our closest neighbours, were very differently constituted from Swat.

In Dir, the Nawab himself belonged to one of the tribes, the Akhund Khel branch of the Painda Khel. So the Painda Khel and Sultan Khel used to fight for him, protect him, install him as Nawab of Dir, do everything for him. Over the generations, the Nawabs also acquired much land as their private property. And the ruling Nawab did not take rent from many of those lands, but gave them instead to persons who rendered service to him. They occupied that land without paying rent, because it was given in lieu of payment for their services. When the merger came, and after Bhutto came into power, those people who were occupying the land, without paying rent to the Nawab, claimed that it was their original land and that the Nawab only forced them to fight for him, and out of patriotism they went out fighting. So the Nawab has lost his rights to all those lands.

In Swat, on the other hand, my father never sought to acquire land apart from what he inherited from his ancestors and some lands that he bought afterwards. I myself had no land — I still have none, because the Government has not alloted us any, and the case regarding my father's will is still going on in court. But the State, in any case, was never based on our private lands; and our authority was never based on tribal connections.

Now in Chitral, the Mehtar claimed all the lands for himself, and his family ruled in this fashion for two hundred years. It was not a benevolent rule. If he got angry with X, he confiscated his property and gave it to B. After a while he got angry with B, and so on — so it rotated. Basically, it was considered state land, and the State was the Mehtar. Now it has all been distributed to the people who were tilling the land. As for his army: there was a militia of 5000, and they were not paid at all. Only 200 came to serve at a time as bodyguards, in rotation; and those 200 were given some pay, plus food and clothing. It was quite a different system.

In respect of bodyguards, Dir and Swat were a little similar. People of good families would send their sons to become orderlies and bodyguards — they felt elated that their sons were serving the Wali or the Nawab; it was a source of *izzat,* honour. Then they were trained here, and we gave them promotion. Some served for twenty or ten years; but then if there was some vacancy in the Army, I made it a point that 25% went to these people, 75% to people from the Army. And these people, on a whole, proved more disciplined.

As I have said, our whole policy of education and development was very different from that of the other States, whose people remained undeveloped. That is one reason why Swat people grumble now: they complain they are not being given the same attention as the people in Dir and Chitral. And the Pakistani officials' answer is: "You *are* already developed. Let them come up to your level first, and then you can go on further together." Those other states had institutions that were inherited from ancient people. My father knew more about the people in Mardan and Peshawar and modernization. So he acted in this way.

Within the family, among his own sons, my father also did things very differently. In Chitral, there were always successional struggles and fratricide in the old days.

In Dir, for the last three generations, three Nawabs have made the same mistake: they made the elder son Waliahad, Heir Apparent, and the younger sons dukes or governors of Jandul (cf. 59, 133). So again and again they aspired and intrigued, and threatened the continuity of the State. My father *never* allowed my younger brother Sultan-i-Room to play any part in the State. He used to pamper him and take him out shooting; whenever he wanted a car, he could have one. If he wanted to go out of the State for a holiday, he could go. But my father never allowed him to have authority, or to mix with the people. And my father told me to do the same with my sons, so that after his death there should be no rivalry. He was very strict on that. In the same way I designated Aurangzeb as my successor, and I never allowed my other sons to play a role in State affairs. My second son, unfortunately, is blind, so he did not matter at all. But number three, Amir Zeb, was never allowed to interfere in state affairs, not by any chance. I encouraged him as a private person, but not in any official role. Not till after merger was I free to disregard this limitation, and let him play a political role in Pakistan.

Now after my father's death, there is a conflict between my brother and me about the estate. My father made a will in 1939, attested by the Government. Now Sultan-i-Room claims that this will was changed by my father; but he cannot prove it. And the commission has not been able to resolve the question. Meanwhile, he has had control as executor of the estate, and he would not give me a single relic of my father — not his stick, not a single chair that he had used, all were sold. There was much bitterness on the part of my younger brother, that I was born before him. But that was hardly my fault!

Yet our conflicts did not impinge on the ordered administration of the State, not even during those difficult years when my father and I were somewhat estranged.

Not only has the structure of the State undergone continuous development and change: society itself has changed profoundly. In the old society, and still for a while after the State came about, what really mattered was land. And politics were feudal politics of big Khans and the two *dǝllas*.

To gain power the Khans have to be aggressive and assertive. If people saw that a Khan was weak, and could not do anything, then they would abandon him and never follow him. It is in human nature everywhere, that everybody wants to rise to some position; or if they can't do that, then naturally they want to become rich, at least. But what people really wanted, in the old days, was glory! Now, nobody is going to kill, unless they have some special vendetta with other people. But still, such people prefer to go followed by two or three retainers with rifles and pistols: it shows the *position* of the person. Wealth used to be secondary, it was mainly a means to achieve position. Even now, if I had no wealth, and did not have my allowance, I would not be able to maintain my position.

The Khans used their grain and their wealth to have these retainers and followers, and to have influence. So in the old days they had very little *money*. When my father brought peace to the country, those big Khans could dispose of their servants and followers, and they kept only five or six retainers. In that way they got income from their land and bought more land and more land, and became richer. And then, according to their recommendation and favouritism they used to bring their *dalla* people from their village to be enlisted in the Army. And they gave their sons education, and tried to get them into good positions in my State or outside.

Other people, those Parachas, they used to be poor people, and they had very little to spend, for entertainment or daily needs. When they started earning money, they could save everything, as they were safe from the Khans thanks to the State. In that way they multiplied their properties; so now some of them are far richer than any Khan. And they would also give their sons education. So the presence of the State turned people's ambitions in new directions.

In 1951 when those Khans turned against me, they realized that my policy was that the Khans should not be so powerful that they could remove me or upset my politics or usurp the land from other people. They were fighting for their old positions, but they lost and became powerless, when I made everyone malik of his own land. And for this reason, all those small landowners and even tenants thought that I was the liberator for them — the *kalangzai* as they have sometimes been called — and the masses were with me. And now, more Pukhtuns and even Khans are opening shops in Mingora; so they are also going into business, over the last ten years.

By the changes that took place, during my Rule, it was really the new upper middle class that was most favoured by circumstances. Yet at the end of the State, they were the ones who agitated against me, even those who had been my close companions. I have said already that gratitude does not create loyalty.

My father used to comment on this. Many people would come to him to ask for loans — not from the State, but personally, from him. He used to tell me — and I still observe these rules myself — that one should calculate how much interest a person would have to pay on such a loan. Then *give* him the sum of that interest, and tell him to use it to take a loan from the bank! Because this man is never going to pay you. So why annoy yourself, and him? Otherwise you will always be thinking how you gave him the money and he is not giving it back — it is better to give him less, as a gift. People who do not pay back a loan easily start feeling aggrieved, as if you were wanting *their* money. There is an Arabic proverb about this: *Al qardu miqraz ul hubb* — "A loan is the scissors of love!"

Being a Ruler, one has to be careful about everything, reflecting over the consequences of everything you do. Not careful in the sense of being fearful for your life. Quite the contrary; I never took great precautions of that kind. Either it was fatalism, in which every Muslim has some belief; or else I felt I heard an inner voice, saying that as long as I am needed, God will protect me. I had my bodyguards, but I exposed myself in the bazaar, though people told me not to go to the bazaar. I answered: "Why not? If I am afraid of my people, I cannot rule them!" I used to walk across from my house to my office, at the regular times. People said I should make an underground passage. I said: "No! When that mistrust comes, you cannot rule." And you can never be safe from a madman's bullet, never, no matter what precautions you take.

It is not that kind of physical danger, or the pressure of work, that forms most of the burden of being a Ruler — I have always liked to work. It is the loneliness. From when I was a very small child, I have felt that. Being a Ruler, I feel different, apart. People respect me, and they still look to me as their leader. Yet I feel the distance. People fear that their words might have an adverse effect on me, and thereby rebound on them. So a subject and a Ruler can never become friends. And your closest associates, people you have worked with your whole life: when circumstances change, they change. For example Ataullah: he was my tutor, I knew him since 1923. I trusted him, my father trusted him. I knew he was with me through the difficult years of my estrangement with my father. For all these years he worked closely with me, up to the *end* of my rule he was close, I trusted him... People turn about, I don't know why. Either they cannot get more benefit, or something. — He is still living; he is a multi-millionaire from the business he developed here, under my protection. But now he never comes to me.

My father was in the same position, but he was a different sort of person; he did not care about the loneliness. He kept himself busy, as I said, with the Holy Koran, or playing chess and cards with his staff. And at night, most of the night, he used to pray. So he did not feel lonely. He never believed in caste. Though there are no castes in Islam, in practice the poor people were treated as having less dignity than the rich people. Never by my father — he respected the man as he was. The greatest thing about him: he was never pompous, and he was not a fanatic. It is admirable that he was so open-minded. He grew up in a religious family when Swat was a very isolated place. He grew up even without the guidance of his father. He was only eleven years old when his father died. Yet he was very wise, very quick, and most liberal — he used to tell me: "You are more conservative than I am!"

In an outer sense, he changed his life very much after retirement: he used his old age for religious disciplines. In the early years, while creating the State, he acted very forcefully and ruthlessly. The reason was, he had to. Religion and morality in Swat in those days were very subordinate; if someone committed a crime, then all the *jirga* would support him, and tell my father *not* to fine him. So if he had not demonstrated his force of character, they would not have respected him and he would have been eliminated. But he was *always* very particular about his prayers. Ever since I have known him, he was always punctual about it. Though he told me that during his youth, when there were battles and all those troubles, he used to miss his prayers. But not when he became Ruler; he observed it and made us observe it.

In his old age, he had nothing else to do; so he read the Holy Koran, to keep himself busy. There is no truth in the view that he was in any sense doing penance for earlier acts. He did not repent, rather he took *pride* in what he had done. As for religion, he observed his prayers always, he fasted, he went on pilgimage, he was a good Muslim — but I would not call him a religious man, in that sense, as he was never a fanatic. But now he had to while away the time, so he said: "Instead of reading other books, let me read the Holy Koran!" His ideas were always the same, and he had perfect belief in God and the Prophet and the Holy Book.

My own attitude has always been that of a practical man. I cannot give time to religious studies, except my prayers. But I have great faith in God, and I believe strongly in Islam. Everyone says that his own religion is better: but the fundamental things in all religions are the same — except the mode of praying. You may pray to your God in a different way, but we are praying to the same God. And no religion believes in robbery, untruthfulness, debauchery, and such things. I have never been a bigoted man; and whether I dealt with a Hindu or a Christian or anybody, I looked to the man as he was — in the same way as my father did.

Some people have an ideal, a person they admire and emulate. I do not think I have ever had such an example before me. I have the greatest respect for my grandfather and great-grandfather, but I never knew them personally. And one has one's father. But with my father, I became so close and like a friend — and then you know too much of each other. But he has certainly served as an example for me, in many ways, as has that mullah with whom I boarded as a child, despite the misery he caused me. I have great respect for both of them. I have also admired the qualities that I have seen in the British people I have met, in the service and administration of British India. Their integrity and self-discipline were remarkable. I won't say that there are no more good people as there used to be. I will put it in another way: everything is detoriating — day by day. In democracy, especially in Oriental countries, the jobs are given more by favouritism, or one's relationship to a minister or somebody high up, instead of by quality and competition. In Bhutto's time, all the people were selected by himself, without going through examination or selection board. Discipline and quality in a whole organization are created only slowly, with great effort; but you can destroy it quickly, as by putting a match to it. It is impossible now to go back on the one-man-one-vote principle; but there should have been a standard: of property, or education, to be a voter. Now, most of the votes just depend on slogans and party affiliation, and the administration deteriorates.

My life work for this State has depended very much on traits of my own personality, my character. And as far as I think, I was born with it. Thanks to education, I could read and write and converse, and I continued to read books — one's education never finishes. By reading books you develop ideas; I always say about everybody: whatever is good or bad character is inborn from childhood. If one thinks about one's own childhood: no one has changed very much from that, over the years.

On the other hand, one can see that people are sometimes spoiled, by circumstances or bad treatment. And in that way, my father has been very important to me. Because he showed me discipline. To be regular in time, to get up at certain hours, go to sleep at certain hours, have one's meals at set hours. If I fixed a time with somebody, I was always ready. That is a sort of discipline my father had himself till the end. You are influenced by your parents.

There will be a tendency for a person in a very powerful position to be tempted to use that power for his own pleasure, to indulge himself and become unprincipled. I never did that. The reason was: my father was the first Ruler. If we had held power for generations, it might have had some effect, making us progressively more pompous and wielding more arbitrary power. But my father never had any vanity and was never pompous. He behaved just like any human being. And so I was brought up in that atmosphere; I thought of myself as a human being. I learned to put myself in their position, and that always gave me more insight. Even from the criminals, when I was hearing cases, I used to learn from them too, because I put myself in their position: If I were like him, how would I feel about myself?

I have always been inquisitive, and eager to learn more — from all people I have met. I have read, and thought about everything I read. I have observed everything, very closely, and learned to judge by small signs. I have tried to orient myself in the larger world, so I could anticipate, and go with the times. My only regret has been that I had no higher education. The circumstances were such that my father was alone. He had those two loyal Wazirs, but after all I was his son. So he wanted me to be trained here with local politics, rather than be sent to the U.K. Though he was very broad-minded, he did not believe that foreign education would be of more benefit. And it is true, if I had spent many years away, I might not have been able to handle people here. But I still think — and have suffered from this mentally — that I should have graduated from Oxford or Cambridge.

My father, in any case, was not going to send me abroad. And then the two Wazirs might have become very powerful; if I had not been here they would have wielded more power, and in the end they might have been in such a position that it would have been difficult for me to deal with them. The first time I went to Europe was in 1954, when everything was peaceful. Experience may be the best education of all. And knowledge is quite a different thing from education. I have seen people with degrees from the best colleges, who know very little about the world and have very little general insight.

In my father's time, physical courage was very important; and one of the factors when he was chosen as Ruler was his fearlessness. But he was not reckless in wars; he always took his precautions; he told me so himself. He did not want merely to show his followers and himself how brave he was, and jump at the other trench and risk being shot. He calculated. About myself, I cannot say, because I never had that experience. By the time I had authority, it was peaceful, so I do not know how I would have behaved.

But in my relations with people, I have always been swift to judge their character, interests, and purposes, and I have always felt confident of myself.

And also, I had confidence in the future, because I knew I had a task in this State. That stimulated me always to think ahead, to prepare myself mentally for what might happen, to anticipate and think further ahead than those who might be opposing me.

There is a kind of realism and honesty in this, which I think must be inborn in a person. First, I owe it to that. Secondly, I owe it to my father — he was always honest and truthful — and to that mullah teacher, who was a very honest person — though he gave us little food, but that was simply because he was a miser; it was his nature. Since he treated his own children in the same way, I can't grumble about that. He was a great disciplinarian. Then later, I came into contact with the British, and saw their integrity. All these influences went together with my own character, and made me *always* believe in truthfulness. If you tell the truth, it will not harm you — rather it will provide the basis for your own quality. So whenever I made a promise, I kept it. I never gave false hopes to people, that I will do such and such good things for you when I come into power — never. Even those people who were dismissed at my downfall, I never promised that I would bring them back. One or two of them tried, pleaded with me, they said: "I don't know what will happen when you become the Ruler!" "We will see, when the time comes." I said. I never informed a person that he would be promoted tomorrow, or in a month. I watched him, judged him for six months, asked this person and that person how he was working and so on. When I had made up my mind, only then did I tell him, and promote him, instead of tempting and promising.

The present administration functions very differently from mine. Cases must wait for years before they are decided; security has become poor, maintenance of public facilities is poor. Officers in charge come and go; they never have time to learn, or to see any project through. The different branches of Government do not coordinate. At the time of the State, one mind and one purpose controlled it all; we could coordinate all the efforts and pursue persistent and long-term policies.

Many people suffer under present conditions — I feel for them.

For me personally, it would be much better to live somewhere else, outside the State. I could have a smaller house, just four or five bedrooms, five or six servants — middle class! But I cannot do that. Most of all, because of the family: it would be finished! My four sons and my half-brother do not get together enough so as to cooperate. The perpetuation of some kind of position for the family depends on me. Nor can I do away with so many servants who depend on me unless I pension them off. I don't want any pomp — as I said, there was never a foundation stone laid by me, and never an opening ceremony performed. No propaganda for myself. People used to tell me: "You must advertise!" I said: "This is my duty, I am doing." Now, I have no official duties.

But despite delays, one day there will be elections again — sooner or later they will be held. Then I will be again involved; and some people will accuse me, that I am indulging in politics. Though there is no ban on me, from the Government's side. I can stand myself, I can support anybody I like, and I can back any party I like, there is no ban on me. But still — one son against the other, one friend against another, so it makes my position difficult. Therefore, I wish I could go away from the State, on a long journey, at the time of the next election. But I do not know whether I shall be able to get away. People would say: "You didn't support me! You ran away!" Again complicated. When the State was merged — by mutual agreement, though it would have been merged in any case, I am glad I anticipated it and acted — at that time, I thought I would be left in peace, living quietly here, and having a few outside friends occasionally come and visit me, to spend two or three days together, now and again. And the old officials who had remained loyal to me, they would come, and be welcome. But this did not happen: There is too much turmoil, and I am still very busy.

In Persian, they say: for a King there is *ya takht, ya takhtah* — either the throne, or the grave. There is no middle way. But for me there should be the middle way of a peaceful and contented life.

Epilogue
by Fredrik Barth

In the presentation of the preceding material I have chosen to retain and emphasize its character as the Wali's own account. It thereby becomes an account of Swat history and politics as seen from the inside and from the centre, and as much the story of a life as the story of a State; and this, I feel, enhances its value. But the account also contains materials and insights on general themes of importance to anthropologists and political scientists. To bring out those that I judge to be most important — though without entering into the more extensive analysis needed to treat them exhaustively — I have elected to highlight some of these general themes. To this end, I shall discuss briefly the origins of the State, the functioning of its central organs, the nature and bases of the Ruler's authority, and the relationship between his policies and the course of social and cultural change in Swat.

Origins of the State

The State of Swat emerged in a territory which before 1915 had no centralized political system. To the extent that it represented an endogenous development, the present text will constitute one of the few contemporary accounts in social science literature of the emergence of a state organization in a previously stateless society. The situation is not, of course, pristine and fully comparable to the formation of historically early states in the Near East or Meso-America: the actors who participated in Swat were all familiar with the idea of a centralized state, and had some greater or lesser knowledge and experience of the structure and mode of operation of other states. Yet the creation of Swat State was in no way the establishment of an offshoot of a pre-existing state, by conquest or invitation; nor was it simply the adoption in a new locality of a centralized system modelled after a pre-existing one elsewhere: it was a new and emergent structure. These points deserve some elaboration.

Firstly, on the question of the endogenous character of the development. I have given brief analyses of the emergence of Swat State elsewhere (Barth 1959a, and especially 1981:172 ff). The Wali's account in chapter 3, above, clearly substantiates the view that the fusion of a nuclear area in the Swat Valley into a centralized state was a truly endogenous development. The *jirgas* of the Pakhtuns took repeated, if indecisive, initiatives to achieve a union under the Miangul brothers, Badshah Sahib and Shirin Sahib, in the years 1910–14 (p. 30); they then turned to Abdul Jabbar Shah; and again in 1917 they turned to Badshah Sahib and acclaimed him their Ruler (p. 32). Throughout these years, there is no evidence of British (or any other external) complicity, encouragement, or even significant awareness of these events and their import; the initiative arose and was realized endogenously. Any argument to the contrary would have to produce its own data for support.

The next question is *where* in endogenous society the impetus to centralization can be located. Ostensibly the *jirgas* invited Badshah Sahib to rule — what covert part did the successful founder himself play in formulating and eliciting the request? The known facts are somewhat contradictory but not incompatible with the Wali's disclaimer that his father sought actively to become Ruler. Badshah Sahib had shown marked effort and ruthlessness to forestall the ambitious Miangul cousins (pp. 26 f.), presumably because of his own interests in the matter. Yet the *jirgas* must have acted without his instigation when they invited Abdul Jabbar Shah and set up that first attempt at a state. By then at least, the initiative must have lain in their hands.

What were the reasons that propelled the assemblies of autonomous tribesmen to give up at least some of their autonomy to a central power of their own creation? Two main considerations emerge very clearly: the urgency of united military defence, and the need felt to constitute a different polity capable of new functions.

Unity of military defence has traditionally in these societies been achieved in the form of *jehad,* under the extra-institutional unitary leadership of an inspired mullah or fakir. Though most effective against self-designated infidels like the British (and sufficient to withstand their imperial thrust in most of the Tribal Areas throughout the whole colonial period), the *jehad* could be and was also used for resistance and rebellions against native rulers (cf. its use against the Khan of Khar, p. 43, and against the Badshah himself, p. 63). The presence of the Sandakai Mullah in Swat at the time was no doubt to service this demand (cf. p. 29). However, the Nawab of Dir was too close and too persistent to be withstood on such an *ad hoc* basis. There was a need for a stable, institutionalized unity of command in defence of territory: urgently on the West Bank, but in the slightly longer run also on the East Bank of the Swat River.

The need to reconstitute the polity can also be seen in part in terms of defence. The Nawab had shown considerable skill in insinuating himself, particularly into the Nikpi Khel area, by utilizing the factional divisions between the *dalla*s. The tribes on the West Bank clearly realized that *dalla* factionalism was inherent in the political constitution of their society. It was not sufficient that all collectively had a will to keep the Nawab outsider at bay: internal conflicts of interest would perpetually generate situations where the option of seeking support from the Nawab was temporarily more attractive to some than sustaining a loss at the hands of the opposed faction. The only way they could see to break out of this systemic weakness was by reconstituting the political organization around a central King — though there is no evidence that they had a clear picture of how such a Kingship was to function, or indeed what the Badshah's plans were for the state that they launched.

Independent evidence that I have collected from the older Khans on the East Bank indicates that, quite apart from the threat from Dir, there was also a pervasive wish to counteract a steady increase in the intensity of factionalism and insecurity that was generated by the operation of *dalla* politics in the stateless society. A plausible reason given for the steady deterioration of security and order was the development of arms technology that was taking place: from mostly swords and axes in the mid-nineteenth century, through increasing prevalence of matchlocks, to an extensive arsenal of breech-loading rifles by 1915.

The population that articulated these purposes and acceded to the kingship of the Badshah was the landowning ruling stratum or caste of Pakhtun tribesmen, — the dominant approximately one quarter of the total population, organized in an acephalous system of lineage councils. There is no evidence as to what the interests of the property-less majority of the population may have been — nor indeed is there any evidence of institutions that would make these strata capable of formulating a distinctive, collective view in the matter.

In no sense was Swat a "conquest state", since no element of force was brought in to create the situation that found its expression in September 1917, when leaders representing a population of about 100,000 assembled and tied the turban of kingship around Badshah Sahib's head. Nor did the continued existence of the State depend on further expansion, though such expansion did in fact take place.

I have asserted that the State represented a new and emergent structure, that its organization was not simply copied and introduced from elsewhere. I shall return below to the intricate and changing manner in which Swat State's government organization interpenetrated with the organization of local society, and thus necessarily represented an emergent structure. Here, it is sufficient to point to the absence of any neighbouring states with a similar organization. Certainly, most or perhaps all of the elements can be found represented in various organizations in the larger region: the bodyguard pattern shared with Dir, the tax auctioning known from Moghul India, the Tahsil divisions and officers of British India, the Islamic institution of *ushur,* etc. Abdul Jabbar Shah's procedure for the swift creation of a popular Army may have been innovative — at least it was unknown to the Badshah (cf. p. 52), but it may well have been an introduction from Amb. But the essential structure of Swat State, which assured its survival, did not emulate the pattern of any other state: not the pluralistic and coercive Khanate of Dir (p. 143, Barth 1981:174f), the intricate centralized feudalism of Chitral (Biddulph 1880, Barth 1956:80ff), the ritual absolutism of Hunza (Lorimer 1934, Müller-Stellrecht 1979), or the colonial bureaucracy of British India.

The boundaries of the State

After the first founding of Swat State, its territory expanded rapidly over some years. What were the determinants of the direction and extent of this expansion? First and foremost, it depended on the will and force of the Ruler of Swat, and of the territories concerned: the Badshah was given no military, material, or moral assistance from third parties in taking possession of these territories. Both the expansion and the subsequent retention of each area tended to depend on the invitation of one, normally the temporarily weaker, of the local *dallas,* in combination with the military force of the State. It thus seems plausible to say that a precondition of conquest was the existence, in the area, of a pattern of two-party *dalla* factionalism, and of a pro-Swat faction. The size and strength of such a faction in the case of Indus Kohistan is, however, in some doubt (pp. 93 f., Story of Swat 1963:102f).

Secondly, an idea of cultural and geographical unity was clearly also present, enshrined in the state's identification as "The Yusufzai State of Swat". As a program for expansion, however, this idea was never realized: closely related Yusufzai segments were *not* incorporated, while some more distant segments, and even territories occupied by entirely unrelated peoples, *were* incorporated. A main reason for this was British Indian interference. A simplified diagram showing the inter-relations of the main Yusufzai segments according to the traditional Pakhtun genealogies is given below.

Starting with the core area (of Babuzai, Aba Khel, Musa Khel, Maturizai, Shamizai, Sebujni, and Nikpi Khel), the areas of Azzi Khel and Jinki Khel were quickly incorporated, and the Nawab of Dir was engaged over the control of Shamozai. Thana village, on the other hand, the closest collaterals of the Musa Khel, could not be approached, as they were within the bounds of the protected area of Malakand Agency, established by the British after 1895 — though Thana was in no sense occupied or administered by British India. The Badshah likewise was prevented from making good his claims against Dir to Adinzai because of British third party interference.

Expansion into Buner, on the other hand, was left open to him through British non-interference. The main groups in Buner, though mostly Yusufzai, belonged to more distantly related segments and were both geographically and sub-culturally discrete. Yet he succeeded in eliminating the influence and armies of Amb from that area, and also incorporated some smaller, non-Yusufzai groups, including some Gadun villages that are probably not originally Pathan. Other similar groups, however, in a narrow zone along the Indus, were put out of bounds by being declared protected tribes by the British.

The mountain zone which he conquered between the Swat valley and the Indus was partly settled by mixed Yusufzai tribes, partly controlled by Mian families comparable to Badshah Sahib's own, and were thus essentially similar and related to areas already under his control. But further up the Indus valley, and in the northern mountain valleys, large areas were conquered belonging to entirely distinct Kohistani populations, speaking languages unrelated to Pashto, and practising cultures very different from that of the Swat valley. Similar areas to these across the Indus, on the other hand, were declared out-of-bounds by the British

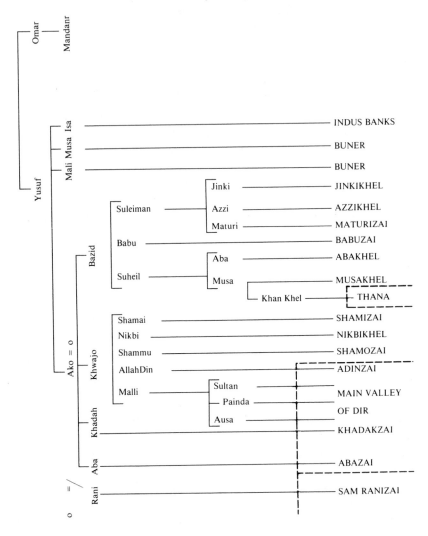

Indian authorities, despite the fact that they themselves exercised no administrative presence whatsoever in the less accessible parts till the very end of British India.

The end result was thus a fairly arbitrary creation, containing a majority of closely related groups, and a considerable accretion of other, in part quite distinctive, peoples. It would seem that the State's territorial expansion simply proceeded in all directions up to the limits introduced by the dominant imperial power.

Membership

Once this territorial unit was created, what kind of grass-roots membership attitudes did it elicit in the population? Beyond a doubt, most citizens of Swat by the 1950s felt in a certain sense like "Swatis", and indeed identified themselves as such to the extent that the older usage of the name "Swati" for certain tribes in neighbouring Hazara district was being displaced. On the other hand, the form of the question, catering as it does to issues raised in attempts to generalize about identity in "new nations", is poorly designed for the present case. To begin with, local society — particularly in the core areas of the Swat valley — is composed of a diversity of social groups, in many ways comparable to castes, with distinctive variants of culture, and unequal social rank (cf. Barth 1960, reprinted 1981 ch. 2). Political alignments were traditionally conceived in terms of the positions taken by the Pakhtun landowners, who served as patrons for the rest of the population, and not directly by that population itself. When the landowners joined or were assimilated to the State of Swat, their tenants and clients ipso facto became "Swatis". Yet, as modernization and development received increasing emphasis — and were increasingly achieved — there was a distinctly growing awareness and pride in a "Swati" identity. However, the articulate elite that would most clearly be identified with this membership was almost as aware as the Wali himself of the ultimate inevitability of merger. As a result, a growing sense of nationhood was focused on the larger unity of Pakistan — and also, in the heady atmosphere of the creation of an Islamic state out of the Muslim parts of British India, on membership in the Islamic world. At the same time, affirmation of these wider memberships was confused by the debates about provincial autonomy — connected with language issues — versus the One Unit organization of West Pakistan, and the other rhetoric connecting Pashto-speakers in an identity shared with most Afghans. In this confusing field, there was no question of Swat emerging as a "nation" of ultimate, exclusive identification, either for the Wali or his subjects. Nor does the pre-existing division between Pashto-speakers and Kohistanis seem to have been overcome, as indicated by the voting pattern after merger (p. 141).

159

Ideological bases of the State

It has been argued that the emergence of Swat State should be understood in the context of millenial movements in general, and Sufi Islam in particular (Ahmed 1976). There seems to be no evidence in the above account, and little evidence elsewhere, to support this contention. In the Wali's account, as in the Badshah's own (Story of Swat 1963), there is a strong affirmation of the Badshah's civilizing task, his bringing of peace and order to an anarchic area, and his desire to base public and private morality on the fundamental precepts of Islam. But no claims are made to extraordinary sources of authority (in contrast to the inspired leaders of *jehad* that he evicted), no visionary rhetoric is used, and no demand or encouragement are given to the creation of a devotional following. Finally, the continuity of any elaborate theological tradition or knowledge from the Saintly ancestor is expressly disclaimed by both the Wali and his father. We must therefore look more deeply at the key features of the administrative system, and its articulation with other features of the organization of the local society, to understand its remarkable success.

The functioning of the central administration

Because of the swift development that took place during the State's fifty-two years of existence, it might appear difficult to characterize its organization in general terms. But if we try to formulate statements that hold true for most or all of its history, we can expect them to bring out features that have been fundamental to its constitution.

Autocracy

Most conspicuous was the marked concentration of power and initiative in the person of the Ruler. At no time during the existence of Swat was the Ruler's authority balanced or otherwise curtailed by any other formally constituted body. The "State Council" established in 1954 along lines imposed by the Pakistani authorities (p. 110) never exercised significant influence, as one could indeed predict from its composition and organization; and my own observations during fieldwork in 1954 and 1960 fully agree with the Wali's own minimization of its importance. Nor was there any endogenously instituted assembly of councillors, advisers, or other representatives, formal or informal, of tribes, areas, or population categories. Indeed, even in the ceremonial sense there was nothing that might be called a "court" surrounding the Ruler, and no office was associated with the *right* to perform a particular function, ritual or practical. The same concentration of all authority in the hands of the Ruler is reflected in the incomplete and somewhat superficial division of functions as between his closest senior officials: since they all acted merely as his executives performing functions that he was continually free to supervise and resume, any strict division of authority between them would tend to be artificial. Thus, they all took cases for settlement, and all of them could pass orders down to lower echelons of the administration. There was a designated commander-in-chief of the Army, but all appointments and promotions he wished to make had to be approved by the Ruler; he had other functions, such as settlement of cases, and the permanent settlement of land after *wesh* in Nikpi khel; and as illustrated in the Wali's account there was nothing irregular in the Heir Apparent's suddenly taking him off on an apparently impulsive journey of several weeks outside the State without prior arrangement (p. 80). Perhaps the most striking image of the character of this administration is the daily scene of the Badshah himself, at his telephone, conversing with leaders and notables throughout the State (p. 63). Despite more bureaucratized routines under the Wali, the same focus on active direction by the Ruler personally was certainly equally characteristic of his whole period of rule: "I was the pivot of it all" (p. 120). It is in this sense that the Wali characterizes his administration as a "family affair"; but he is far too modest when he explains such a concentration of power in terms of the small scale of the State (p. 121). Such command over a freedom-loving and turbulent population of initially several hundred thousand, growing to seven hundred thousand by the end of the State, can only be achieved by a combination of well-designed and well-attuned organization and great political skill. Let us try to identify key features of this organization.

Articulation with local society

The Wali's account emphasizes the settlement of cases as the most essential function of the Ruler. This was true both under his father (p. 80) and himself (p. 126). Such an emphasis is consistent with the ideological focus on peace, order and security as flowing from the presence of the

State, and thus with the original mandate for the creation of the State. It could be argued that this also reveals the class basis of the State: The administration of justice, with focus on the protection of life and private property, seems above all a service in the interest of the established and propertied class; and so through this service the state administration secures the necessary support, from those who have the power, to sustain itself. Such a view of Swat State is also sometimes formulated by Pakistani students and intellectuals. The Wali does not address it directly in the preceding text; but it is quite clear that he does not see the State as an organ of a pre-established class, but as an instrument of his father's and his own policy. Indeed, the thesis as formulated is much too simplistic, and a proper analysis requires (i) a closer scrutiny of the policy that guided the settlement of cases, and thus determined the consequences that accrued from that activity, and (ii) an explanation of the steady erosion of the power and prominence of Pakhtun landowners that has taken place through the history of the State. I shall present the view that the settlement of cases was the most important way in which the State sought to regulate local level politics, and thereby secure its own survival in the context of deep and powerful political processes generated on the village level. I see the management of this articulation of the State apparatus with other aspects of society in Swat as critical to the success and growth of the State.

To appreciate this, the reader needs to have a clear picture of certain aspects of the locally-based social and political system with which the State administration articulated (cf. Barth 1959, 1981). From before the State and throughout its existence, local society was built on a system of economic dependence and political clientage, whereby property-less tenants and craftsmen obtained land and labour contracts from landowners, and both they and the smaller landowners aligned as the political followings of bigger Khans, alternatively of Mian leaders in the marginal and less fertile areas. The alignment of persons in such followings was a result of pragmatic choices made under a number of constraints and pressures: persons sought to obtain the security that sprang from being the follower of a strong and competent leader, and they sought advantageous contracts for labour and land. Leaders on their part were dependent on having large and effective followings, especially in the times before the State, to serve them under threat and in battle; and so they sought to transform relations of economic dependence, house tenancy contracts, and the poor man's need for spokesmen and protectors, into comprehensive relations of political clientage. To enhance this the Khans practised a suitable mixture of protection, coercion, hospitality and largesse, focussing on feasting, companionship, and group control in the *hujra* men's house of the Khan. Khans were judged against ideals of "weight", "solidity", "forcefulness", "hospitality", and "manliness" (Barth 1981:160). Since the common man's relation to any particular Khan was optative and a follower's benefits from the relationship were highly dependent on his patron's effectiveness and goodwill, great attention was given to the Khan's current performance and success. Generally, followers were quick to abandon a loser and flock to a rising leader (cf. pp. 23 f., 145). The result was a striking combination of strong leaders and volatile followings.

Neighbouring Khans were generally rivals for land, followers and influence (especially *tarburs,* i.e. cousins/enemies, see p. 25). Besides pitting their local followings against each other, each Khan also sought reciprocal promises of support from other more distant Khans against his close rivals, and thereby formed large coalitions where one's enemy's enemies became one's natural allies (p. 80). By a compelling systemic logic these alliances built up into the two grand, dispersed parties — *dəllas* — which have characterized all Swat politics, whereby both *dəllas* are represented in most localities by the locally opposed rivals. If no other powerful political factors intervene — as for example under pre-state conditions — there is simply no way that a local Khan and faction can remain outside this big bipartite alignment: a local third party can be dominated and exploited with impunity by both the larger *dəllas,* and must join one or the other for protection. But the compelling bi-partition is sometimes an imperfect mold for more complex and individual interest alignments: one may find rivals *(māriz)* locked by regional political necessities in a common *dəlla.* There were also divided interests as between leaders within the *dəlla* arising over particular issues, settlements, and general competition for influence.

Such divisions represent potential lines of cleavage within the *dəlla.* They become highly consequential because of strategic properties inherent in the pattern of two-party coalitions. I have sought to demonstrate this elsewhere by means of a Theory-of-Games analysis (Barth 1959b, 1981). Briefly, in any one area, one of the two *dəllas* will have the edge and be dominant. This advantage its members exploit by pressing the weaker *dəlla* to give way in conflicts, relinquish disputed lands, etc. This weaker party, increasingly at a disadvantage, seeks to bolster its position by (a) seeking alliance with the dominant *dǝlla* in the neighbouring area, and especially by (b) enticing disgruntled leaders and subfactions in the opposing *dǝlla* to defect and thereby swing the balance of power (ultimately, the number of mobilizable fighting men) in favour of the formerly weaker *dǝlla*. The negotiating counters in such attempts are: offers of leadership in the combined *dǝlla;* priority for land conflicts of particular interest to the defecting group; support against the defector's *māriẓ* in their *dǝlla* of former membership. The result of these circumstances is a tendency for groups to split off from the dominant *dǝlla* and cause a see-saw change of dominance between two regional *dǝllas* of shifting membership. In the process, some particularly fortunate and shrewd leaders will tend to shift opportunely and grow swiftly, while the followings of others may come unravelled equally swiftly, and their positions and properties be lost.

It was this see-saw game which allowed the Nawab of Dir for a time to insinuate himself into the politics of the West Bank of Swat (p. 29), and which represented the systemic weakness which the Khans could not repair by their own institutional means (p. 155). But at the inception of the State, this vast organization of society and politics was not overthrown. All that happened, was the introduction of an imprecise charter for the centralized, moderating and co-ordinating activity by a "King", to be pursued by a new pretender in the person of the Badshah. His problem was how to provide this centralized institution with some force, and even more difficult: how to defend it against a potentially growing coalition of Khans once it started emerging with some effectiveness. The operation necessitated "riding the tiger" — participating with superior skill in the two-party game while increasingly asserting a covert control over all the leaders in *both dǝllas* (cf. pp. 65ff.), regulating their careers and alignments through the balancing of *dǝllas* and interference in the leadership of both parties. It is *here* that the settlement of cases plays a crucial role. The "cases" to be settled by the Ruler and his officials are precisely the stuff of *dǝlla* politics: land disputes and disputes between persons variously aligned in factions. Thereby, the Ruler achieves two purposes: (1) the State increasingly invades and takes over those functions which *dǝlla* activities previously served, and thereby reduces the importance of the patronage which local leaders provide, on which they based their authority; and (2) by influencing the outcomes of disputes, the Ruler can variously strengthen and weaken competing leaders and thus affect their alignment and the patterns of local and regional power.

By this crucial process the Ruler was able to practise an essential economy of force: whereas each *dalla,* unopposed, would through much of the history of Swat have commanded a force considerably stronger than that of the State apparatus, the power of Khans was perpetually balanced mainly by the power of *other* Khans, and the State only needed to command the marginal force always to hold the balance of power between the *dallas.*

In the earliest years of the State, this must have been a very precarious business; but the very real threats from the outside, from Dir and Amb, also no doubt relieved the Badshah of some of the internal pressures. But also in later periods, perpetual adroitness and vigilance were needed. The discussion which the Wali refers to between himself and his father regarding feudalism (e.g. p. 111) is primarily concerned with the underlying principles guiding this vigilance. The Wali's policy from 1954 represented a conscious shift from a policy of basing the State's control of Swat directly on the *dalla* structure through a careful balancing act, to one of progressively localizing and pulverizing the *dallas.* But both these policies were achieved above all through the constant flow of cases which were settled by State organs, most critically by the Ruler himself.

Thus, the emphasis on peace, order and justice in no way represents a policy of defence of established class dominance. Leaders before the State were to some extent above such constraints: might was right, and the protection of person and property which the State started performing entailed a *reduction* in their privileges. The Badshah, and later the Wali, continually encroached, contained, and progressively eliminated the power and prominence of Khans. In other words, the policy of the State in its exercise of law and order undermined the previous position of the dominant class. A nearly universal praise of the State from older members of the non-Pakhtun strata for protecting the integrity and property of smallholders and poor people also bears witness to this. Yet there is no basis for identifying the State's policy as one of class liberation of the client class, the *"Kalangzai"* (p. 146). Pre-established wealth was secured, men of influence were coopted into the State administration, and new inequalities were allowed to emerge (p. 146, and below). Other issues than social policy were primary: an articulation of State organization with local organization in a way that secured the survival of the State in a complex field of powerful local politics.

The design of State organs

A similar economy of means is characteristic of a number of the institutions composing the State organization. Rather consistently, they show a design which might be characterized as self-regulating or self-animating when placed in the context of local society in Swat. Perhaps most simply and basically, this can be seen in the tax auction system of *ushur* (pp. 53f.). Given the *dalla* organization and the rivalry for dominance and influence between local leaders, to win the tax rights to an area must of necessity come to be regarded as a major prize and symbol of local ascendancy. Local pretenders were therefore motivated to go quite high in their bids, and even risk considerable losses, to secure this prize; and the organization of the collection of *ushur* from each field in one's area was not considered by them so much as an outlay to obtain returns on one's bid but rather as an intrinsically valuable public exercise of symbolic hegemony over the area. Consequently, by merely fixing the rate of *ushur*, setting up the annual auction, and providing a framework of local courts to which farmers can appeal in the event of abuse, the State maximized its land revenue. At the same time it escaped the costs and complications of making tax assessments, organizing the tax collecting agency and the necessary controls against graft and embezzlement, or directing against itself the inevitable displeasure aroused in each farmer for having to part with the full amount of his tithe.

In a more complex way, the organization of the Army exhibits similar features (p. 55). Its local and regional basis assured a political division of officers and men in all echelons into *dalla* factions, which precluded that the Army could be employed for purposes of separatism, rebellion, or coup. The prestige of rank, arms, and martial activity was harnessed in the service of an organization mainly employed in public works, as a functional equivalent of corvée labour. Commissions provided officers with a highly valued source of legitimate authority and command, and thereby with the outer forms of the influence and status — the "glory", cf. p. 145 — so eagerly sought in Swat society. Among the poorer households of the population at large, ordinary soldier contracts provided a significant marginal addition to subsistence, and thus a valued source of commitment to the regime. It all added up to an elaborate system whereby 6000–8000 men were individually enrolled in the State apparatus. It composed a formidable force for internal use in defence of the authority of the State without being open to subversion as a danger to its Ruler. It had the useful capacity to perform extensive public works. And last but not least, it constituted a large store of bonuses and perquisites to be widely dispersed in politically opportune ways (cf. p. 108).

The mode of collecting fines was similarly "self-animating" (p. 57): at the cost of one third of the fines imposed by the Tahsildars' courts, the State obtained the services of the local Khan in collecting such fines, provided a reward for acting as Khan and an incentive for him to involve himself in reporting breaches of State law by locals to the State's officials, and divided the authority of imposing fines from that of collecting them and thereby prevented abuse.

And perhaps the simplest prototype of this organizational pattern was the Wali's finesse of rewarding teachers in proportion to the relative performance of their pupil average in objective exams (p. 113). By this means he went a long way towards solving one of the perpetual weaknesses of third world public educational systems, and enhanced the performance and career options of a whole generation of Swatis in the wider Pakistan.

Finally, to obtain the information and intelligence necessary to defend the regime, both the Wali and his father depended simply on the commentary, rumour and gossip that reached them through holding the channels of communication to the Ruler open for all persons.

In these various ways, it is characteristic that the organizations that composed the State were designed to articulate with the larger society in a manner suited to regulate and sometimes stimulate activities, but mainly to assure its own perpetuation by harnessing the local-level organizations, divisions, and energies for State purposes. Its revenue likewise depended on the taxing of the fruits of private activities: tithe on agricultural production, fees on the extraction of timber, tolls on imports and exports, and licence fees on various activities. Public works were concentrated on providing an infrastructure for transport and communication, and educational and welfare services. Though much of Swat is intensively irrigated, the State never involved itself in hydraulic works or the control and distribution of water (p. 118). It thus shows none of the typical features ascribed to "Oriental Despotisms" (pace Ahmed 1976:126). A framework of administration was set up, subdividing the territory into regions and Tahsils; but the State was not segmentary in its deeper structure or mode of functioning. The Ruler acted on any and every matter he might wish, directly or through any person he might choose, towards any person in any echelon or locality; and channels of communication were open from any person direct to the Ruler. In these ways, the whole State organization may be seen as an instrument of the central Ruler. While increasingly expanding its field of influence and control through its history, and thereby contributing profoundly to the reshaping of society in Swat, it is yet most instructive to see the State not as a framework for that society but as an organ or body within it, perpetuating itself while affecting its environment.

Bases of authority and legitimacy

In choosing the words to describe the bases in Swati ideology and culture for the State and the Badshah's and Wali's rule, it is difficult to avoid a vocabulary which presumes precisely that which should be explored. We need to question the extent to which the foundations of Swat State and the Wali's rule are retrieved by a concept of legitimacy, and not merely what might constitute the sources of legitimacy; we should not merely analyse the sources of authority of the Ruler over his subjects, but ask how — and how significantly — membership and participation in a centralized State were conceived by Swatis, and how this specifies the senses of "authority" which are meaningful in a discussion of these political relations.

This exploration is made particularly difficult by the multiplicity of easy and superficial answers that might be adopted. A diversity of ideologies have been at least partly known and employed in political discourse in Swat, deriving variously from (1) formal education, perpetuating a British syllabus from colonial times, (2) Islamic tradition, in relatively archaic and parochial interpretations, and (3) current political rhetoric in Pakistan. It might be tempting to adopt one of these viewpoints and vocabularies for a discussion of the ideational base in the broader Swati population for the ascendancy of Badshah and Wali, and their state. However, even careful balance of all three would provide a most questionable basis for analysing the emergence, growth and perpetuation of rulership and the State. Familiarity with British concepts, and with modern political rhetoric, certainly post-date the establishment of the State and most of its history, and so cannot provide a proper template for understanding its foundations. Nor can one lightly assume the Islamic theory of the State to provide such a template. Local conceptions of person and polity surely derived — and possibly still derive — from the broad and deep folk substratum of ideas and institutions characteristic of local, stateless society. In its terms, relations of in-equality, power, and participation were interpreted in a framework of very different premises from those embraced in a society based on the State.

The basic premise of stateless society was precisely that other people's political relations were their separate concerns, not a collective respon-sibility. Independence and personal sovereignty were highly, perhaps in-ordinately, valued; but they were conceptualized as goods for each to seek for himself, not as rights for all, to be collectively safeguarded by all. A person who commanded effective and sufficient sanctions to dominate and exploit others was not particularly condemned and his acts were not collectively resisted — indeed he would rather be admired and sought as ally and leader, unless he was so feared for the threat he might pose to one's own autonomy that one sought to build a defensive faction against him. Even such exceptional, general social obligations as were codified by Swat custom were not seen as responsibilities to or for society so much as ways for persons to excel. Thus the obligations of asylum *(nanawati:* the obligation to receive and defend anyone who sought your home or *hujra* as refuge), hospitality *(melmastia:* the obli-gation to feed and not molest a visitor/guest), and charity *(zakat:* the obligation to give economic support to the poor) were not so much seen as rights of the recipients, springing from a collectivity of membership, but as sources and standards of honour, self-respect, and excellence in the man who disbursed them. *Jehad,* holy war, — that collective action which had been assimilated so deeply into Pathan custom — was like-wise conceived not as a collective defence of independence (though it frequently functioned as such), but as a merit-giving response to specific impieties and breaches of God's law. As against the British, it was a reaction against the gross impiety of profaning the Dar ul Islam with Kafir armies and claims to rule; against a local tyrant, it was in punish-ment of particular forbidden acts on his part.

In other words, at the time when the State of Swat was founded, people in the valley knew of states but in large part did not employ con-cepts or embrace values in their daily lives which were so designed as to provide a basis for ordered political relations in a centralized state sys-tem. To the extent that such concepts and values are found at later times, and may provide support for the perpetuation of the State, they have probably been progressively adopted or developed, or at least re-ceived new and increased emphasis. The two questions (a) What factors favoured the creation of centralized rulership and the Badshah's candidature as Ruler?, and (b) What modes of legitimation of state organization and the Badshah's and the Wali's authority were made use of once the State was established?, are two distinct questions that must be treated separately. What is more, the reconstruction of an answer to the former question must be highly tentative, and it is particularly important to be on guard against contagion from (b) to (a).

Let us first focus on the role of Badshah Sahib in establishing a viable state, and the factors that provided the necessary bases for his candidature and success. I read the evidence provided in the preceding chapters as follows:

The election of Abdul Jabbar Shah to Kingship in 1915 demonstrates that the will among Pakhtun leaders in Swat to unite in a State was in principle independent of the candidature of Badshah Sahib as pretender. The reasons that motivated these Pakhtun leaders have been discussed above (pp. 155ff.). Their conception of this option was no doubt coloured by the fact that the revered Akhund of Swat had sponsored state formation in the previous century; but that did not link descent from the Akhund with a unique task or capacity to realize the new project.[21] Indeed, the account gives ample evidence of the ambitions of a diversity of pretenders to sovereignty: besides the Badshah's uncle and his two cousins, there were also the son of Sayyid Akbar Shah, and his daughter's son Abdul Jabbar Shah; there were the attempts at independent smaller statehood on the part of Mian Hamzallah of Sardari (pp. 45f); and I would also see the various struggles and successes of Khans in the neighbouring areas (Dir, Nawagai, Khar) in the same light. I therefore conclude that a pervasive struggle for hegemony between the most powerful leaders of the region has been a general feature of political life. It is thus not the Badshah's candidature to kingship, but his success in obtaining wide acceptance *and* retaining centralized control, which is exceptional and requires explanation.

It is also essential to note that, besides the traditional Khanates of the Western areas,[22] there are *two* basic modes of establishing regional hegemony, one representing a stateless pattern, the other through state-building. The former is exemplified by Saidu Baba the Akhund of Swat, the junior Miangul Abdul Khaliq (Badshah Sahib's father), and more temporarily and on a smaller scale by e.g. Sandakai Mullah (pp. 29f., 47). The state-building mode is exemplified by Sayyid Akbar Shah, his daughter's son Jabbar Shah, and attempted by the senior Miangul

Abdul Hanan (p. 15), the Badshah's two cousins, etc. The Wali makes a clear distinction between these two forms of hegemony in his account of the early period. Saidu Baba and the junior Miangul ruled by "spiritual power" (p. 16). Their authority was a development from that of the ubiquitous Mians who serve as spiritual advisers and *ad hoc* mediators in conflicts in the stateless framework. The distinctive mark of hegemony in an area, sought by the most ambitious of these and achieved by Saidu Baba and his junior son, lies in setting up Shariat courts and monopolizing judicial functions within a territory, not merely operating as mediators. Likewise, it was by establishing such a court in Upper Swat that the Sandakai Mullah became a challenge to the Badshah's hegemony (p. 47). There seem to have been at least seeds of a whole theory or vision of a polity in these Saintly efforts to establish the rule of law through spiritual influence — an alternative realization of Islamic society in a stateless version, which, however, it is very difficult to retrieve today in any detail.

The Badshah's program and mandate, on the other hand, was of a different kind: to set up a State. This entails, in the Wali's account, an organization which opposes anarchy not by spiritual force but by superior force of arms (p. 16), ideally by monopolizing the use of coercive force. The key to its functions lies in an army (cf. pp. 52, 96). Its distinctive character from the polity over which Saidu Baba prevailed is intimated in the apocryphal petition of the tribesmen to Saidu Baba (p. 14): the existence of a theocratic state is implicitly denied; its practicability under Swat conditions is negated; a secular form of state is requested. Saidu Baba himself could not serve as Ruler in such a state and did not encourage his sons to do so (p. 15). Likewise, the Sandakai Mullah, with spiritual ambitions, brought Abdul Jabbar Shah for the task rather than attempt it himself (p. 30). Badshah Sahib, conversely, having lost the religious tradition of the family through the early death of his father, and having entered the civil wars at the age of 13 (p. 16), was a most suitable candidate for Kingship.

With this clarification of what a project of state-building did and did not entail in the particular historical and cultural setting of Swat, I judge it to be fairly straightforward to formulate the major strengths and qualifications of the Badshah as pretender to kingship. In the way of positional and material assets, he was firstly the owner of *large lands*. Through inheritance, and the subsequent elimination of his agnatic cousins, his properties placed him initially in the highest echelon of political leaders, an equal participant with the biggest Khans in local war and politics. Secondly, being of *non-Yusufzai descent,* he was yet outside the constraints of having any particular tribal and segmentary position: this gave him both greater freedom of political maneouvre and, as pretender to kingship, greater universal acceptability. Thirdly his descent from Saidu Baba gave a great bonus of *influence,* extending over wide areas of the Frontier outside as well as inside Swat (p. 16); this influence deriving from descent has persisted through subsequent political changes (cf. e.g. p. 103) and is still reflected in the flow of pilgrims from as far away as Bannu and Waziristan who pay their respects to the Wali after visiting Saidu Baba's shrine.

Equal or greater emphasis must be placed on the Badshah's personal qualifications as reflected throughout the preceding account, both in the acts and events that have been described, and in the characterizations of his person formulated by the Wali as son and observer. These might be summarized under four headings: (i) exceptional tactical foresight and swift intelligence, (ii) great personal force, courage, and ruthlessness, (iii) unusual openness, adaptability and pragmatism, and (iv) a remarkable gift of candid and compelling expression, whereby he was able to assert much influence over others in council and informal conversation.

Without such a powerful combination of qualifications and qualities, I think the course of events recorded above indicates that the Badshah might never have come to the point where he was chosen for kingship, and surely would never have been able to gain and retain the control so as to make his state more than one more of those brief episodes which the attempts of his most successful predecessors had been.

Throughout the history of Swat State there has been very little effort invested in formulating and publicizing any official version of the bases of the State's and the Ruler's claims to legitimacy, nor have the State's subjects been drawn into activities which might serve to confirm such legitimacy. This is most clearly seen in the remarkable absence of State ritual (cf. p. 119), the very limited formality associated with access to the Ruler and his administration, and the pragmatic purposiveness of the Ruler's own behaviour in public and private. In part this reflects a situation where the effectiveness of State and Rulership were undeniable and authority was amply demonstrated. In part I would also see it as reflecting basic forms of political consciousness perpetuated in the culture from pre-state times, as noted in the opening paragraphs of this section. Even in the 1960s, the existence of a centralized State was not given the kind of constitutive primacy in Swati conceptualization of society that it tends to have e.g. in European consciousness. Rather, the Ruler and his State were simply acknowledged as a dominant fact in the political field. But the desirability or otherwise of this fact was an individual, pragmatic judgement, depending on the balance of advantages and drawbacks which one felt its presence entailed for oneself and one's own interests — sometimes tempered by a realistic judgement of what might be the possible alternatives. In these terms, some of the Khans whose sovereignty had been so dramatically reduced might sometimes feel that the many benefits they also obtained still did not compensate their loss: some members of new, ascending elites might find their exercise of new powers or privileges too curtailed; and some members of the poorer classes might occasionally feel that the State's demands on them had merely been added to those of the landowners. The criticisms formulated by such malcontents may be used as a lead to what is accepted as a significant source of legitimacy. Thus, disgruntled Khans would sometimes argue that the Badshah's rule was based on his acclamation by the Pakhtuns in *jirga* in 1917 — i.e. it rested on a political contract not unlike the traditional forms of contract concerning political agreements and alignments. But, they would complain, whereas the *jirgas* merely recognized him as a central coordinating and peace-making mediator, the Badshah had by cleverness and ruthlessness transformed his position into one of absolute rulership (cf. Lindholm 1982:42 for a statement of this view, apparently reflecting that of his informants). In my experience, others were little impressed by this argument, pointing out that such manoeuvring is inherent in political negotiation and contract, and that the Khans had only themselves to blame for what they had thereby lost of power.

Another objection, voiced by the new elite and published in Pakistani newspapers outside of Swat during the 1960s, concerned "the dictatorship of the Wali" (cf. p. 132). This appeal to principles of legitimacy derived from contemporary Pakistani political rhetoric was particularly apposite at a time when martial law was being brought to an end in Pakistan (1962) and forces were mobilizing to overthrow its regime and change the structure of the state (cf. pp. 132, 134). Judging from the Wali's argumentation at his meetings with Pakistani representatives in Kalam in 1953, I understand him to take the position that his rule was *not* properly subject to validation by electoral test, but that if it were so tested, there would be no doubt about its being confirmed (p. 109), as also shown by electoral results after merger (p. 139). But the more central point to note is that his own and his supporters' responses to challenges to his legitimacy are not to meet them with counterclaims, or references to other abstract principles of legitimacy. Most striking, in view of the origins of the ruling family, is the absence of active religious, Islamic validation. Such references as are made to Islamic principles and rules by the Wali are simply those of the common sense of everyday morality in this cultural context, and those of his father likewise reflected no more than the idioms and consciousness of his generation.

The most frequent form of praise heard in Swat concerning the Badshah's and the Wali's rule refers to the functions and services provided by the State, and it is in the emphasis on these services that we come closest to an explicit legitimization of state organization and rulership. *Roads* are used, both by the common man and by the Wali, as a concrete symbol of progress and achievement: the bridges; the penetration of communications into all parts of Swat; how (before merger) the main road from Malakand improved in quality as one passed through Landakai into Swat State; the deterioration of maintenance and quality after merger. But other themes are also stressed. Educational and health facilities are praised. Personal security under the State is contrasted to insecurity under pre-State conditions, in the stateless tribal areas, and even in neighbouring administered areas. After merger, the deteriorating conditions of security are commented on, and a contrast is drawn between the speed and sureness of justice under the Ruler, and the endless delays and indecisions of present court practice. In these terms, Swat State was cast as the way to progress and modernity, and each bridge, school and hospital served as a monument to the Ruler (p. 112).

Another component of possible legitimization lies in the formal recognition of the State by an outside power. It is clear that such recognition was sought and valued throughout the history of the State. However, it can hardly be an essential component of legitimacy, since the State did without it during the first and no doubt most critical 9 years of its existence. The Wali's account gives no indication that he or his father thought in terms of legitimization when they valued recognition so highly: their reasoning is explicitly strategic. Saidu Baba is lauded for his ability to see that the British were in the ascendancy and that this was a fact one would have to accept. The Badshah built up his position in a manner designed to avoid their displeasure while maximizing his local position, and thereby in time to compel them from a position of strength to recognize him. The purpose of this was to secure good relations and avoid possible subversion from the outside, not to gain legitimacy. The Wali likewise judged the supplementary instrument of accession in pragmatic and tactical terms (p. 110) and not as support in legitimization.

The picture that emerges is one where it is the fact of effective control and ascendancy — not its formal confirmation or justification — that is consistently pursued. Neither Badshah nor Wali were unaware of the communicative value of political acts and events; but what they sought to establish were object-lessons rather than elaborate symbols. This is certainly consistent with how political relations were perceived in pre-state Swat, as noted in the opening paragraphs of this section. It also has wider distribution in the Middle East in the zone between state and non-state organizations. Thus, one analyst of Morocco in the nineteenth century perceptively notes how "strength did not have to be represented as other than what it was" (Geertz 1977:161). In demonstrating new forms of control, the Badshah certainly had the more spectacular task, and solved it with brilliance. But one should not underestimate the great skill likewise exercised by the Wali, in a situation when the limits were far narrower. After the advent of Pakistan, the continuation of Swat as a State was perpetually in the balance, and much of the time even a small disturbance, with local and temporary loss of control, might have been sufficient to precipitate a takeover. On the other hand, any ill-considered attempts to rally too strong support, and any independent experiments in reform and popular participation, might likewise not have been tolerated by Pakistan (p. 110). It is a measure of the Wali's political abilities, fully equal to those of his father, that he observed these limits and consistently prevented any internal coalition or minority faction from emerging with sufficient coherence to produce such an incident.

In 1969, however, there was a sudden failure of this ability to govern effectively. One may wonder whether this reveals a weakness in the bases on which the State was built, whether a stronger ideology of legitimization, and mobilization in collective symbolic participation, might not have made the regime more resistant. But the question is purely academic, since no amount of internal strength could have made the State of Swat immune to pressures and major shifts in the general Pakistani population, or to decisions made by the Government of Pakistan. It is again a measure of the Wali's exceptional realism that he saw this so unemotionally, and acted to facilitate rather than resist merger.

As seen from the centre

In a state so strongly centred on the person and office of the Ruler, the concepts and images by which the Ruler understands his environment and himself become powerful determinants of how the State operates as an organization. The Wali's account therefore deserves to be briefly analysed from this perspective.

Both in his evaluation of his father and himself, the basic quality of statecraft which the Wali consistently emphasizes is that of foresight. To rule effectively is to be able to anticipate, to judge correctly what is feasible and can be successful, and what is inevitable and therefore must be accepted and accommodated, and preferably turned to the Ruler's and State's tactical advantage. In the immediate context, this ability is apparent in the Wali's remarkable perspicacity and swiftness in anticipating and identifying correctly the purposes and interests of the innumerable persons who still seek him for advice and support, and the far larger numbers who used to seek him as Ruler for conflict resolution, requests, and attempts at manipulation. One prerequisite for this ability is the detailed knowledge of persons, their genealogies, rivalries, and current and ancient disputes. Another is a great ability in adopting the position of other persons (p. 150) and seeing how they perceive their situation and options. A third requirement is no doubt a swift, unsentimental and analytic mind, kept sharp by continuous practice. But the mere exercise of this in the daily and immediate context, though necessary, is in no way enough. A longer, strategic view is likewise necessary: it is only in terms of such long-term foresight that change can be turned to advantage, and consistency and stability of policy can be achieved. In these terms, the Wali praises his great-grandfather the Akhund of Swat for recognizing the inevitability of a British presence and the value of mutual non-involvement, and his father for his persistent attention to overcoming the suspicions of the British and establishing good relations with them. His own policy of abandoning his father's practice of maintaining the two *dǝllas* and balancing them, in favour of progressively pulverizing the *dǝllas* e.g. through making small landowners "maliks of their own land" (p. 146) represented one such major and timely shift in basic strategy. Another was his awareness of the consequences of increased educational facilities for political participation (cf. p. 111). A third example was his apparent understanding of the wider strategic preconditions for the State's survival. Caught in the cross-pressures of conservative, localized interest groups naturally gravitating to his abdicated father, and the national, modernizing interests both internal to Swat and represented by the Pakistani authorities, he seems to have cultivated each in a manner to obtain its support against the other, thereby wresting a considerable area of manoeuvre for himself and his State from this constellation. He saw to it that no one could find fault in his peacekeeping and development achievements, and also pre-empted the local new elite's access to national Pakistani fora by cultivating close personal relations with Pakistani leaders. On the other side, he cultivated his father's goodwill and defended the separateness and identity of Swat. Against undue pressures from Pakistan he could point to the indisputable potential presence of his father and the dangers of conservative Pakhtuns and religious backlash; against local pressures he could point to the threat of merger. Through this form of statecraft, the opportunities inherent in an otherwise unfavourable situation could be realized.

A concomitant of such a view of statecraft, with its emphasis on realism and the primacy of self-perpetuation, is that conceptions of program and goal must become more contingent and unspecific. The Ruler does not work towards a detailed vision of the society he wishes to create; rather, it becomes a matter of "going with the times" (pp. 111, 150). Such a view, however, entails less, and is less pragmatic, in a fundamentally Muslim society than it might be elsewhere. Islam provides a charter, once and for all, for the right society; to articulate the goals of social policy appears as a less meaningful political task, given this premise, than it would in another cultural context. In this, I am not arguing that the Wali, or indeed the Badshah, functioned as Islamic fundamentalists in their policies, but only that many premises of policy will appear to greater extent given and unexceptional in an Islamic setting. The Ruler's statecraft was thus pursued within a set of value standards — both Islamic and modern — which could remain largely unquestioned and thereby unfocussed, never specified as a program. As a result, the trajectory of social change in Swat under the State seems to have been largely unplanned, a product of external and internal forces and in part of unsought consequences of the State's own activities. But, though unsought, the changes in society in Swat were closely observed and judged by the Ruler, and early trends anticipated in their consequences, through his exercise of statecraft. As one of the parties to a perpetual, complex and changing political contest, the Ruler thus sought to maintain his edge by staying informed and prepared for the changes as they unfolded.

Yet it would seem unperceptive to conclude that the Wali as Ruler had no purpose in his policies, other than that of perpetuating his rule. I understand this purpose to be most directly expressed in his own summing-up of his achievements: "everybody respects me" (p. 142). Let us reflect briefly on what is retrieved by this concept of respect. To identify how it might direct the activities of the Ruler, we must first give some precision to its content, in this culture: what must a person be and do to "be respected"?

Various comments in the Wali's preceding account will have given the reader some sensitivity to the concept's local nuances. To my understanding, essential components are as follows. Firstly, respect is more a question of an attitude and an associated way of acting towards a person, and less a question of a moral judgement on that person. To respect a person requires that you take that person seriously, give weight to his presence, opinion, interests, and above all his *will*. It entails accepting the validity — though not necessarily the morality or desirability — of his positions and acts; it implies a confirmation of his value, in terms of ideals of strength and wholeness. It is incompatible with a record of failures or ineffectiveness by the person; whereas it is fully compatible with fear of the person — thus the Badshah's ruthlessness in the early days is explicitly justified by the Wali as being necessary to produce respect (p. 148f.). To secure the respect of others one must be capable of monitoring and disciplining oneself: only by maintaining an objective and realistic view of oneself and compelling oneself to act with consistency and force can one hope to act so as to elicit the respect of others.

To be respected in this sense by one's *subjects,* a Ruler must avoid acts of purposeless injustice, indifference, or capriciousness. Order, responsibility, reliability, and impartiality are desirable; force, will and effectiveness are essential; benevolence and humanity are almost irrelevant. Respect from one's *opponents* is won by swiftness, skill and ruthlessness; its presence is revealed or expressed by the care which one's opponents show in their dealings with one, and their reluctance ever to try to take advantage of one. Respect from *equals* or others outside one's own realm of activities reflects a more comprehensive evaluation, and depends on a relatively consistent record of competence, courage, and the moral defensibility of one's acts.

Besides these *realia* there will be, in any effort to create respect, also a significant tactical component of impression management. A Ruler can enhance the impression of his force and effectiveness by not revealing his plans and programs, and indeed not wishing (or at least never showing that he wishes) that which cannot be realized. If such a Ruler is relatively successful, and his occasional failures are not revealed or acknowledged as such, he will also benefit from a strong tendency for a self-confirming circularity to develop. Whatever happens, the interpretation can be fostered that it came about in conformity with the Ruler's will, as the result of a covert scheme too complex to unravel. Such interpretations are widely adopted by the public in Swat, even to the extent that the period of estrangement between the Wali and his father is often represented as a ruse to tempt the Badshah's opponents to reveal themselves to his only apparently estranged son.

What direction would it give to the activities of the Ruler of Swat if he were to conceive the goal of obtaining universal "respect" as his primary objective? It strikes me that its intelligent pursuit would indeed motivate all the notable features of the Wali's policies and style. It would give that shape to his practice of government and conflict settlement which has been described, and it would provide guidelines for how he has indeed handled his internal opposition. Most interestingly, it would also supply a template for controls and checks on the Ruler's autocracy which have seemed to be structurally absent in the political organization of Swat State. I have noted above (p. 161) the absence or insignificance of any constitutional constraints on the power of the Ruler, the absence of formal representatives or bodies who might act against possible abuses of power by the encumbent. Admittedly, I have suggested that major sectors of the population of Swat have subscribed to values of honour and autonomy, and retained patterns of organization, so that the politics of maintaining a centralized state in this society has had the aspect of "riding a tiger". This in itself represents a major check on the abuse of power: the Ruler must act so as not to catalyze his own overthrowal. Yet, compared to most regimes the Rulers of Swat have practised an exceptional responsibility and restraint, while at the same time their rule through most of the State's history has not appeared sufficiently precarious to explain such care. If, on the other hand, the Ruler has conceptualized his program as one of securing the *respect* of all major sectors of Swat society, this would engender a comprehensive sensitivity to a host of culturally defined limits and standards for the exercise of power and privilege. What is more, Swat has throughout its history been a small part of a larger world — of free Pakhtun tribes, other States, cultural and political influence from Kabul, and above all the dominant presence of British India and subsequently Pakistan. The Badshah, and the Wali to an even stronger and more well-informed extent, have clearly regarded it as a major, highly desirable aim to be respected in these latter circles; in many ways the governing of Swat can have been experienced by the Wali as an exercise to prove his own worth by winning the respect of a British Indian civil service and a changing succession of Viceroys, Generals, Presidents, foreign Monarchs, and distinguished visitors. Given an interest in the pursuit of such prizes, combined with the personal qualities of intelligence and self-discipline, there has been no need for other controls to enforce high standards and forestall abuses. In this cultural and ideological sense, even more than in the social and organizational sense, Swat can only be fully understood when analyzed *both* locally and in its wider regional setting.

The strain of integrating such a diversity of social systems, scales, and cultures falls squarely on the person of the Wali, and must be a major force in generating the feeling of loneliness which forms so persistent an undercurrent in his self-awareness (e.g. p. 147). I understand it to have numerous components. Most obviously, the relationship between a man in a position that structurally comes so close to being that of a despot, and other men who are his subjects, can never have the qualities that would relieve loneliness. Faithfulness, where it occurs, is overwhelmed by dependency and inequality in a simple-minded relationship of servant to master. As events and life stories unfold, the cases demonstrating how people are governed by their (current and future) interests only multiply; even the most long-lived relationships wither when their bases in personal advantage disappear (cf. e.g. p. 147). This experience must become all the more poignant with the awareness that one's own position and responsibilities as Ruler compel one to act likewise. Note the passing acknowledgement of priorities in the Wali's description of his close relationship to General and President Ayub Khan: it was President Iskander Mirza who was his friend, ever since 1927, whereas Ayub Khan he first met in 1944 (p. 130). Yet the moment Iskander Mirza made his fatal political misjudgement of abrogating the constitution in 1958, only to lose his position within 10 days to General Ayub, the interests of Swat State depended on the Wali's relationship to Ayub, and Iskander Mirza disappears from the account. Only a few friendships, to higher echelon civil servants in Pakistan, seem to have survived from the Wali's youth by never having been subject to the strains of political necessity.

Finally, there was the most essential relationship of the Wali to the

Badshah. There can be no doubt but that the Wali judges this relationship correctly when he characterizes it as one of great love, and in adult life also one of friendship. Badshah Sahib's abdication, while still relatively young and with entirely unimpaired vitality, in favour of his son is the most unequivocal expression of these feelings. Yet the years spent under the shadow of suspicion were equally true, and reveal other strands in their relationship comparable only to those between rivals and successors to the Moghul throne. At no time in his life, after his earliest childhood, can the Wali have been in a position to rest at ease in acceptance and trust of his father's intentions and acts: as with all others, there was always the need to observe, judge tactically, and act guardedly also in his relations to his father. Surrounded by flatterers, opportunists, and enemies, and also many honest and competent associates who yet were in positions totally unlike his and had above all *their* own interests to defend, and with the greatest powers and highest stakes always located in the closest relations, including brothers, sons, and above all father, he would always find that he was entirely alone in his final judgements of what must be done, whom to trust and whom to fear, what was the portent of events, and where lay his best options. Read as a life story, this is an account of a person whose fate was dominated by *one* status and the considerations that sprang from it in a way that is most unusual. It entailed a life of intense and perpetual vigilance, judgement and choice, often brilliantly pursued; and it led to a position of great eminence and power. To all of us who, not knowing such a position, have reflected less on its implications, perhaps its most unexpected aspect is the picture we are given of complex decisions without equally elaborate goals, and great power without enhanced freedom.

Gazetteer of persons mentioned in text

Abdul Ghaffar Khan: leader of Red Shirt Movement and member of Congress Party during British rule in India.

Abdul Ghafur, Akhund of Swat: great-grandfather of Wali, born 1795 or 1796; became renowned religious leader with strong spiritual and secular influence in Swat; died 1877.

Abdul Hanan: "Masher Miangul", the senior son of the Akhund of Swat, died 1887.

Abdul Jabbar Shah: a sayyid from the village of Sitana in Buner, elected Ruler of Swat in 1915, expelled in 1917; for some years subsequently engaged in attempts on behalf of the State of Amb at conquering parts of Swat.

Abdul Khaira Khan: a khan of the village of Kambar; made *munsif* judge by Wali.

Abdul Khaliq: "Kasher Miangul", the junior son of the Akhund of Swat and Wali's grandfather; died 1893.

Abdul Matin Khan: ruler of Jandul; the son of Omara Khan.

Abdul Qayyum, Nawab Sir: prominent politician of N.W.F.P. during British rule, died 1957.

Abdul Qayyum Khan, Khan: prominent Pakistani politician, sometime Governor of N.W.F.P.

Abdul Rashid, Sardar: schoolmate and friend of Wali.

Abdul Wadud: *see:* Badshah Sahib.

Abdul Wahid: founder of the Miangul family in Swat; father of the Akhund of Swat.

Afzal Khan: son of Darmai Khan (Habib Khan) and local leader of the faction opposed to Wali in Shamizai; elected to Provincial Assembly in 1970.

Ahmed Ali: the younger Wazir brother, prominent administrator in Swat under Badshah; commander-in-chief of Swat Army till 1940; left Swat in 1943.

Ahmed Zeb: youngest son of Wali.

Akbar Khan: intelligence officer in Pakistan Army in 1969; later Pakistani Ambassador to England.

Akbar Shah: first ruler of Swat in 1849–57; of Sayyid family descended from Pir Baba.

Akhund of Swat: *see:* Abdul Ghafur.

Akhund Darweza Baba: influential Hanafi theologian in Pathan area in the 16th century.

Alamzeb: second son of Wali.

Alamzeb Khan: second son of Nawab Badshah Khan of Dir.

Ali Shah Tarmezi: *see:* Pir Baba.

Aman-ul-Mulk: Mehtar (Ruler) of Chitral, a princely state north of Swat; father of Wali's grandmother.

Amir Badshah: Miangul Abdul Wahid; cousin and rival of Badshah Sahib before the founding of Swat State; son of Abdul Hanan; killed in 1907.

Amir Khan: prominent Khan in lower Nikpi Khel (brother of Zarin Khan); allied to the Wazir's faction; reduced in influence in 1943.

Amir Nawab: khan in Babuzai; brother of Jamroz Khan.

Amir Zeb: third son of Wali; elected to National Assembly as P.P.P. candidate in 1974; married daughter of President Ayub Khan.

Aslam Khan Khattak: schoolmate of Wali at Islamia Collegiate School; later Governor.

Ataullah: chief secretary to Badshah and subsequently to Wali until merger of State; born in Gujranwalla, Panjab; resident in Swat since 1926.

Aurangzeb: eldest son of Wali, born 1928; officer's career in Pakistan Army; married daughter of then General, later President Ayub Khan in 1955; elected to National Assembly in 1970.

Ayub Khan: President of Pakistan, deposed in 1969; friend of Wali since 1944; daughters married to Wali's sons Aurangzeb and Amir Zeb.

Badshah Gul: Mian of Sar (q.v.); Commander-in-Chief of Swat Army; candidate to Provincial Assembly in 1970 election.

Badshah Khan: Nawab of Dir; ruled 1905-1925.

Badshah Sahib: Miangul Gulshahzada Abdul Wadud, the Founder of Swat; born 1882, died 1971; Ruler of Swat 1917-1949; father of Wali.

Bahramand Khan: son of Shirin Sahib; cousin and brother-in-law of Wali.

Baradar Khan: khan of Takot by the Indus; opponent of Badshah in 1920s.

Best, Leslie William Hazlet Duncan ("Archie"): Political Agent in Malakand 1935.

Bhutto, Zulfikar Ali: Prime Minister of Pakistan 1971-77; executed by Pakistani authorities in 1979.

Bolton, Sir Norman: Chief Commissioner of N.W.F.P. 1923-30.

Brierly, Sir Charles: Colonel, medical officer in Peshawar in the 1930s.

Caroe, Sir Olaf: British administrator with extensive experience in the N.W.F.P.; Governor of N.W.F.P. 1946-47.

Cobb, Col. E.H.: Political Agent in Malakand in 1947.

Cunningham, Sir George: Governor of N.W.F.P. 1937-46.

Darmǝi Khans: see: Habib Khan; Masam Khan.

Diamond, Col.: medical officer, Peshawar, in the 1930s.

Doste Khan: khan of Manglawar village in Babuzai; son of Nowsherawan Khan.

Dundas, Ambrose: Political Agent in Malakand 1932; Deputy Commissioner Peshawar 1935.

Glover, William Thomson: Political Agent in Malakand, established Government rule in Kalam.

Griffith, Sir Ralph: Chief Commissioner, thereupon Governor, N.W.F.P. 1931-37.

Habib Khan: younger of Darmǝi Khan brothers, influential khans of Shamizai; died 1927.

Habibullah Khan: locally influential khan of Jinki Khel, with stronghold in Miandam; sought to establish independent principality during early years of Swat State.

Hamzallah, Mian of Sardari (q.v.): local leader of Saintly family, belonging to Badshah Sahib's faction during early struggle; developed ambitions for a separate principality shortly after the founding of the State.

Hay, W.R.: Political Agent in Malakand in 1932-33.

Hazrat Ali: elder Wazir brother, key administrator in Swat under Badshah; Chief Minister of Swat until June 1943; left Swat in October 1943.

Holland, Sir Henry: missionary doctor in Quetta, specialist in eye diseases.

Humayun Khan: Political Agent in Malakand in 1969 at time of merger, when he was also made District Commissioner of Swat; later Pakistan ambassador to Bangla Desh.

Irwin, Lord: Viceroy and Governor General of India 1930.

Iskander Mirza: President of Pakistan until deposed in 1958; friend of Wali since 1926.

James, Col. E.F.S.: Political Agent in Malakand in 1925.

Jamroz Khan: prominent khan of Babuzai and leader of the faction opposed to Badshah there; son of Malak Baba.

Jamshed Khan: prominent khan of Kuza Bandei, Nikpi Khel; son of Zarin Khan and close supporter of Wali.

Janes Khan: khan of Babuzai and leader of pro-Badshah faction there; son of Malak Baba.

Jeffrys, Cpt.: British Army engineer; later first Chief Engineer of Pakistan Army.

Johnson, Harry Hall: Political Agent in Malakand in 1936.

Kamran: prominent businessman in Swat; one-time associate of Wali but active critic of Wali rule during last years of the State; candidate for Provincial Assembly in 1970 elections.

Kasher Miangul: *see:* Abdul Khaliq.

Keen, Col. J.W.: Acting Chief Commissioner N.W.F.P. in 1926.

Khan Bahadur Sultanat Khan: Khan of Jura, prominent landowner and leader in the Sebujni area; close associate of Badshah and later also of Wali.

Khan Sahib: brother of Abdul Ghaffar Khan; moderate politician and intellectual of British Indian times.

Khurshid, Sahibzada: Political Agent in Malakand in 1939; governor of N.W.F.P. in 1949.

Khusro Khan: Nawab of Dir, ruled 1960—69; son of Shah Jehan Khan.

Latimer, C.: Political Agent in Malakand in 1928.

Lewanai Fakir: alias Sartor Fakir; leader of jehad against Malakand in 1897.

Liaqat Ali Khan: first Prime Minister of Pakistan, assassinated by a fanatic in 1951.

Malak Baba: Taj-al-Nur Khan, a very prominent Khan of Babuzai in the latter half of the 19th century; a close supporter of the Akhund of Swat.

Masher Miangul: *see:* Abdul Hanan.

Mallam, Major: Political Agent in Malakand in 1939.

Masam Khan: elder of Darmai Khan brothers, influential khans in Shamizai.

Mazoob Mullah: religious leader in Indus Kohistan; launched an attempted jehad against Badshah in 1926, in which he was killed.

Metcalfe, H.A.F.: Political Agent in Malakand in the 1920s.

Mianguls: the family of the Wali of Swat; used particularly of the two sons of the Akhund of Swat, Abdul Hanan and Abdul Khaliq.

Mians of Sar: locally prominent Saintly family from the village of Sar in the hills east of Saidu; *see:* Badshah Gul, Sharab Gul.

Mians of Sardari: locally prominent Saintly family from the village of Sardari in the hills east of Saidu; *see:* Hamzallah; Shah Madar.

Mir Abdullah Khan: prominent khan of Babuzai belonging to Badshah's faction; son of Malak Baba.

Mohammed Ali Shah: maternal uncle's son of Wali; candidate to National Assembly for Muslim League in 1970 elections.

Mohammed Rahman: businessman in Mingora; elected to Provincial Assembly as Muslim League candidate in 1970 election.

Mohammed Rasool Khan: younger son of Habib Khan of Darmai, Shamizai.

Mohammed Sharif Khan: Nawab of Dir during conflict with Omara Khan and after; died 1905.

Mufti Mohammed Yusuf, Col.: Political Agent in Malakand in 1950.

Nawabs of Dir: rulers of the State of Dir, adjoining Swat to the west; by descent members of Akhund Khel of Painda Khel, Malizai, Yusufzai. Mohammed Sharif Khan, died 1905; Badshah Khan, 1905-25; Khan Bahadur Shah Jehan Khan, 1925-60; Khusro Khan, 1960-69.

Nazim-ud-Din, Qazi: Governor General of Pakistan 1949.

Nowsherawan Khan: khan of Babuzai, the son of Mir Abdullah Khan; local ally of Badshah.

Omara Khan: expansive ruler of Jandul in latter part of 19th century; conquered Dir and besieged Chitral in 1895.

Parsons, Sir Arthur: Acting Governor N.W.F.P. in 1939.

Parvez Khan: prominent khan of lower Nikpi khel; the favoured son of Amir Khan; married to the daughter of Wazir Hazrat Ali.

Patel: Prominent Congress leader in British India; Home Minister of India after Partition.

Pears, Sir Steuart: Chief Commissioner N.W.F.P. 1930–31.

Pir Baba: Sayyid Ali Shah Tarmezi, prominent scholar and religious leader during latter half of 16th century; his grave in Pacha in Buner is a major shrine.

Pir Mohammed Khan: commander of the Swat Army in the 1950s, later made *munsif* judge by Wali; son of Janas Khan of Babuzai.

Pirdad Khan: influential khan of Kana; close friend and ally of Badshah.

Qaid-i-Azam: Mohammed Ali Jinnah, the leader of the Muslim League and founder and first Governor General of Pakistan; died 1948.

Rahim Shah: son of Wali's maternal uncle; elected to National Assembly in 1970 elections.

Rashid Khan: khan of Odigram, Babuzai; affinal relative of Badshah.

Robertson, Sir George Scott: British Agent in Gilgit, besieged in Chitral Fort by Omara Khan in 1895.

Said Badshah: Miangul Abdul Razak; cousin and rival of Badshah before the founding of Swat State; son of Abdul Hanan, the Masher Miangul; killed in 1903.

Saidu Baba: *see:* Abdul Ghafur, the Akhund of Swat.

Sandakai Mullah: prominent religious leader, born in Chakesar; active in Swat in the period 1910–1920; sometime sponsor both of Abdul Jabbar Shah and Badshah Sahib as rulers; later expelled from Swat by Badshah.

Sar Mians: *see:* Mians of Sar.

Sardari Mians: *see:* Mians of Sardari.

Sartor Fakir: *see:* Lewanai Fakir.

Shaghalai Miangul: the "False Miangul"; purported posthumous son of Abdul Hanan, the Masher Miangul, by a concubine.

Shah Durran: khan of Manglawar, Babuzai, and professor at Jahanzeb College; son of Doste Khan.

Shah Jahan Khan: Nawab of Dir, son of Nawab Badshah Khan; ruled from 1925 till 1960 when he was deposed and exiled to Lahore by Pakistan authorities.

Shah Madar: Mian of Sardari; prominent political leader of one faction in the mountain valleys between the Swat and Indus rivers; military commander under Badshah; died in battle in 1918.

Shah Room, Fazal Qadir: half-brother of Wali; deceased in 1929 at age of 17.

Shahibuddin, Khwaja: Governor of N.W.F.P. in 1953.

Shaikh Mahbub Ali, Nawab: Political Agent in Malakand in 1943; previously Oriental Secretary to Sir Francis Humphrey in Kabul in 1928 at the time of King Amanullah's fall.

Shaikh Malli: prominent religious leader in Swat in 16th century, credited with constructing the system of *wesh* (shared tenure) among the Yusufzai.

Shazad Gul: Mian of Sar (q.v.); Naīb Salar of the Swat Army.

Sher Ali Khan: khan of Nalkot in lower Nikpi Khel; son of Amir Khan.

Sher Mohammed Khan: Wazir-i-Mal (Secretary of Finance) in Swat, retired in 1967; son of Janas Khan of Babuzai.

Shirin Sahib: Miangul Abdul Manan, younger brother of Badshah Sahib; leader of faction opposed to Badshah before the accession of Abdul Jabbar Shah; Commander-in-Chief of the Swat Army until he was killed in the war against Dir in 1918.

Shuja-ul-Mulk: Mehtar (ruler) of Chitral installed by the British at the time of the siege of Chitral in 1895.

Sultan-i-Room, Fazal Mabud: half-brother of Wali, born 1927.

Sundia Baba: religious leader in Chakesar; arrested for subversive agitation in 1931.

Taj-al-Nur Khan: *see:* Malak Baba.

Taj Mohammed Khan: prominent khan of Arkot in Sebujni in the early 20th century; sometime ally of the Nawab of Dir.

Taj Mohammed Khan: prominent khan of Nikpi Khel; Mushir of Lower Swat until 1954.

Wali Khan: prominent politician, largely in opposition, during the existence of Pakistan; son and successor of Abdul Ghaffar Khan.

Wavell, Lord: Viceroy of India in 1946.

Wazir brothers: prominent administrators under Badshah Sahib, *see:* Hazrat Ali (senior), Ahmed Ali (junior).

Yahya Khan: general in Pakistan Army; President of Pakistan 1969-71.

Zarin Khan: khan of Manglawar, Babuzai; executed for murder of his *tarbur* Doste Khan.

Zarin Khan: prominent khan of lower Nikpi Khel; brother of Amir Khan; his daughter was engaged to the Nawab of Dir before the creation of Swat State.

Ziaullah: candidate to Provincial Assembly in 1970 elections; son of Ataullah.

Notes

1 According to Hay, who has his information mainly from Plowden, and orally from Badshah Sahib in 1933—34, "He began his religious life at the age of 18, and eventually, about the year 1816, settled down as a hermit at Beka, on the banks of the Indus in Swabi Tahsil. Here he remained for 12 years, after which he became displeased on account of an incident connected with local politics, and migrated. He wandered from place to place, and it was not until about 1845 that he settled in Saidu, where he remained till he died." (Hay 1933:3).

2 Pir Baba, i.e. Sayyid Ali Shāh Tarmēzi. Pir Baba's shrine at Pacha in Buner is probably the most frequently visited shrine in the Province. Sayyid Ali Shah himself (cf. Caroe 1958) was the son of Qambar Ali of the town of Tarmez on the Amur Darya river. His father came to India in the service of the Emperor Babur (1526—1530). Ali Shah became a religious student, and after a while he settled as a Pir in the Doaba on the Peshawar plain, around 1550, and later moved to Pacha. He married a Pakhtun woman, and most of the prestigious Sayyid families in the area are his descendants. His theological position was one of strict Hanafi orthodoxy against the extreme heterodoxy of his contemporary Bayazid Ansari, founder of the Roshani movement. The ultimate defeat and elimination of this heterodoxy from Pakhtun consciousness was probably mainly achieved by Pir Baba's disciple Akhund Darweza Baba around 1580 in two great debating confrontations, the latter of which took place in Katelai in Babuzai, Swat (Badshah 1963: xxxiv). Very few traditions of these controversies are known to those who today visit his shrine, beyond the general acknowledgement that he was an outstanding pious, orthodox Pir.

3 According to Caroe 1958, Sayyid Akbar Shah's rule in Swat extended from 1849 to 1857.

4 The Ambela campaign was a major military operation. Fighting in the Ambela Pass lasted from 20 October 1863 to 16 December 1863, and involved in the order of ten thousand men on each side. It has been extensively described and discussed in previous literature. It is summarized in Caroe (1958:360—69); a first-hand British account is given in Roberts (1897, Vol. II:1—22). The Badshah's account contained in Muhammed Asif Khan's "Introduction" to The Story of Swat (1963:xlviii—lv) is somewhat at variance with these. British sources insist that "The Akhund stood aloof... But when hostilities were prolonged he too came in, and in the eyes of the Sayyids (of Sitana, the objects of the British attack) usurped a credit which they claimed should have been theirs" (Caroe 1958:366). Badshah Sahib's account, on the other hand, gives the Akhund a central place from the beginning: "...he responded to the call for assistance by setting out from Saidu Sharif on October 14, 1863, all alone. The news that Saidu Baba was going for *jehad* spread like fire and hundreds of people joined him on the way, with the result that when he reached the battlefield at Ambela on

October 26, there were four thousand volunteers on foot and one hundred and twenty-five on horseback with him." (Story of Swat, 1963:xlix).

5 British sources reporting on political conditions in the area deny any secular influence to the Junior Miangul.

6 In the Badshah's memoirs, this is commented on as follows: "... our differences (i.e. between him and Said Badshah) caused us to go without any formal education and also put a stop to our spiritual leadership; this was a source of greater regret to me." (Story of Swat 1963:3). "My present occupation is study and the acquisition of knowledge. I began my education at the age of 68 years and have continued it ever since." (Story of Swat 1963:132).

7 For an account of this episode by the British representative himself, see Robertson 1899.

8 A firsthand account, from the British side, is given in Churchill 1898.

9 Hay, on the other hand, gives a more equivocal account. "In 1897, when the troops advanced to Mingora, they fled to Miana, that is the present Murghzar, whence they sent many letters containing protestations of innocence and offers of submission. In August a letter addressed to the Khan of Dir, and asking him to join the tribes in their struggle against the Government, came into the hands of the Political Agent. It bore the seal of Abdul Wadud (Badshah Sahib)." (Hay 1933:7). Other sources give an even less friendly picture: "In July 1897, a full jirga of Upper Swat came to express friendly feelings, but 3 weeks later led by the Mianguls, joined Sartor Fakir's (the Lewanəi Fakir) attack..." (Memoranda, 1938:201).

10 A fuller account of customs, politics, and economic organization is provided in Barth 1959 and elsewhere, see bibliography.

11 Various, contradictory, accounts are given of this event by persons who were alive at the time (personal communications to me in 1954). One version is given by Badshah Sahib himself (Story of Swat, 1963:9). However it actually happened, it apparently caused considerable consternation at the time. Badshah Sahib and his closest associates had to seek refuge and hide for the first ten days after the event (ibid., p. 10). Hay describes the situation as follows: "On December 28th 1903 the other Mianguls conspired together and murdered [Said Badshah] with the intention of dividing up his property amongst themselves. The tribes resented their action and they were compelled to fly. Their houses were burned, but within a fortnight they were back in Saidu. Their greed was baulked for the time being by the birth of a posthumous son to the murdered man. The child, however, only lived for just over a year." (Hay 1933:9).

12 Badshah Sahib's own, slightly more detailed, account is given elsewhere (Story of Swat 1963:13). Hay makes the following comments on the event: "His excuse was that he fired in self-defence. The tribes were indignant at first and his lands at Thana were confiscated by the local jirga. But it was not long before his excuse was accepted and the matter blew over. Amir Badshah left no son, so that with him the elder branch of the Akhund's family became extinct. Having disposed of his cousins, Gulshahzada had only his younger brother Shirin to deal with, and the next few years were largely taken up by their quarrels and reconciliation, until the rise to power of Sayyid Abdul Jabbar Shah caused them finally to unite." (Hay 1933:10).

13 According to Hay, a confidential payment of Rupees 500 per annum was made, irregularly, to the Mianguls from 1902. (Hay 1933:9). In view of the extensive allowances that were regularly disbursed by the British in the whole area, this is an expression of rather extreme reserve, rather than acceptance. British political and military reports from the period likewise give expression to the strife, chaos and anarchy of the area, the deviousness of the Badshah's activities, and the limitations on his influence (e.g. Memoranda, 1938:201f).

14 For other data on Malak Baba, see Barth 1959:60, 113, and Barth 1981:166, 179f.

15 On the death of Shirin Sahib, Badshah Sahib himself comments: "The sudden death of Shahzada Sherin Jan, my only brother, was a great loss and cause of unbearable sorrow to me. That the Shahzada for whom I was ever prepared to lay down my own life was no more amongst us, I could not possibly get over; yet, for the love of truth, I should confess that henceforth being unencumbered with the necessity of listening to someone else's suggestions and proposals, I could proceed according to my plan with the work of reorganizing the army on a firm footing." (Story of Swat 1963:50).

16 "The Swatis got wind of the impending movement and occupied positions on the line of retreat. As a result, the Nawab's lashkar suffered a reverse which must have been unprecedented in tribal warfare. From 500 to 1000 men were massacred, while 800 rifles and 250 horses fell into the hands of the Swatis." (Hay 1933).

17 Originally, it seems to have been one soldier for each *brakha* of land, but this was reduced at an early point to one man for every two *brakha* by the Badshah (cf. Badshah p. 111) with a view to reducing the number of armed servants directly under the command of the Khans.

18 Wali Sahib comments: "In fact, there was another reason. In their relations to the British Indian Government, there was a precedence between the States, depending on their times of recognition. So Chitral was No. 1, then Dir, then Amb, and our State came last, being the newest. But my father said he felt embarrassed sitting below those other three. So he made a point, whether they attended or not, he would not go. He would send me — that way, it would not matter, if sometimes they sat first, and I sat last. Though the Nawab of Dir never attended *any* function, but used to send his son, and he took precedence *below* me. Eventually, I had the matter of precedence redressed, in the 'sixties. I put the simple question to the (Pakistan) government: What are the criteria? There should be criteria for these things, either population, or area, or degree of development of the State, or loyalty to Pakistan, or service to Pakistan. Now during the first World War Chitral made some effort to reconquer some part of Afghanistan. So the Mehtar of Chitral was given the title of His Highness; but we were not called that — by Pakistan! I wrote a long letter — drafted by myself and polished by my secretary for its English: "I don't mind if he is called His Highness; but when he dies, his son is His Highness and I am not. That means Pakistan is recognizing the institution — then what will be the method whereby we can gain that position?" There was the other factor, which I knew, that they did not want to give the Nawab of Dir first place. So I said: "I don't mind if the Nawab of Dir ranks higher than the Mehtar of Chitral: he has more population, and more area." So they changed it, and Chitral was given a salute of 11 guns, while Swat and Dir were given 15 guns. Following that letter's reasoning. These things were important, even in Pakistan, because when there was a big congregation, people noticed where you were placed, and thought you were below that man if you sat somewhere else."

19 The National Awami Party is identified with the old Congress Party of British Indian times, because the leadership is in the hands of Wali Khan, the son of Abdul Ghaffar Khan, the "Frontier Gandhi" of British Indian times, and leader of the "Red Shirts". The Wali comments as follows: "It was a big mistake of Abdul Ghaffar Khan to remain with Congress. But that again is *Pukhtunwali:* a Pakhtun, if he makes a mistake, he is stuck with it. He always says he is right, it is very shameful to abandon his party. At the time of Partition, Abdul Ghaffar Khan was the leader — he still is leader though he said he was no more. But he is too old, and away from it, living in Afghanistan (1979). The sons were young in 1947, and went by his direction. But Wali Khan I think is a more sensible person; he can see the world in a modern way. So his disadvantage is his father, because he cannot deny him, and yet cannot obey him to the extent that Abdul Ghaffar Khan would like."

20 Khan Abdul Qayyum Khan started his political career in the Congress Party of British

India, as a close follower of Abdul Ghaffar Khan. But 2—3 years before Partition, he joined the swiftly growing Muslim League. The Frontier Province had a Congress ministry headed by Doctor Khan Sahib (Abdul Ghaffar Khan's brother) at the inception of Pakistan, but since they were hardly representative of the mood of the population with the emergence of Pakistan, they were removed and Abdul Qayyum was made chief minister of a minority government in the province. He persuaded some members of Congress to join him, built up his power base, and ruled autocratically till he was moved to the Central government — formally an advance, but actually a reduction in his power (cf. p. 108). He tried to retain his hold on provincial politics through protegées, but ran into complications because of reluctance and rebellions. On his return he built up his personal influence again within the framework of the local Muslim League party, as in his dealings with the Wali and others described here. After the 1974 elections he joined Bhutto, having been rebuffed in his attempts to arrange a temporary alliance with Wali Khan (cf. note 19). After Bhutto's fall, he again sought to establish a united Muslim League front.

21 The whole subsequent account goes fundamentally counter to the argument developed by Ahmed, who in a particularly opaque and I think generally misread passage (Ahmed 1976:110—121) depicts the Badshah at once as a charismatic leader, a historical antithesis to the millennial leaders of *jehad,* and a perpetuator of the Akhund's religious and political influence. The reader who wishes to go more deeply into this disagreement should turn to Ahmed's own text, and confront both his facts and his interpretations with those provided above by the Wali, and by myself elsewhere (Barth 1959, 1981).

22 I have elsewhere (Barth 1959:126, 1981:172ff) suggested an explanation of why these Khanates have developed in Dir and Bajaur but not in the Swat valley. Briefly, the smaller scale of the Western valleys makes it just possible for a traditional Khan through the course of a particularly successful lifetime to obtain control of the whole natural unit composing the valley, and thus create a bounded centralized unit. These valleys also have the advantage of being located on the very fringe of Pathan lands, so a significant fraction of a Khan's following may be composed of (politically more malleable) non-Pakhtun smallholders.

References

Ahmed, Akbar S. 1976: *Millennium and Charisma among Pathans*. Routledge & Kegan Paul, London.

Asad, Talal 1972: "Market model, class structure and consent: a reconsideration of Swat political organization". *Man* (New Series) vol. 8 no. 1:74-94.

Barth, Fredrik 1956: *Indus and Swat Kohistan — an Ethnographic Survey*. Universitetets Etnografiske Museum, Oslo.

Barth, Fredrik 1959a: *Political Leadership among Swat Pathans*. The Athlone Press, London.

Barth, Fredrik 1959b: "Segmentary opposition and the Theory of Games: A study of Pathan organization". *Journal of the Royal Anthropological Institute* vol. 89 part 1; 5-22.

Barth, Fredrik 1981: *Features of Person and Society in Swat: Collected Essays on Pathans*. Routledge & Kegan Paul, London.

Biddulph, J. 1880: *Tribes of the Hindoo Koosh*. Superintendent of Government Printing, Calcutta.

Caroe, Sir Olaf 1958: *The Pathans*. McMillan & Co., London.

Churchill, W.L.S. (Sir Winston) 1898: *The Story of the Malakand Field Force*. Longmans, Green & Co., London.

Embree, Ainslie T. (ed.) 1977: *Pakistan's Western Borderlands*. Carolina Academic Press, Durham N.C.

Fautz, Bruno 1963: *Sozial Struktur und Bodennutzung in der Kulturlandsschaft des Swat*. Technische Hochschule, Karlsruhe.

Geertz, Clifford 1977: "Centers, Kings and Charisma: Reflections on the Symbolics of Power" *in* Joseph Ben-David & Terry Nicholo Clark (eds.): *Culture and Its Creators*. University of Chicago Press, Chicago & London.

Hay, W.R. 1933: *Confidential Report on Swat State*. Government of India Press, Simla.

Jansson, Erland 1981: *India, Pakistan or Pakhtunistan? The Nationalist Movements in the North-West Frontier Province 1937-47*. Studia Historica Upsaliensia 119 Almqvist & Wiksell, Stockholm.

Lindholm, Charles 1982: *Generosity and Jealousy: The Swat Pukhtun of Northern Pakistan*. Columbia University Press, New York.

Lorimer, D.L.R. 1935-38: The Burushaski Language. Instituttet for Sammenlignende Kulturforskning, Oslo.

Meeker, Michael E. 1980: "The twilight of a South Asian heroic age: a rereading of Barth's study of Swat". *Man* (New Series) vol. 15 no. 4:682-701.

Memoranda on the Indian States, 1938. Manager of Publications, Government of India Press, New Delhi.

Müller-Stellrecht, Irmtrand 1979: *Materialen zur Ethnographie von Dardistan Teil 1:*

Hunza. Akademische Druck- u. Verlagsanstalt, Graz. 1981: *Teil II & III: Gilgit, Chitral und Yasin*.

Roberts of Kandahar, Field Marshal Lord 1897: *Forty-One Years in India*. 2 vols. Richard Bentley & Son, London.

Robertson, Sir George Scott 1899: *Chitral — The Story of a Minor Siege*. Methuen & Co., London.

"Story of Swat" — see Wadud, Miangul Abdul.

Wadud, Miangul Abdul (Badshah Sahib of Swat) 1963: *The Story of Swat, as told by the founder to Muhammed Asif Khan* (translated): Ashruf Altaf Husain. Ferozsons Ltd., Peshawar.

Index